Prosper Mérimée

Currents in Comparative Romance Languages and Literatures

Tamara Alvarez-Detrell and Michael G. Paulson
General Editors

Vol. 124

PETER LANG
New York • Washington, D.C./Baltimore • Bern
Frankfurt am Main • Berlin • Brussels • Vienna • Oxford

Prosper Mérimée

Plays on Hispanic Themes

TRANSLATED, EDITED, AND INTRODUCED BY
OSCAR MANDEL

PETER LANG
New York • Washington, D.C./Baltimore • Bern
Frankfurt am Main • Berlin • Brussels • Vienna • Oxford

Library of Congress Cataloging-in-Publication Data

Mérimée, Prosper, 1803–1870.
[Plays. English. Selections]
Prosper Mérimée: plays on Hispanic themes /
translated, edited, and introduced by Oscar Mandel.
p. cm. — (Currents in comparative Romance languages and literatures; v. 124)
Includes bibliographical references.
1. Mérimée, Prosper, 1803–1870—Translations into English.
I. Title: Prosper Mérimée. II. Mandel, Oscar. III. Title. IV. Series.
PQ2362 .A26 842'.7—dc21 2002041131
ISBN 0-8204-6308-6
ISSN 0893-5963

Bibliographic information published by **Die Deutsche Bibliothek**.
Die Deutsche Bibliothek lists this publication in the "Deutsche
Nationalbibliografie"; detailed bibliographic data is available
on the Internet at http://dnb.ddb.de/.

Cover design by Lisa Barfield

The paper in this book meets the guidelines for permanence and durability
of the Committee on Production Guidelines for Book Longevity
of the Council of Library Resources.

© 2003 Peter Lang Publishing, Inc., New York
275 Seventh Avenue, 28th Floor, New York, NY 10001
www.peterlangusa.com

Printed in the United States of America

Table of Contents

Foreword

No fewer than seven out of Mérimée's thirteen known plays are set in Spanish-speaking countries—in Spain, Cuba, Peru, and Colombia; while an eighth, though it takes place on a Danish island, concerns a Spanish garrison stationed there. We have also from his hand a substantial number of critical and historical writings on Spanish themes. Indeed, Mérimée made his literary debut in 1824 by writing four articles on the Spanish drama of the seventeenth and eighteenth centuries. His best-known work, of course, is the tale of Carmen, published in 1845 and turned into an opera by Bizet thirty years later. Mérimée also travelled wide and deep in Spain; rejoiced in bullfights, executions, and the company of ruffians in the sierras; published lively accounts of his experiences and impressions; and made friends with the Count of Montijo and his family, one of whose members was the little girl who became Empress Eugénie, wife of Napoleon III, and never wavered in her devotion to him. He never crossed the ocean, however, and remained content with thoroughgoing if lightly applied documentation for his Hispano-American plays. That faraway world seemed to provide even better ground than Spain for the display of fierce passions in picturesque settings that he favored for his dramas and comedies.

Our interest in Hispanic matters has, if anything, increased since Mérimée's lifetime; hence I have thought it especially attractive to select some of his Spanish and Spanish-American plays for the present collection. Five out of Mérimée's eight Hispanic titles are included here. I have translated another, *The Spaniards in Denmark,* in a separate volume. The seventh, *Heaven and Hell,* is no more than an amusing skit (it does, however, deserve translation) and the eighth—*A Woman Is a Devil*—is an immature playlet that can be ignored in good conscience.

Because no genuine overall study of Mérimée's plays has yet been published in any language, and because his plays are for all practical purposes unknown in the English-speaking world (and very nearly so among the French themselves), I have provided a critical and even at times polemical introduction to his dramatic works. Readers who are indeed unacquainted with the plays should perhaps take possession of the latter *before* turning to the essay so as to meet my arguments fully armed. My hope, of course, is that they will take up arms together with me in the conviction that the best plays of this classic author should be inserted at long last into the mainstream of our theatrical culture.   O.M.

Prosper Mérimée, Playwright

Mérimée, famed as a storyteller, is so nearly unknown for his dramatic work that a basic account of the principal publications, productions and English translations of his plays is in order before we proceed with a discussion of their character and merits.

Publications

During Mérimée's Lifetime

In 1825, when Mérimée was 22 years old, he published six plays under the title *Le Théâtre de Clara Gazul*, pretending that the plays were the work of a spirited Spanish actress, an amusing life of whom he invented as an introduction to the book. The six plays were as follows:

- *Les Espagnols en Danemarck (The Spaniards in Denmark)*
- *Une Femme est un diable (A Woman Is a Devil)*
- *L'Amour africain (African Love)*
- *Inès Mendo ou le Préjugé vaincu (Inès Mendo or the Defeat of Prejudice)*
- *Inès Mendo ou le Triomphe du préjugé (Inès Mendo or the Triumph of Prejudice)*
- *Le Ciel et l'enfer (Heaven and Hell)*[1]

In 1828, Mérimée published a volume containing *Scènes féodales*: *La Jacquerie,*[2] followed by *La Famille de Carvajal.*

In 1829, he published two plays, *Le Carrosse du Saint-Sacrement (The Coach of the Blessed Sacrament)* and, a few months later, *L'Occasion (The Opportunity)*, both in *La Revue de Paris.*[3]

In 1830, in the same journal, Mérimée published a short play, *Les*

---

1. The two Inès Mendo plays can be regarded as a single play consisting of a prologue and the main action. I have so joined them in this volume, but at the same time I count and comment upon them separately.

2. The name refers to a bloody peasant uprising in 1358. Mérimée used the rare spelling "Jaquerie."

3. In the present volume, the first of these is titled *The Gilded Coach.*

Mécontents, 1810 (The Malcontents, 1810).[4] He reprinted it in a miscellany called *Mosaïque* in 1833.

Again in 1830, a second edition of *Le Théâtre de Clara Gazul* appeared, including, in addition to the original six plays, *Le Carrosse du Saint-Sacrement* and *L'Occasion.* At this point we can speak of eight "basic" Clara Gazul plays.

In 1842, a third, corrected edition of the eight Clara Gazul plays was published, but now it was followed by *La Jacquerie* and *La Famille de Carvajal.* This larger collection (which did not include *Les Mécontents*) was reprinted with slight corrections in 1850, then with somewhat more significant ones in 1857. The latter edition, on which the translations in this volume are based, was reprinted in 1860, 1865, and 1870.

In 1850 a drawing-room comedy, *Les Deux héritages (The Two Legacies),* appeared in *La Revue des Deux Mondes.* It was reprinted in 1853 in a volume which also contained Mérimée's translation of Gogol's *The Inspector General,* along with a set of dramatic scenes concerning the rise of the so-called False Dmitri: *Les Débuts d'un aventurier (The Beginnings of an Adventurer).*[5] Altogether then, Mérimée wrote and published thirteen dramatic texts—a substantial portion of his total literary production.

After 1870

The first important twentieth-century edition of the eight Clara Gazul plays is that of Pierre Trahard (Paris: H. Champion, 1927). It includes four early articles by Mérimée on the Spanish theatre, notes and variants for the plays, and a reprint of a number of reviews published from 1825 to 1830.[6] Eugène Marsan edited these plays for Le Divan in 1927, Pierre

---

4. This was spelled "Mécontens" in Mérimée's time, but I have used the modern spelling throughout.

5. Mérimée called the first of these a "Moralité à plusieurs personnages" and gave it the subtitle "ou Don Quichotte." We are told that two playlets, *La Charade* and *Le Cor au pied (The Bunion),* were performed by guests at Compiègne for Napoleon III and his circle, and that the second of these was printed for the first and last time in *L'Information* in 1920. No evidence exists that any writer on Mérimée has seen this text, and I have been unable to trace either the play or the periodical in question.

6. It should be noted, however, that the full story of the reception of Mérimée's published theatre in his lifetime remains to be written by someone willing to dredge the materials out of the periodicals of the times, as well as the letters, diaries, articles, etc. As for the critical pieces on the Spanish theatre, these were published anonymously in *Le Globe* in

Martino did so for F. Roches in 1929, and Gilbert Sigaux added *La Jacquerie* and *La Famille de Carvajal* for Le Club Français du Livre in 1963.

A volume containing *Les Deux héritages* and *Les Débuts d'un aventurier* was published in 1928 under the imprint of Le Divan, with an introduction by Eugène Marsan.

L'Occasion was edited as a separate work by P. Valde for Le Seuil in 1949.

A paperback edition of the eight plays, followed by *La Famille de Carvajal*, was edited by Pierre Salomon for Garnier-Flammarion in 1968, using the texts of the 1842 edition.

The Pléiade edition of Mérimée's works: *Théâtre de Clara Gazul, Romans et nouvelles*, edited by Jean Mallion and Pierre Salomon (Gallimard 1978), based itself on the 1857 edition but omitted *La Famille de Carvajal*. Like Trahard's edition, it included notes and variants.

All of these editions are currently out of print.[7]

The only edition of the *Théâtre de Clara Gazul* in print at this time is that of Patrick Berthier, in a Folio paperback published by Gallimard in 1985. Unfortunately, it contains only the six plays of the 1825 edition.

A few of the plays are still in print individually: (1) *La Jaquerie, suivie de La Famille de Carvajal*, edited by Pierre Jourda with abundant notes and variants (Paris: H. Champion, 1931); (2) *Les Mécontens*, in an annotated new edition of *Mosaïque* by M. Levaillant (Champion 1933); (3) *Le Carrosse du Saint-Sacrement* (Paris: Librairie Théâtrale, 1980); (4) The same play, in the "Collection du petit mercure" (Paris: Mercure de France, 1998). It should be noted, however, that the Champion editions are anything but readily available.

Productions

The information I have been able to gather is limited to Paris with only one or two exceptions.

In 1827, *L'Amour africain* was performed as one of the acts of a "divertissement" by Edmond Rochefort and Paul Duport, *Les Proverbes au château,* produced at the Théâtre des Nouveautés.[8]

1824. It was Trahard who first proposed Mérimée as their author, an attribution which is now fully accepted.
7. As of the date of publication of the present volume.

In 1850 *Le Carrosse du Saint-Sacrement* was given six performances at the Comédie-Française.

In 1898 *Une Femme est un diable* was performed at the Odéon—apparently as a single so-called "popular Saturday" event.

In 1918 Georges Pitoeff staged *L'Amour africain* in Geneva and again in Paris at the Théâtre des Arts, namely in 1926.

Le Carrosse du Saint-Sacrement came to life again in 1920 at the Vieux-Colombier with Jacques Copeau and Louis Jouvet in the cast.

Charles Dullin produced *Une Femme est un diable* and *L'Occasion* at the Atelier in 1922 and again in 1924.

In 1926 *Le Carrosse du Saint-Sacrement* returned to the Comédie-Française. It remained in the repertory until 1970, totalling 213 performances during these 44 years.

In 1940 Dullin produced *Le Ciel et l'enfer* at the Atelier.

Also in 1940. *Inès Mendo* was produced at the Charles-de-Rochefort playhouse under the direction of Jan Doat.

In 1944 *L'Occasion* was produced at the Théâtre du Temps.

In 1948 *L'Occasion* entered the Comédie-Française, with Jeanne Moreau in the leading role. Fourteen performances were given that year, and another 14 in 1949.

Also in 1948, the Comédie-Française staged 22 performances of *Les Espagnols en Danemarck*, followed by five performances in 1949.

In 1952, G. Arest adapted *La Jacquerie* for the Charles-de-Rochefort theatre.

In 1958 Jean Vilar produced *Le Carrosse du Saint-Sacrement* in Bordeaux, with George Wilson as the Viceroy and Maria Casarès as La Perichole.

A television adaptation of *Le Ciel et l'enfer* was broadcast in 1969.

Le Carrosse du Saint-Sacrement was performed in 1974 in the Théâtre Firmin-Gémier in Antony, a suburb of Paris.[9]

I have been unable to find any "live Mérimée" after 1974, but, of course, other productions may have taken place, perhaps in and around Paris, and a little more probably elsewhere in France.[10] Unfortunately, full

---

8. For a description of this literary curiosity, Pierre Trahard 1925, Volume 1, pp. 234–6 may be consulted.

9. "Massacre de Mérimée à Antony," reads the headline of the review in *Le Monde* of March 8, 1974.

10. The Pléiade edition mentions a production of *Les Espagnols en Danemarck* in Mans in 1967 and, without further information, "une émission télévisée."

information of this kind is almost impossible to obtain, but it appears that two of Mérimées's best works, *La Famille de Carvajal* and *Les Deux héritages,* have never been performed; instead, his two juvenile trifles, *Une Femme est un diable* and *L'Amour africain,* have been staged by distinguished directors. Even *Le Carrosse* seems to have vanished from the stage though it remains easily accessible in print.

English Translations

There are no productions in the English language to report. However, a few printed translations do exist, as follows:

The 1825 volume of *Le Théâtre de Clara Gazul* was anonymously translated in that very same year as *The Plays of Clara Gazul* and printed in London by G. B. Whittaker. It may be guessed that Stendhal was instrumental in arranging for this publication, but I am not aware of its making any noise in the English-speaking world then or later. The translations are stilted though fairly accurate.

The Coach of the Holy Sacrament, a translation by L. A. Loiseaux, was published in 1917 (Paris-New York: Collection du Vieux-Colombier).

An anonymous translation of *Les Mécontents* as *The Conspirators* appeared in Volume I of *The Golden Book Magazine* in 1925. *The Conspirators*, translation by Paul Vaughn (Bath: Absolute Classics, 1997), is distributed by the Theatre Communications Group in New York.

The present writer published his translation of *Les Espagnols en Danemarck* in *Two Romantic Plays: The Spaniards in Denmark by Prosper Mérimée and The Rebels of Nantucket by Oscar Mandel* (Los Angeles: Spectrum Productions/Books, 1996).

The Playwright

All but unperformed in his own lifetime, Mérimée's theatrical fortunes failed to improve decisively in the hundred years following his death in 1870 and have, unfortunately, declined since then. His only genuine post-mortem success consists in a long run of *Le Carrosse du Saint-Sacrement* at the Comédie-Française; and even though the play dropped out of the repertory after 1970, it survives as the only dramatic work by Mérimée which is fairly widely known, or at any rate recognized, by the educated French public. *Les Espagnols en Danemarck* was given its turn at the Comédie-Française as well, but 1948 and 1949 were probably bad years for the display of a boldly unpatriotic work that exalts resistance *against* the French. Still, in the 40s it might have been predicted that Mérimée's stock was on the rise at last, for it was possible in that decade to attend

performances not only of the two plays already mentioned, but also of
L'Occasion—an early vehicle for Jeanne Moreau—*Le Ciel et l'enfer* in
the hands of no less a figure than Charles Dullin, and even *Inès Mendo*.
However, the tide receded as swiftly as it came in, and, with the exception
of *Le Carrosse*, Mérimée's plays have lapsed into a condition which
closely resembles oblivion.[11] Of course, we are concerned with an author
whose position is secure as one of the classic writers of the nineteenth
century, but he owes that place almost entirely on the strength of *Carmen*
and a set of other tales which easily retain their place of honor in the
canon. He is also remembered with gratitude for his contribution, as
General Inspector of Historical Monuments, to the preservation and repair
of a great number of decayed architectural masterpieces throughout
France.[12] But even though most of his plays were lately in print in France,
and, together with his narrative fictions, basked in the sunlight of a Pléiade
edition,[13] they remain stubbornly absent from public consciousness in
their own country and, *a fortiori*, everywhere else. Whether in French or in
English, the critical literature, sparse to begin with, is largely hostile to
them; even the plays' editors usually denigrate the very works they are
editing, so that one wonders why they have bothered to undertake the
task. They have done nothing, indeed less than nothing, to stimulate
curiosity about these plays in the minds of theatre professionals, general
readers, or other students of literature. It must be confessed, therefore, that
strong minds might quake at the thought of choosing this moment in
history to beat the drum for Mérimée the playwright and proclaim, *envers
et contre tous*, that a grievous and lasting miscarriage of literary justice
has been committed.

---

11. *Le Carrosse du Saint-Sacrement* has inspired several imitations and adaptations: an
operetta with music by Offenbach called *La Périchole* (1868), a versified version of
Mérimée's play by one Maurice Vaucaire, performed at the Odéon in 1893, and *Le Carrosse
d'Or*, a film by Jean Renoir (1952). It is also a minor source for Thornton Wilder's *The
Bridge of San Luis Rey* (1927): see, for this, Walther Fischer (1936, *passim*).
12. From 1834 to 1852, Mérimée travelled extensively, often in great discomfort and
with large helpings of exasperation, in order to report on work needing to be done.
Among many other accomplishments, he is the savior of the Madeleine at Vézelay
(Burgundy), a favorite of modern tourists.
13. This edition, which recently went out of print, omits *La Famille de Carvajal*, *La
Jacquerie*, *Les Mécontents* and *Les Deux héritages*. The editors' evaluations, as shown
indirectly by their inclusions and omissions and directly in their introductory "Approche
de Mérimée," differ drastically from the present writer's.

Two things are needful at this point: the emergence of a daring producer who will resurrect one or more of these plays or, better yet, stage a series of Mériméan plays in what will amount to a coherent Mérimée festival of his most stageworthy works and a publisher who will select Mérimée's best plays instead of following his predecessors, who have lazily reprinted the six or eight plays of Mérimée's original *Théâtre de Clara Gazul*, indiscriminately mixing the bad and the good, and ignoring the important plays outside that volume. It is a little odd, to be sure, that these hopes or demands, and altogether the attempt to rescue Mérimée's plays from critical misunderstanding and near-oblivion, should be conveyed in English, and in English-speaking countries, rather than in Mérimée's own language and land. Odd and yet, I hope, admissible—a modest instance, perhaps, of globalization. Besides, the enterprising producer of Mériméan drama I am calling for might just be lying in wait in London, New York, Toronto, or Los Angeles.

Be that as it may, my purpose in the present volume is to place before the reader part of the evidence for my claim that, a couple of adolescent skits aside, Mérimée's plays entitle him to a lofty place among the dramatic authors of nineteenth-century Europe. A complete Mériméan florilegium would consist of the works printed here, to which would be added all thirty-six scenes of *La Jacquerie, Les Espagnols en Danemarck, Les Deux héritages*, and as light desserts, *Le Ciel et l'enfer* and *Les Mécontents*—in other words, all but two or three of Mérimée's plays.[14] Here surely is enough bulk and enough quality to pull Mérimée the dramatist up from the cellarage, and place him on a pedestal next to the profusely recognized Musset: the two finest and most original French playwrights of the first half of the nineteenth century, though it takes some brushing away of cobwebs to see this for a fact.

*

The 1825 edition of the *Théâtre de Clara Gazul*, addressed exclusively to readers, established Mérimée as a respected writer and significant voice in support of the anti-classical movement in drama, which was gaining momentum in that decade, for he had implemented in actual dramatic

---

14. The first *Inès Mendo* playlet would probably join two other titles in the original Clara Gazul collection—*A Woman Is a Devil* and *African Love*—as expendable juvenilia (though all three have their good points), but it gains admittance to the mature set as a necessary prologue to the larger play that follows.

texts most of the reforms his older friend Stendhal had called for in his
manifesto *Racine et Shakespeare*. Hence Mérimée's plays are usually
discussed in the histories as curious precursors to the *performed* Romantic
plays of writers like the elder Dumas, Vigny, and, above all, Hugo. Indeed,
Dumas, in his preface to *Henri III et sa cour*, acknowledged Mérimée as a
model, and Hugo printed a dedication to "M. Prosper Mérimée, the
master of us all." For Mérimée had planted the flag before anyone
else—five years before the Romantic theatre triumphed, amidst catcalls
and plaudits, with the production of Hugo's *Hernani*. We mark with
Mérimée the beginning of the end for the neo-classical drama—its iron-
clad unities of time, place, action and tone, its balanced Alexandrine
couplets, its language purged of all low and most concrete references.
Nevertheless, after tipping our hats to the precocious forerunner, barely
out of his adolescence, we can proceed on the assumption that the other
plays of the Romantic movement would have been written even if he had
never been born. Historically speaking, Mérimée can thus be thought of
as a dispensable precursor. The standard innovative plays of the
age—*Hernani* and the others—bear no resemblance to his work except
for their common divergence from the tired rigors of the classical model.

The revolt against the ways and means of drama immortalized by
Corneille and Racine, perpetuated by the less-talented Voltaire, and
reaffirmed as eternal theory by La Harpe, had become irresistible in the
post-Napoleonic atmosphere of Paris, where it fused with the political
opposition to the reactionary regimes of Louis XVIII and Charles X. To
be a Romantic was to be a liberal in politics and a liberator in literature.
Now, Mérimée was one of the young Turks of that epoch, and he
contributed his noise to the brouhaha that accompanied *Hernani*, but
other sources and resources for the movement were plentiful. We cannot
even claim for him the role of indispensable source for Musset, the other
truly eccentric playwright of the epoch. Musset without Mérimée is
perfectly thinkable. The truth, finally, is that Mérimée the playwright is to
be viewed as an outsider, a free-floater: the high road passes him by.
Neither the Hugo-Rostand line of creators, nor the school of blunt realists
(with Henri Becque as its master), nor the great writers of farce of the
century, nor the Symbolists are in his debt. Accordingly, the vindication I
call for in these pages has nothing to do with demonstrating that he
deserves a place in the development of French or world drama. Writing
remarkable plays—eminently stageworthy remarkable plays—is his only
claim to importance. It is, however, for artist and public alike, the one
importance that really matters. An advantageous position in the *history* of
a type or a form does not in itself attract us to a work of art.

*

Why, it may be asked, did Mérimée turn from drama to fiction after 1830, when he was only twenty-seven years old, returning to playwriting only for a moment around 1850? Alfred de Musset (1810–1857) would have had a stronger reason than he to turn his back on drama. The second edition of the *Théâtre de Clara Gazul* had appeared in September 1830. In December of the same year, Musset's first play to reach the stage was performed at the Odéon, and this, flatteringly, at the specific request of its director. But *La Nuit vénitienne* lasted for only two performances: neither the public nor the press liked it, and the disappointed poet followed Mérimée's example for the following seventeen years in creating his plays for armchair readers only.[15] We do not know whether Mérimée had, from the beginning, foreseen and feared the same outcome for his own work if a director had asked for it. But it seems that no director came hat in hand, nor do we know of any move by Mérimée himself to solicit performances for any of his Clara Gazul plays. Unlike Musset, he was neither flattered by producers or actors nor humiliated by an audience.

If, lacking the motive of a public defeat, we question the man by combing through the seventeen volumes of the *Correspondance générale*, or the anecdotes gleaned from his contemporaries, we draw another blank. Mérimée turns out to be singularly self-effacing not only *in* his works but also *about* them. He does not expound theories, trumpet his talents, backbite rivals, analyze his motives for writing one thing or not writing another, or, astonishing to report, complain of ill-usage.

Neither do we have from him a published body of literary criticism from which we might deduce an answer to our question. As mentioned before, his very first published work consisted of four short critical articles on Spanish drama, and they tell us something about his own way of writing plays—his predilection for terse endings, for instance—but very little in that vein was to follow. Mérimée had no ambition to become another Sainte-Beuve, and in any case his observations on literature reveal nothing about the windings of his own literary career.[16]

---

15. *Un Spectacle dans un fauteuil* was the charming and significant title of his first two volumes of plays (1832 and 1834). Incidentally, Mérimée's titles (and subtitles) tend to be distinctly less inspired than those of Musset.

16. Besides the articles just mentioned, Mérimée published a substantial number of critical essays or review articles about the works of others, and his opinions about other writers and questions of literary craftsmanship are scattered throughout his

Might the reviews of his book of plays have fallen secretly short of his expectations? This is highly unlikely, for the reception could hardly have been more encouraging—encouraging to any author but *a fortiori* to a beginner. While it is true that Mérimée belonged to a coterie of ardent reformers in the arts and would-be reformers in politics, these friends and comrades did not hesitate to criticize each others' works, personally or in print. Their praise was not to be dismissed as friendly back-patting. Besides, there was commendation in journals that stood outside the fraternity and no lack of admiring words from truly disinterested readers. A few examples should be cited:

> ....These six comedies, where, for the first time, I have seen men of our time speak as they speak and act as they act. (Anonymous subscriber in *Le Globe*, June 18, 1825).

> Although we are far from approving all the literary licences [the author] has allowed himself, we believe it to be our duty to recommend the *Théâtre de Clara Gazul* to our readers, not as a model to follow, but as a very original and successful attempt [un essai fort original et très heureux] and one that suggests the highest hopes for the man or woman who composed it. (Anonymous writer in the *Revue encyclopédique*, June 1825).

> Every one [of the six plays] is notable for its deep knowledge of the human heart, for an uncommon verve and energy and a dialogue both concise and natural.... Too young to have had much time to study [human] nature, he seems to have sensed it ahead of time. We have no doubt that these compositions, which the rigors of the censorship will necessarily keep from the stage, would have earned the same success in production which they obtain when read. (Anonymous writer in *La Pandore*, June 7, 1825).

> While the partisans of classicism persisted in imitating Euripides and Racine, their opponents were content to discuss without producing. Now at last, under the name of Clara Gazul, an original and independent spirit has arrived to fight in favor of the new system by means of examples; and we do not fear to say that

---

correspondence. R. C. Dale has sifted through all this material and shown that a coherent aesthetic can be fashioned from Mérimée's utterances. Not surprisingly, Mérimée's views about how writers should and should not write mirror his own "instinctive" practices. Dale's excellent study confirms, however, that Mérimée is close-mouthed about himself as *littérateur* (Dale 1966, *passim*).

since Monsieur Lemercier's *Pinto*, nothing so remarkable as several of these six plays has appeared. ("A" in *Le Mercure du XIXe siècle,* 1825).[17]

This last critic, who expressed the wish, amusing to us, that Clara Gazul had been a French author, acknowledged that Madame Gazul's proclivity to see the *ugliness* of things might be accounted a crime by many readers; "but, let a person look about ever so slightly, is it so rare to see something else than beautiful nature?"[18] Even Goethe, from afar, admired the author of *Le Théâtre de Clara Gazul,* as we know from his conversations with Eckermann, duly reported to Mérimée.

The most perceptive critique of Mérimée's plays and tales came from Sainte-Beuve, writing in *Le Globe* in January 1831, when Mérimée was almost done with playwriting. Since Sainte-Beuve's observations have never been bettered, and since they demonstrate more clearly yet that Mérimée had every encouragement to continue as a playwright, I will cite somewhat more extensively.[19]

> himself to substitute anything for it.... He has allowed system-makers of every conviction to have their say; he has neither rejected nor embraced any of them, maintaining his silence, not always listening The artist has usually thrust upon [his characters] the most vigorous and simplest profile, a language as curt and strong as possible; in his fear of being effusive...he has preferred to stick to what is most certain, most graspable in the real.... Positive in spirit, an

---

17. The comparison with *Pinto* would not sound like much of a compliment today, but this cheerful if clumsily amateurish historical drama about the Portuguese uprising of 1640 against Spanish domination, produced in 1800, was an early slap at the classical unities of time, of place, and, above all, of tone. The censors prevented a production in 1825, but the play was well known, and Lemercier had it reprinted in 1827. In 1834 it became a sensational hit, partly because of its eloquent attack on tyrants. The censors, defying popular outcries, suppressed it in 1836. See the critical edition by Norma Perry, University of Exeter Press, 1976.

18. However, Jean-Jacques Ampère—friend but no sycophant—rightly pointed out in 1830 that although Mérimée liked to depict "a class of feelings which are not ideal," nevertheless, his tableaux showed "that the human heart is seldom without some spark of virtue, and the most abject lives, the coarsest passions are not entirely bereft of a certain admixture of loyalty, generosity, even grandeur, which ennobles their wretchedness and consoles us for their waywardness." I will be coming back to this accurate assessment. The comments cited so far are printed in Trahard 1927, but a comprehensive survey of the reception of Mérimée's published and performed works remains to be undertaken.

19. Sainte-Beuve's comments on Mérimée are usefully collected in the Notes to *Les Grands écrivains français,* Volume 2, edited by Maurice Allem in 1927, pp. 282–4.

observer, curious and studious of details, of facts, of everything that can be shown with precision, the author early shook off the vague metaphysics of our critical age in religion, in philosophy, in art, in history, without taking it upon, abstaining from any judgment.... He kept close to facts, questioned travellers, inquired into savage customs and civilized anecdotes alike; he was interested in the form of a dagger or a tropical creeper, in the color of a fruit, in the ingredients of a drink; he went back without repugnance and with a nervous suppleness of the imagination to earlier mores, turning himself freely into a Spaniard, a Corsican, an Illyrian, an African, and in the present giving preference to rare curiosities, singular passions, strange cases, remnants of the mores of old which stand out best in the midst of our *blasé* and levelling epoch: adulteries, duels, stabbings, good scandals to our etiquette-based morality.... His execution is altogether what one might expect: perfect simplicity, continuous force; no pomposities, no chatter; no philosophizing [*point de réflexions*] and no digressions; something that goes straight to its goal... no vapors on the horizon, no half-tints, but rather clean lines, strong and sober colors... every reality closely followed and rendered with severe exactness...concentrated and virile in his passions, even the women; and behind these characters and these scenes, an author who effaces himself, whom one neither sees nor hears...and who intervenes at most only at the end, under a false air of not caring and a half-ironical smile.[20]

Mérimée's book of plays was no best-seller, either in the original edition or the augmented one of 1830, yet the critical reception it enjoyed could not but encourage him; even the negative opinions were respectful. Everyone recognized the author's boldness, independence, and originality. He had not to stomach the hostility and (let me be plain) the mediocrity of most of the twentieth-century commentators who have examined his plays. Indeed, there is indirect proof that Mérimée was satisfied, for in 1833, when he published the miscellany he titled *Mosaïque*, he signed it "*par l'auteur du Théâtre de Clara Gazul*," even though his bulky new book contained only one little play, *Les Mécontents, 1810*. All in all, then, it is safe to say that neither blame nor indifference pushed the young playwright, dejected yet ambitious, into the direction of the narrative arts. A more credible motive might be found in the efficient severity of the censors who kept the theatre in line. It was in any event clear, as one of the reviewers I have quoted remarked, that plays like those Mérimée was able to publish could not hope to receive

---

20. In 1840, in the course of an article on George Sand, Sainte-Beuve spoke of Mérimée as possessing one of the most fundamentally dramatic talents of his time (Allem 1927, p.

the censors' permission to be produced. *Les Espagnols en Danemarck* was an easily perceived attack on the French policy of coming to the aid of the odiously reactionary Spanish king Ferdinand VII, besides showing a most unpatriotic attitude to the French in general.[21] But that was nothing to the ferocious anti-Catholicism of several of the other plays. Mérimée detested the Church, going so far as to convert to Protestantism at life's end in order to be buried in non-Catholic earth.[22] This passion shows in his plays, and when ambition finally got the better of him and he "allowed," with feigned reluctance, *Le Carrosse du Saint-Sacrement* to be performed in 1850, its anti-clerical persiflage sank it after six performances, even though, after the second one, the role of the bishop of Lima had been prudently deleted. Mérimée's disrespect for the ruler of a land, a viceroy, almost a king, did not help either. The censors who watched the playhouses under Louis XVIII, Charles X, Louis-Philippe, and Napoleon III did not sleep at their desks, whoever wore the crown. When, for instance, an English company visited Paris in the 1827–8 season, the king and queen in *Hamlet* had to be demoted to duke and duchess. Victor Hugo's problems with the censorship were notorious. Musset was not spared either. The wronged husband of his *Andrea del Sarto* is guilty of the sinful delicacy of blessing his wife and her lover (who has inflicted a mortal wound on him in a duel) as they run away to be married. This was worse than Mérimée! In 1850, the year in which *Le Carrosse* came to grief, the offended censors forced Musset to kill the lover along with the cuckold in order to avert the scandal to morality. One wonders what operation Mérimée would have been obliged to perform in order to make a shocker like *Carvajal's Family* fit for the theatre.

My guess, however, is that a deeper cause was at work in turning Mérimée away from drama. We can, after all, imagine him fighting or—more likely—fooling the censors, and two or three of his plays (*Inès Mendo,* for instance) might have received official assent without much trouble; but Mérimée could not help perceiving that even without censorship, his plays could not be transferred from page to stage; they strayed too far from the range of what was expected and accepted in the theatres of his time. The reviewers had it right: he was "*un génie*

---

285).

21. I have noted already that the play failed in 1948–9 probably for this very reason. This was also the opinion of Louis Aragon: "What infuriated our critics, apparently,...was that the French here play the ugly role before the Spaniards," etc. (Aragon 1954, p. 190).

22. His grave is in the Protestant cemetery of Cannes.

indépendant et original"—a compliment perhaps too readily bestowed by critics but truly applicable in this instance. He crafted his work as far from the new wave of enthusiastic Romantics as from the retreating tide of classicism. Like Dumas, Hugo, and others, he was fighting for fresh air in the theatre. But when we examine any of the plays performed in Paris in the period we are considering, it becomes obvious at once that Mérimée was writing as if for another age. Neither his subject matter nor his form takes the practical stage of his day into consideration. The hypothesis I would advance, therefore—one that rests on the idea that it often takes at least two causes to produce one result—is that a combination of stoical resignation to the impossibility of a living stage for his plays and an already applauded gift for narrative story-telling led him to concentrate his literary forces on the genre for which an outlet existed—the one for which he is honored to this day.[23]

Whether or not this hypothesis is correct, it invites us to continue the task, begun by the reviewers and critics of 1825–30, of inquiring into the astonishing differences between Mérimée and those contemporaries of his who, despite their shortcomings, play leading roles in the events and trends that constitute the history of the French theatre.[24]

*

Victor Hugo was a year older than Mérimée. Both were eager beginners when they wrote their first ambitious play, each one, by coincidence, creating a *Cromwell* of his own—Mérimée in 1822, Hugo in 1826–7. Typically self-critical and clear-eyed, Mérimée destroyed his play and spared posterity the unpleasant need to insult it. "You cannot imagine," wrote this boy of nineteen to a correspondent, "how painful it is to reread with a mind in repose what one has made in a fit of enthusiasm.... Disenchanted now [*désenthousiasmé*], I discover nothing but what is absurd, fake, and ridiculous in my sublime tragedy." Mérimée could not foresee that these adjectives apply exactly to Hugo's interminable

---

23. In 1829 alone Mérimée published a novel, *1572—Chronique du temps de Charles IX*, and several short stories, among them the powerful *Mateo Falcone* and *Tamango*—all very favorably received.

24. One recent history is the multi-authored two-volume *Le Théâtre en France*, edited by Jacqueline de Jomaron (Paris: Armand Colin, 1988). The chapters dealing with the theatre after Napoleon I are written by Anne Ubersfeld. The only work by Mérimée she mentions at all is *La Jacquerie*, though it is to her credit that she calls it the masterpiece among the *scènes historiques* of the time (Volume 2, p. 44).

hodgepodge on the same subject; but Hugo proudly published instead of burning and set a path of self-satisfaction for himself from which he never deviated. Critics remain perplexed to this day by the cohabitation in his plays of wonderful short scenes, passages of enchanting poetry, plots ludicrous even for the operatic libretti they have famously spawned, and stretches of drama mired in juvenile ranting and rambling—"floods of sonorities," as Remy de Gourmont put it. Gustave Lanson, equally hard on Hugo, called the latter's plays childish—"*enfantins*"—in his *Histoire de la littérature française*, and declared, with some exaggeration to be sure, that "the most complete unintelligence rises from them." Such was, indeed, Mérimée's own opinion: "This is a man who gets drunk on his words and no longer bothers to think."[25]

However, the nineteenth-century public loved sublimity, loved it, as we know, in all the arts, and no writer revelled in it more than Hugo. Sublime ideals and virtues, sublime renunciations, sublime reconciliations, sublime clemencies, sublime self-abnegations, sublime defiances, sublime points of honor, sublime devotions, sublime death-throes, even sublime crimes[26]—along with every other device known to melodrama, including heart-stopping dilemmas and far-fetched diabolical machinations. Hugo's plays, ostensibly historical and true to life, are in fact a product of his literary fantasies, very imperfectly correlated with reality, but luckily for him, reality was not the commodity most people shopped for when they entered the playhouse.

My purpose, however, is not to repeat what even Hugo's admirers have always admitted, nor to deny Hugo's indomitable verve ("Victor Hugo," said Théophile Gautier in one of his naively admiring reviews, "has a quality that is the greatest and the rarest in all the arts: force!") nor to ignore his strong colors, his fine lyrical passages, the occasional eloquence that truly works. These qualities deservedly keep his work from dropping into the oblivion of Pixérécourt's melodramas, even though the latter are no more absurd in their plots than Hugo's. Rather, I am trying

---

25. Letter to Jenny Daquin, September 27, 1862.

26. Here, however, the prize goes to Dumas' *Antony* (1831), where the hero (who lives without a last name, apparently undisturbed by the police) stabs his virtuous mistress at the end of the play rather than expose her to the shame of discovery, and then, as the husband appears, throws down the dagger and cries, "She resisted me, I killed her!" in order to protect her reputation. The tears the audiences shed kept them from noticing that Antony's sublime last words had no chance of fooling the new-made widower, since Dumas had shown that all Paris was aware of the liaison between the two lovers.

to bring out as starkly as possible the staggering difference between the two coeval authors. In contrast to Hugo, Mérimée is self-critical, his eye rests on reality rather than on fancied ideals, he eschews rhetoric, ignores the sublime, keeps the actions of his major plays brief, simple and credible, understands humanity, and writes as Stendhal had asked dramatists to write, in "a simple, correct prose without ambition."[27]

Even a frightening drama like *Carvajal's Family* is free of the bombast that mars its predecessor, Shelley's *The Cenci*, and that any writer of his generation but Mérimée would have pumped into it. Consider the play's finale. Catalina has stabbed her father to prevent him from raping her. He falls to the ground. Enter her lover who is supposed to rescue her. The dying Carvajal accuses his daughter of murder. The lover shockingly turns from her in moral outrage and leaves her to die in the jungle. All this in a few terse brutal lines of dialogue. No arias here, no tirades, no *in extremis* repentance, no forgiveness, no reconciliation, no redemption, and no moral reflection. Not even poetry! The play's uncompromising cruelty denied the reader even that consolation.

Scenes of this kind show Mérimée's almost uncanny modernity. For better or for worse we are hard-nosed when it comes to literature, and so was he.

True, in *The Opportunity* Maria expresses her horror after the crime, and she pleads for forgiveness before rushing off to drown herself. But this happens in less than a minute of time on stage. It is not a scene, it is a cry, and besides, it is a cry that her victim, Francisca, does not hear. The latter dies not knowing that Maria had been her rival and why the girl has poisoned her. There is no touching, redeeming scene of forgiveness and reconciliation. Violence so devoid of edifying sentiments—so true to the probabilities of life rather than the fantasies of idealism—was unheard-of

---

27. See the sixth letter of Stendhal's *Racine et Shakespeare*. But I doubt that Mérimée needed his friend's advice. His independence is shown by the fact that he ignored the latter's call for national historical tragedy when he composed the plays of *The Theatre of Clara Gazul*. Furthermore, the national historical tragedy he did eventually write, *La Jacquerie*, does not in any way adhere to the Stendhalian model, exemplified by the plot of *Le retour de l'île d'Elbe* that Stendhal sketched out in his treatise. Mérimée simply agreed with Stendhal's derision of the unities and bloated tirades as well as with his call for a full everyday vocabulary expressed in prose. Note, in this connection, that the most sensational aspect of Hugo's revolution of French drama was precisely his use of an everyday modern vocabulary—but in Alexandrine verse! Every writer followed his own

on the public stage before the invention of the avant-garde experimental theatre.

In 1862, conveying his impressions of Flaubert's *Salammbô* to Jenny Daquin, Mérimée spoke of "a lyricism copied from the worst of Victor Hugo" and told her that he hated "*l'emphase*," that is to say, bombast—it made him furious.[28] Even he, however, had given in to "*emphase*" on one occasion in his short playwriting life, and in the spirit of fairness we ought to catch him *in flagrante* before absolving him. *The Spaniards in Denmark*, most of which is delightfully crisp, treats us to a girl's conversion to virtue and a larmoyant confession of sin in the "best" sentimental tradition. Elisa has been spying on the Spaniards in company with her ruthlessly enterprising mother. But she has fallen in love with Don Juan Diaz, their intended victim. A page-long soliloquy of remorse ensues ("He's lost! And undone because of me, miserable woman! Curse the day I set foot on this island!" and so on). Later, when Don Juan proposes marriage, her anguish only increases ("There is a terrible reason that prevents me from marrying you. I love you too much to marry you without revealing it to you. But don't ask it of me if you want to love me. Adieu, Don Juan, I will think of you as long as I live"). Of course, this leads to a confession and to a counter-access of virtue ("Elisa, you are my wife!").[29] Not surprisingly, these scenes were much admired by Mérimée's contemporaries. Mérimée himself, however, knew better and never indulged in bombast again.

Audiences, however, revelled in pictures of repentant and forgiven sinners.[30] In 1829, for instance—the very year of *Carvajal's Family*—Casimir Delavigne's *Marino Faliero* ran successfully at the Théâtre de la Porte-Saint-Martin. Old Faliero has joined a conspiracy to overthrow the government of Venice because of an unpunished slur upon

---

predilections in picking from the many innovative literary ideas that flourished in the writings and conversations of the Restoration.

28. *Ibid.,* Volume 11, p. 251.

29. Casimir Delavigne imitated this episode in an interesting scene of his *Don Juan d'Autriche* (1835), set in the Spain of Charles V under the menace of the Inquisition, when the young lady confesses to her most Christian lover that she is—Jewish. He too sweeps the objection aside, giving Delavigne an opportunity to express his liberal views on this subject. Unfortunately, the play as a whole remains an amusing swashbuckling machine.

30. The pattern had been established with sensational success in 1788 by August von Kotzebue's *Menschenhass und Reue* (Misanthropy and Remorse). See, in this connection,

the virtue of his young wife Elena. The poor greybeard is unaware that she has sinned—one time only, the audience is relieved to hear—with his own beloved nephew, Ferdinand. Ferdinand is killed in a duel with the author of the slur. Elena, devoted after all to her husband and remorseful from the start (sentimental heroines failed to enjoy their fling as long as the nineteenth century lasted), confesses her fault to him, for she hopes that, by nullifying his motive for leading the conspiracy, he can be persuaded to keep away from it. It is too late, however. Faliero is arrested, and duly curses his wife as he is dragged off to prison and present execution. However, such a near-Mériméan blow could not be allowed to conclude a stageworthy play. In Delavigne's finale, Faliero forgives his wife and saves the day for the box office.

> ELENA: What! you forget everything!
> FALIERO: No; for I remember that you made me love my burdensome life. Your care prolonged it, and, in my sorrow, I feel that you sweeten death for me.

He then gives her a document: it is her inheritance. But how can she, guilty wretch that she is, accept it?

> FALIERO: Accept out of virtue: it is noble, sometimes, to endure a gift.

Besides, Elena will use all that gold to help the children of the other condemned conspirators.

> ELENA: But may I die after I have given everything away?
> FALIERO: Worthy of your husband. And your supreme judge, indulgent as well, will also forgive you.[31]

By giving up this *topos*, Mérimée all but locked himself out of the theatres of his time. He must have been strong-minded indeed to resist such larmoyance when, as we have seen, he had shown himself quite capable of indulging in it.

---

the present author's *August von Kotzebue: the Comedy, the Man* (University Park and London: The Pennsylvania State University Press, 1990, pp. 5 ff).

31. The play was written in classical Alexandrine couplets, though it disregards the unities of time and place. Delavigne was a worthy poet and deserves to have had a fine street of Paris named after him. Mérimée, less favored, gets only a tiny one in the sixteenth *arrondissement* (far from his home and haunts), which runs, o disgrace! parallel to the broad and noble one named after Victor Hugo.

Ardent, bombastic declamation a propos of almost anything was still a requirement for serious drama, just as the aria formed the basis of opera. In this respect the new Romanticism kept faith with the classical model. Authors now allowed their characters to declaim—and frequently to rave—either in prose or in Alexandrine couplets, but either way the spoken aria continued to prevail. When Mérimée's friend Jean-Jacques Ampère, welcoming *Le Théâtre de Clara Gazul* in the pages of the *Globe* in 1825, announced that "we" had tired of "the heavy declamations of so many dramatic personages," he was unwittingly anticipating the twentieth century rather than defining his own. In *Hernani* Hugo opened the hitherto closed couplet and marshalled everyday words into the alexandrine, but far from giving up the tirades of old, he even lengthened them. Don Carlos' soliloquy in the presence of Charlemagne's tomb rumbles on for several hundred lines. Here, however, is a shorter sample. I take it from Pierre Lebrun's verse drama *Le Cid d'Andalousie,* produced a few months before the appearance of Mérimée's first volume. The play is set in thirteenth-century Seville, where the doomed Don Bustos resists a newly arrived tyrant:

> I too honor the hereditary right of kings, but without invoking heaven for something that is of this earth. Are they evil? That right is profane and vain. Only by doing good does a king make his right divine. If he is just or merciful, if he forgets or forgives, ah! then he has his crown from God! So before obeying I examine.... After the reign of the last Moorish king, I saw, as a boy, days of freedom shine in this noble and valiant city. It is something one remembers for a long time. You could not know the unutterable well-being of living without a master, of being equal one and all, of obeying only the laws!... This credulous and fanatical loyalty, this blind devotion without rule or law, this religion of vassal to the king, have too often transformed the noblest and bravest men into guilty slaves. (Act I, Scene 2)

Altogether, Don Bustos' oration takes up 46 lines of exemplary alexandrines as yet untouched by Hugo's hammer—although I suspect that the great bard was not a little indebted to the now-forgotten Lebrun. It is typical of the oratory that audiences expected and relished. Oratory was still prized in the forum, and playgoers enjoyed it in their fictions too; they liked characters who mounted tribunes and displayed a high eloquence about principles rather than muttering half-phrases about their innards. I hasten to add that our ancestors may have been wise to enjoy the best of these arias, whether metaphysical, political, or personal. Our muttered half-phrases and our grunts do not necessarily indicate a cultural summit. The point here is simply that Mérimée, knowing that people do not in fact converse in Demosthenes orations, defied the general taste and made do without them. A few of the speeches in *The Opportunity* are long and overlong, but they are not tirades, they are not declamations on a platform, they are personal, intimate, and concrete. Indeed, read in the context of his contemporaries, the *humility* of Mérimée's dramatic works is truly touching.

This humility extends to his refusal, exceptional for his time, to use characters to vehiculate his own *Weltanschauung*. Don Bustos emerges from the thirteenth century to express Lebrun's liberal thesis. Hugo's Charles V speaks for Hugo. In *Antony*, Dumas managed (rather cleverly) to insert a disquisition on modern versus historic subjects for drama. Mérimée differs again and proves himself the complete dramatist: the characters speak for themselves, not for him; he has caught them speaking or thinking (he did not discard soliloquies) and has recorded what they said or thought. Here again is Ampère: "One can blame him only for not putting enough of himself into what he does, while there are so many authors who need one's forgiveness for putting too much of themselves into what they have done." Sainte-Beuve too, in the article I have cited, speaks of Mérimée as "the author who conceals himself, whom one does not hear or see, whose sympathy or love never manifests itself through some irresistible outburst."

Even Musset is guilty of too frequently turning his characters into his own vocal cords. He and a reclaimed Mérimée are the two major playwrights of the age, and there is no need to adjudicate between Musset's whimsical woolgathering and Mérimée's harsh, virile force. And yet, for all his virtues, Musset, like Hugo, seldom resists the urge to listen to his own eloquence, which he foists on his characters either as introspective exaltation or philosophical rumination. A passage from *Fantasio* (one of his best and most typical plays) will illustrate my point. The melancholy but humorous hero, sitting in a tavern with his friends, has just invited them to muse about this, that, and the other thing: "*Restons un peu ici à parler de choses et d'autres, en regardant nos habits neufs.*" This "while looking at our new clothes" is purest endearing Musset. But it is also a threat of things to come. Here is a sample:

> FANTASIO. Oh! If only there were a devil in heaven! If there were a hell, how quickly I'd blow out my brains in order to go see it all! What a miserable thing is man! Unable so much as to jump out of a window without breaking his legs! Forced to play the violin ten years in order to turn into a tolerable musician! To study in order to be a painter, to be a stable-hand, to make an omelet! Look here,

Spark, I sometimes feel like sitting on a parapet, watching the river flow, and
starting to count one, two, three, four, five, six, seven and so on till the day I
die.
SPARK. Many would laugh at what you're saying. But it gives *me* the shivers;
it's the history of our entire century. Eternity is a grand eyrie, from which the
centuries have flown like eaglets one after the other to cross the sky and vanish;
ours arrived in its turn at the nest's edge; but its wings have been cut, and it waits
for death while gazing at the spaces into which it cannot soar.[32]

Musset's ruminations in other plays may take different directions
(sentimental self-analysis, for example), but the realization always comes
to the reader or spectator that the character speaking is Musset himself,
Musset baring his soul rather than moving the action forward. Now,
Mérimée's characters never sound like Mérimée expounding his view of
things or of himself, they speak as such characters would speak if alive
and unacquainted with Mérimée, and if now and then a director might
want to shorten a speech—as in *The Opportunity*—still, he will be
shortening a speech that pertains strictly to the character in that particular
place and that particular action, not an outpouring of views dear to the
author.

Mérimée's radical pessimism stands in contrast, too, with the optimism
that shines even through the tragic dramas of the age, except for a
singular work like Musset's *Lorenzaccio*. In the Preface to *Lucrèce
Borgia* (1833), Hugo spoke of himself as knowing "that the drama,
without departing from the impartial limits of art, has a national mission, a
social mission, a human mission.... The masses [*la multitude*] must not
leave the theatre without carrying away some austere and profound moral
point.... And as far as the wounds and miseries of humanity are
concerned, whenever [the playwright] displays them, he will try to throw
over the too odious aspects of these naked truths the veil of a grave and
consoling idea." For it was the poet's duty to participate in what Hugo
called the world's "immense movement of ascension toward the light"
(*Légende des siècles*, 1857). This cheerful world-vision and this view of
the high mission of art were alien to Mérimée's sense of things. I say
"sense of things" because no man of his intelligence was ever less
disposed to philosophize or blather philosophically. The works
themselves reveal his pessimism, as does the occasional remark which has

come down to us in his letters. "Know," he writes to Jenny Daquin in 1832, "that nothing is more common than to do evil for the pleasure of doing it. Rid yourself of your optimistic ideas and put it in your mind that we are in this world in order to do battle against one and all. Let me tell you, in this connection, that a scholar friend of mine who reads hieroglyphics, told me that one very often reads these two words on Egyptian tombs: *Life, War*; which proves that I did not invent the maxim I just gave you."[33] Of course, we should always treat the words of a private letter with prudence, and in this instance very particularly we need to distinguish between pessimism with respect to mankind's destiny or history and pessimism with respect to human character. In 1830, Mérimée's friend Jean-Jacques Ampère had written that in the playwright's darkest dramas, "the human heart is seldom without some spark of virtue, and the most abject lives, the coarsest passions are not entirely bereft of a certain admixture of loyalty, generosity, even grandeur, which ennobles their wretchedness and consoles us for their waywardness."[34] In other words, Mérimée was not in the business of exploding illusions about our nature. A man very much of his own time in this important respect, he believed in the existence of virtue.

*

The performable plays of Mérimée's time were complicated plot-machines which obeyed the advice given two centuries earlier by Lope de Vega, namely, that *comedias* should surprise the audience at every turn. I have found that bare plot summaries typically require two densely typewritten pages, whether they are distilled from the works of "commercial" playwrights like Scribe and Pixérécourt or from those by authors proclaiming higher aspirations. Here is the mere beginning of a typical Pixérécourt entertainment:

> In *Le Pèlerin blanc, ou les Orphelins du hameau* [The White Pilgrim, or the Village Orphans], we see the veneration in which the absent Count of Castelli is held by his tenants and villagers; his castle had burned down fourteen years earlier, leading to the death of his wife, the supposed death of his infant sons,

---

32. From Act I, Scene 2; *Fantasio* was published in 1834 but never performed in the author's lifetime. The ten-years' study to make an omelet is again unmistakable Musset; Mérimée has no such deliciously surprising imagery at the tip of his pen.

33. *Correspondance générale*, Volume 1, p. 175.

34. Trahard 1927, p. 536.

and the Count's own disappearance. The sorrowing villagers presume that he is now dead; and we learn of the tyranny exercised by the present chatelaine, the Baronne (the Count's niece) and her evil *intendant* Roland. Two orphans arrive, and after being hospitably welcomed by the villagers, they are taken off to the castle by Roland. There, when evidence shows them to be the Count's missing sons, they are imprisoned on the Baronne's orders; while Roland administers (as he thinks) poison to the boys. However, he is foiled by a mysterious elderly retainer, who. . .

and so on.[35]

Neither the popular nor the "artistic" playwrights bestowed much care on the correlation between their machines and human reality. I have said as much already about Hugo, but in Hugo's dramas we find but an exaggeration of the norm in his time. "Good theatre," experience had shown, could be almost as independent of life as music was exempt from rendering street noises. Hence the profusion of accidents and coincidences, mistaken and recognized identities, fatal overheard conversations or dropped objects, secret closets and passages, extraordinary changes of personality, and premises of sheer, unmitigated absurdity. Everything, in short, that we label melodrama, a type that should not be confused with the sort of candid *Magic Flute* fantasy we get from Ferdinand Raimund and others. Perhaps the most abused device was that of the "fatal coincidence"—e.g., the youth you killed was, horror! your own son. But all the devices I have mentioned (and, undoubtedly, some I have forgotten to name) had proved themselves efficacious remedies against boredom. It was "good theatre" to make a lackey fall in love with the queen of Spain and wisely govern the kingdom for a few days as the pawn of a sinister villain (Hugo's *Ruy Blas*); to let the Emperor Charles V take a short leave from the monastery of Yuste in order to recognize his illegitimate son, save him from the clutches of the legitimate one, and rescue his Jewish love from the Inquisition (Delavigne's *Don Juan d'Autriche*); to introduce an astrologer who conveys a sleeping duchess into her would-be lover's presence at the touch of a button; or make the lovers come to grief because the duchess forgot her handkerchief (Dumas' *Henri III et sa cour*; in *Kean* the fatally forgotten object is a fan).

---

35. Howarth 1975, p. 65. The play was produced in 1801. I will return to Pixérécourt at a later point.

And where did Mérimée stand? He too had dabbled in melodrama. The scene in the first of the *Inès Mendo* plays where honest Mendo hacks off his own hand rather than Don Esteban's head is melodrama. In *Une Femme est un diable*, we are treated to an ascetic Inquisitor running off with a pretty girl after stabbing a fellow Inquisitor: that too is melodrama. In *L'Amour africain* two hot-headed Arabs of Cordoba fight over a beautiful slave; one of them kills the other, and then, furious at having sent his best friend to the great beyond, stabs the girl to death! More melodrama. Not that melodrama is to be equated with violence. Neither *Othello* nor *Phèdre* is melodramatic. Violence is melodramatic only when it strikes us as overdone, far-fetched, and absurd. And by that definition, once we exclude these three short plays, we discover that Mérimée's plays are remarkably free of melodrama. His violent plots, which can be summarized in a sentence or two, follow the curves of high probability—in plainer English, they are realistic, and in this, once more, they display an artistic humility unknown to his contemporaries.

In a play like *The Opportunity*, for instance, the world of adolescent girls in a convent school excludes, on the one hand, the poetic whimsy in which Musset was to drape subjects of this kind, and, on the other, the melodramatic complications and absurdities every other playwright of the time would have invented for it. Even the violent conclusion delivers a psychological truth, childlike yet deadly—a truth which, to my knowledge, had never before entered literature—with plain directness.[36]

Two of Mérimée's plays are as free of blemishes as drama can be: *Le Carrosse du Saint-Sacrement* and *Les Deux héritages*. The faults one can detect in his other important dramatic works are minor ones. I have already touched on one of them in *The Opportunity*. Here it may also be thought that, inasmuch as Irena and Ximena have other youths than Fray Antonio very much on their minds, the praise they lavish on him and the flattering story they tell about him are dragged in by the author. Worse, their story does not prod Francisca and Maria into a new direction: the action resumes unchanged after the giggling girls depart. To be sure,

---

36. The Pléiade edition reiterates the perfectly absurd notion launched by Trahard that the sources of the play are Moratin's *El si de las niñas* and Lewis' *The Monk*. It is true that we find a Rita, a Paquita, and an Irena in Moratin's sentimental comedy, and that his sixteen-year-old Paquita has just come out of a convent. Such is the extent of Mérimée's "indebtedness." Summoning *The Monk* is even more impertinent. See Mallion and Salomon 1978, p. 1195. The truth is that no source is known for *L'Occasion* and that we are unlikely to discover one outside the author's remarkable imagination.

some readers may argue that we wanted more evidence that Fray Antonio is a decent man, not a vile "gothic" seducer made viler by his priestly habit. Another objection (not everyone may feel as I do) is that Mariquita speaks too much like a wronged woman of mature years after unmasking Fray Antonio ("You understand that conversing with you has lost some of its charm for me," and so forth); for a moment I no longer hear the convincing adolescent she was at the beginning.

In *Carvajal's Family,* the episode of Carvajal's attempt to sedate his daughter may also be questioned. The attempt as such is not, in my view, a literary artifice, a far-fetched invention, in short melodrama; life offers all too many instances of assaults on a woman's resistance by means of drugs or alcohol. Since this tactic also conforms to Carvajal's behavior in other scenes, Mérimée's artistic instinct is sound so far. The fault occurs when Catalina, suddenly remembering that she should fast on that particular day, pours out the glass of adulterated milk. As a result of this contrived coincidence, when Carvajal assaults her, she is wide awake and capable of stabbing him to death. She would, however, have been wide awake if Carvajal had not plotted to sedate her to begin with—if, in other words, Mérimée had dropped the whole unnecessary milk episode, and Carvajal (unlike Lord Lovelace) had wanted to rape a living, struggling girl rather than an unresponding body. It seems, then, that Mérimée inserted into his otherwise impeccable action a minor, parenthetical, flawed episode the action did not need.

Impeccable or nearly so; for the final stage direction, which tells us that Catalina faints as she passes her father's body, is also in my opinion a mistake. Did Mérimée, I wonder, lose his nerve for a second? Surely her last spoken line and even Ingol's epilogue indicate quite clearly that she will walk head high into the jungle and not be carried out by the Indian, limp and unconscious. Fortunately a director can ignore stage directions without the guilt he *ought* to feel when he mutilates dialogue.

One of the flaws of the first *Inès Mendo* play need not detain us, since Mérimée himself has indicated it for us in his Notice: too much happens too quickly. But in fact this little play shows the youthful apprentice playwright at every turn, creating, in effect, an anthology of artistic errors. He appears, for instance, uncertain as to whether Don Luis de Mendoza is a hero or a fool. The horror surrounding Mendo's profession of village hangman is melodramatically exaggerated. It is also structurally useless, since the social disparity between Inès and Don Esteban suffices as an obstacle between them. Another mistake is the extreme unlikelihood that only two of the villagers are aware that Mendo is their executioner. The episode of the chopped-off hand is sheer melodrama, as is, of course, the just-in-time pardon brought in by the king himself. The latter does call magnanimously for a surgeon, but that severed hand seems to shed no torrent of blood nor cause its owner much inconvenience. To go on detailing the flaws of this "undergraduate" work would be fatuous. I have translated and included it not only because of its status as a prologue, but also because it enables us to witness the astonishing leap into maturity that occurred when the young author proceeded to write the second of his two Inès Mendo plays.[37]

Some readers or spectators of this second play may wish that Mérimée had matured so far as to conclude it with a final, bitter separation rather than two corpses spread out on the floor. Of course, a diminution of cadavers could also have been recommended in its day for *Hamlet* and *King Lear*. Racine, late in his career, saw the beauty of ending *Bérénice* without fatalities. However, theatre is theatre, and we run the danger of becoming too grimly austere in our standards. A small opening can surely be allowed a dramatist for overdoing a turn or two and appealing to something a mite below our highest judgment. The second *Inès Mendo* play commands our admiration, and it remains a wonder that a playwright twenty-two years old demands so little indulgence from us.

Any account of Mérimée's few and minor mistakes needs to be balanced by a sampling of his many felicities. I mention a handful at random. Don Esteban, in *Inès Mendo*, caught between his anger at the neighboring gentry for snubbing his low-born wife and his shame because of her native naivete and clumsiness—he must, for instance, bear to hear her ask of the supercilious duchess whether Mercury is the first name of the king's minister. In *The Opportunity*, Doña Maria's anguish over her letter: "that studied handwriting...with its commas and periods! He'll believe that I'm copying phrases out of a novel"; the grotesque contrast between her life-and-death torment and Antonio's eagerness—an innocent one, after all—to have his cup of chocolate with Mother Superior; the grating blend of hatred and generosity in Maria's offer of help to her unwitting rival. In *Carvajal's Family*, Mérimée's depiction of the utter abjection of the victim-wife, and Carvajal's haunted sense that he is growing old and possibly impotent. In *The Gilded Coach,* the Viceroy of Peru unable to recall the names of the provinces he rules—"why don't

---

37. These remarks will explain why I decided to place the *Inès Mendo* plays as the last of the series in this volume instead of the first, where they belong chronologically. By composing a short prologue to the second play, I have also made it possible for a director to dispense with the "Defeat of Prejudice."

all the Indians speak Spanish?"—and that most alive character who never appears on stage at all, the matador Ramon. A large gallery of colorful and believable characters observed with cool precision, brisk dialogue, expert pacing and tempo, riveting actions, penetrating and unsentimental intelligence—such are the ingredients of Mériméan drama. We note, incidentally, that the supernatural element is altogether missing from it; it was only in some of the tales that it began to appear; the plays remain strictly earthbound. Furthermore and significantly, unlike Musset, Mérimée never experienced the urge to be a poet.[38] It is true that he printed—anonymously—a set of fake Illyrian ballads in 1827, but these were "objective" and dramatic poems. Mérimée was free of the fundamental egotism that goes into the making of self-expressive poetry. He inquired into others, not into himself. The fates, in short, had destined him for drama, and he kept the gifts he brought to this art finely honed when he converted himself into a teller of dramatic stories.

*

Mérimée must have been pleasantly if modestly aware of this talent of his, for he quietly returned to playwriting twenty years after the second edition of *The Theatre of Clara Gazul* and eight years after the third. The last surviving plays we have from his pen, *The Two Legacies* and *The Beginnings of an Adventurer*, prove at any rate that his dramatic powers were intact or even, arguably, improved. He saw to it in 1850 that both works were published, and three years later, despite the rout of *The Gilded Coach* from the stage, he had them reprinted. Admittedly, *The Beginnings of an Adventurer* is no more than an admirable prologue to a tragedy about the False Dmitri which he never wrote—one that needed to be as lengthy as *La Jacquerie* in order to be a fully fledged play.[39] Mérimée was working on a straightforward history of the short-lived career of this impostor, who made Russia believe for awhile that he was Ivan the Terrible's son, presumed murdered in his infancy. Since little was known about the early stages of Dmitri's rise to power, Mérimée decided to invent a good story as a prelude to the known facts. And a good story it is, dramatized with the full clarity of intellect, the verve, and the acute sense of the concrete Mérimée had displayed in his account of the French

---

38. In no fewer than three of his plays, songs or ballads are given in prose instead of verse, Mérimée not troubling himself to look for rhymes.

39. Torsos are prized when they are sculptures; much less so when they are plays.

peasant uprising. Still, the dramatic tale is aborted just when we want more of it; hence, although the play is not a fragment in the usual sense, it will perhaps not do for the Mérimée festival I evoked at the start. It remains, however, a rousing *spectacle dans un fauteuil.*[40]

Quite different is the position of *Les Deux héritages*. Here the injustice done to Mérimée by posterity is especially flagrant, for this play has been reprinted only once since the 1853 edition and has never been produced as far as I can determine. Mérimée hoped to interest the national theatre in producing his new *"petite drôlerie,"* but was quickly discouraged by the circle of professional readers to whom he proposed it. Hippolyte Taine, in his fine short study of Mérimée after the latter's death, spoke highly of the play—together, incidentally, with Les Mécontents. "All the details strike home and are loaded with meaning; it is the way of great painters to draw an unforgettable figure with five or six strokes of the pencil."[41] But most writers on Mérimée fail even to mention this comedy, and those who do dismiss it. Two typical comments will suffice to give the general tone. "It is not," says A. W. Raitt, "a very distinguished work, and one wonders quite what impelled [Mérimée] to write this mild domestic comedy."[42] As for the editors of the Pléiade edition, after wondering why Taine admired the play, they write it off as "one of those mediocre comedies of manners, of which the epoch produced so many. The writers of that time imagined that after the temporary reign of romantic drama...the theatre had at last found its equilibrium in a kind of vaguely moralizing bourgeois drama.... It may be that Mérimée shared in this illusion for a moment."[43]

The plain fact of the matter is that *Les Deux héritages* is neither a mild domestic comedy nor a vaguely moralizing bourgeois drama. It is not mild but biting. It is not vague but precise. It does not moralize: Mérimée never moralizes. It does show us the high bourgeoisie (hardly a crime), but one of its main characters is a marquise, and a very important secondary one is a chorus girl. And here it should be noted that, wherever he situates his works—in the Paris of his own day, in deepest Russia, in the

40. In the latter part of his life, Mérimée plunged with enthusiasm into the study of the Russian language, Russian literature and Russian history. He admired Pushkin, translated Gogol's *Inspector General*, was friendly with Turgenev, and published a variety of articles on Russian authors.

41. Taine 1874, p. xxiv.

42. Raitt 1970, p. 248.

43. Mallion and Salomon 1978, p. xxxvii.

Andes, or anywhere else—Mérimée's touch is equally convincing whether he portrays the aristocracy, the bourgeoisie, chorus girls, poor soldiers, ruffians, innocent heroines, trembling wives, the bold, the timid, the devout, the blasphemers, the hypocrites, the fools and even—what is most difficult—the kind-hearted. This felicity does not fail him in *Les Deux héritages*, which offers us an authentic hero, acceptable as such even to the cynical reader of our day. We believe in Colonel de Sacqueville (the Don Quichotte of the superfluous subtitle) because Mérimée does not sentimentalize him and does not put moralizing speeches in his mouth. This gentleman (significantly of or near Mérimée's own age) has returned to Paris after fourteen years of warfare in North Africa.[44] His first visit is to the contrasting character of the play: his nephew, Louis de Sacqueville, a breezy fellow, charmingly unscrupulous in his ambition to be elected deputy for a Breton district he cares nothing about, and make a profitable marriage on the way. This portrait of a young man "on the make," which retains its unfading freshness and relevance, manages to be comical without turning into caricature—without, in other words, involving a loss of realism.

The good colonel has come to Paris at this particular time because the woman he has loved all his life, the Marquise de Montrichard, is recently widowed. The marquise's strict virtue had kept their love from being consummated. Sadly, the colonel discovers that while she is still a beautiful and elegant woman, she has turned into a *dévote*, credulous, conventional, and stupidly attached to a superbly delineated schemer who obsequiously serves himself in serving all the worthy charitable causes dear to the elite. Another exquisitely drawn portrait is that of the Marquise's brilliant daughter, who mocks her mother's pieties and has the good sense to see through young Louis, to whom she has been half engaged, and fall in love with the older man—who has the good sense gently to decline. But Mérimée's pencil is equally at home, on a lower rung of the social ladder, with Mademoiselle Clémence, the chorus girl who looks after her interests more successfully, in the end, than Louis manages his.

---

44. Mérimée shows himself implicitly sympathetic to French colonialism, an attitude that may put off a number of present-day readers or spectators, whose tolerance of political views other than their own in the arts is limited. For Mérimée, at any rate, the simple, tough army life represents an innocence hard to find in the *salons* or streets of Paris.

All this is handled by Mérimée with a profusion of subtle details—telling touches ("five or six strokes of the pencil" as Taine noted) that open large, disquieting vistas to the alert reader. Why then, it may be asked, was Mérimée bluntly told that the play should not be staged? Perhaps he was being too much his well-known self, that is to say, unbearably satirical about religion and its respectabilities. Perhaps, however, a little sentimentality would have made the satire digestible, but that was a concession Mérimée would not offer. When Emile Augier wrote *Monsieur Poirier's Son-in-Law* (produced in 1855), he saw to it that *his* young rogue, the Marquis de Presles, is converted to middle-class virtue in the finale; indeed, the young patrician trembles at the verge of taking an honest job! Louis de Sacqueville, instead, rides off to Baden-Baden, where he will be sponging off Clémence—two irredeemable birds of a feather. Theatre crowds wanted edification, and Mérimée remained unwilling to furnish it. Our own conclusion, in the meantime, is that far from having lost his touch as a playwright, Mérimée had shown that he could exercise it in the here-and-now with full effect and had no need to go to Colombia or Lithuania in order to prevail. To prevail, that is, in a manner of speaking, since, as I have reported already, the world has remained blind and deaf to the play.[45]

At this point a few words about *La Jacquerie* are surely in order, if only because this masterpiece has always oscillated between faint praise, contempt and oblivion. In the words of A. W. Rait, "lack of plot and unity, dispersal of interest, characters who are little better than types, excess of melodramatic devices, crudeness and confusion of local colour, inaccuracy of historical background—these are but a few of the reproaches heaped on a work which has only rarely been reprinted since 1828."[46] Pierre Jourda, the editor of the definitive 1931 edition of the play, gives it a relentless drubbing in his introduction, calculated, it would seem, to kill all interest in a work to which he must have dedicated several years of his life. Here is a sampler: "The reader's attention is too often

---

45. Together, *The Two Legacies* and *The Gilded Coach* would make for a perfect evening at the theatre, but the first of these has yet to be translated.

46. Raitt 1970, p. 70. Raitt himself, however, is one of the few defenders of this work, albeit a timid one. The passage I have quoted continues thus: "Yet when one reads it nowadays, it is strangely fresh in its appeal; that it has shortcomings is undeniable, but taken for what it is, it is more successful than some of Mérimée's detractors—and even some of his supporters—are inclined to allow." I do not know what Raitt meant by "taken for what it is."

dispersed, and, too often, does not know what the author is trying to say.... Not people but symbols are seen in action.... *La Jaquerie* has no action, no characters. One looks in vain in it for a plot or a soul.... [The plays shows] a series of scenes without marked unity, without psychology, where the depiction of customs remains banal and without depth, where the author has not wanted to deprive himself of sure but vulgar means of pleasing the public," etc.[47]

Of these objections, the one most often repeated was voiced early on by Mary Shelley: "We feel the want of one prominent character to concentrate the interest."[48] In my view, however, the absence of a single, or even a pair, of central characters is not in itself a fault; it is merely an unusual characteristic, neither good nor bad until we see the execution. Mérimée created what might be called a vast *field of action*, similar, incidentally, to what we find in typical major works by Bosch and Brueghel (e.g., the latter's "The Fair" at the Hermitage Museum) and many other Dutch or Flemish paintings, for instance the skating scenes of Averkamp. In *La Jacquerie*, the perfectly unified and coherent field of action—of deeply tragic action—is constituted by the doomed uprising of the poor and the victorious resistance of the rich, looked at impartially, without moral verdict, without "historical" tirades, without vacuous philosophizing—horror in all its concrete nakedness. Mérimée was bold enough to show that the poor can be as barbaric as the rich and that one is not a saint just because one is oppressed. At the same time, he made it equally plain that the rich amply deserve the revolts that seek to overthrow them. In any event, the reader remains firmly within the field of action from begining to end; it is the "one prominent character" Mary Shelley wanted. Not only is there no dispersal of interest; surely Mérimée would have made a grave mistake had he focused the action on one, two, or even three central personages or episodes. He chose to be everywhere in order to "prove" that carnage and futility are everywhere.

As for the accusation of melodrama, let it be clear—again—that dramatizing atrocities is melodramatic only if the latter are absurdly improbable, and *La Jacquerie,* however true or false to the documented uprising, is perfectly free of improbabilities. Let us read the daily newspapers for verification.

---

47. P. Jourda 1931, pp. xii–xiv.
48. Quoted in Raitt 1970, p. 84. Another critic calls *La Jacquerie* "a pretentious, heteroclitic accumulation of medieval local color" (F. P. Bowman 1962, p. 3).

Criticism has yet to catch up with this strange, ruthless, powerful work, the vastest and most ambitious product of Mérimée's dazzling outburst of literary activity between 1825 and 1830.[49]

*

Two questions that have agitated scholars since Pierre Trahard began to devote himself—with scant sympathy—to Mérimée's life and works concern, first, the writer's fidelity or indebtedness to the Spanish drama (the presumed family of Clara Gazul's plays), and second, the socio-historical accuracy of the plays he set in the Hispanic world. Let me begin with the second of these so-called problems, typified by the naive remark of the editor of the Garnier-Flammarion pocket edition of the *Théâtre de Clara Gazul*: "The Spanish atmosphere [in these plays] is not perfectly authentic. The lack of respect with which a viceroy of Peru is presented would have shocked the Spanish public."[50] A considerable number of similar observations could be cited, some noting Mérimée's hits, others his misses. Forgetting, without exception, that Mérimée was a playwright and that a playwright is an artist, they fail to inquire into the underlying question whether true, verifiable insights into the genius of an alien culture have any bearing whatsoever on the quality of a work of art. For if they do not—and for the present writer the irrelevance is patent—then the inquiry into the authenticity of Mérimée's depiction of a Peruvian viceroy of the eighteenth century and all other "problems" of this kind take place in an intellectual void.[51]

Mérimée did venture now and then into scholarship on Hispanic subjects; we have from him, for instance, a *History of Don Pedro the First* (1847) as well as scattered writings on the Spanish theatre and Cervantes, and it is obviously pertinent and necessary to judge these efforts from a scholarly point of view. But as far as his plays and stories are concerned, the pertinent questions lie elsewhere. Literary historians will note, for

---

49. One of its few admirers was Aragon, but he misread its bitterly neutral point of view in the light of his own politics. For an extensive study of the "epic" historical plays of the 1820s (to use Brecht's term) into which *La Jacquerie* fits, see Jules Marsan 1910, but Marsan does not even mention Mérimée's work! Anne Ubersfeld, as we saw in an earlier footnote (note 24), rightly calls it the *chef-d'oeuvre* of the genre, but without further comment.

50. Salomon 1968, p. 29.

51. The same observation applies to *La Jacquerie*, for Jourda and others sharply *reproach* Mérimée for historical inaccuracies or omissions in this work.

instance, that although motifs drawn from Spain had been common in French drama since the seventeenth century, the Americas seldom appeared in French plays. However, the War of Liberation led by Simón Bolívar in the 1820s created a fashion in Paris. For liberals, Bolívar was the hero to brandish at Louis XVIII and Charles X. The carving of new independent nations out of a colonial empire excited liberal spirits. At the same time, the accounts of geographers and other travellers were eagerly listened to or read. Thus it is of interest that Mérimée was riding a wave when he set one play in Colombia, another in Peru, and a third—with something of a stretch but still flirting with the Americas—in Cuba. It is also worthy of note that the year of Bolívar's death (1830) marks the time when Mérimée ceased to exploit Latin American settings for his literary work. Be that as it may, it is known, and of interest to the literary historian, that he was a voracious reader who delighted in immersing himself in studies about the places in which he chose to set his plays and stories and, specifically, that he was a friend of Dr. Roulin, who talked and wrote about his travels in and around Peru.[52]

But when all this is recorded, we return to the essential argument that Mérimée's task as an artist was to exploit his materials for works of art, whether or not, in the process, he acted with the responsibility of a historian. He might have claimed with Schiller that history must toe *his* line. Incidentally, though Schiller wrote the grand epic drama of Switzerland, redolent of mountain, pastureland, lakes, and folk, he never set foot in the country; he only read about it and went on to play *very* imaginatively with whatever he had read. And we need hardly dwell on his praiseworthy crimes against English history in *Maria Stuart* and Spanish history in *Don Carlos*. Mérimée's procedure was identical. He did not visit the overseas Spanish possessions, and his first journey to Spain took place, significantly and as though facetiously, *after* publishing all his Hispanic plays. All the same, like Schiller, he succeeded in imparting to his works a sense of place—call it an illusion if you will—that is missing, for instance, from the Messina of *Much Ado About Nothing* or the Poland of *La Vida es sueño*. Mérimée had done his homework and picked successfully the colorful details he needed, or else invented them in the right spirit. Why should we trouble to sift what is true from what is imaginary or erroneous in his accounts? Such truths do nothing to determine the power and intellectual significance of works of art. As far as local color is concerned, Mérimée achieved something more important

52. See my Appendix to *Carvajal's Family*.

than historical or geographical accuracy, namely, the avoidance of operatic prettiness and sentimentality. His imagination sought out the exotic not for opportunities to dream up ideals but, on the contrary, for occasions to paint scenes of unrestrained passion and violence. The artist he was—not the historian—found there what was needed.[53]

The other pseudo-problem is that of Mérimée's faithfulness or faithlessness to Spanish drama. The too widely read Pierre Trahard was the first writer who made this question a prolix part of his life of the young Mérimée. His pedantic array of Mérimée's supposed Spanish sources would have amused its victim. More recently, an article by Jane H. Byers absurdly contends that, after having absorbed a welter of Spanish plays, Mérimée "strove to create a simulacrum of the Siglo de Oro *comedia*."[54] She finds, of course, that he miserably failed, for he did no more than pick up and mismanage from his readings a few superficial odds and ends, along with names, titles, and the like. "The end results...are simplification, willful deformation, and ironical debasement.... All aspects of the imitation are undercut, distorted, and debased to produce a general parody of the Spanish theatre."[55] This onslaught would also have amused Mérimée. Need one say that he strove neither to imitate nor to parody the Spanish *comedia*?[56] The latter is written in a variety of verse forms; it is divided into three acts or *jornadas*; it bustles with actions; it is peopled (to cite the males only) with mercurial, sword-happy youths, whether wicked or good, anxious fathers, and clowning servants; it defers prudently to royalty. None of this, to go no farther, appears in Mérimée's plays. Fortunately; for if our thoroughgoing Parisian author had in fact been possessed by the low-grade ambition to imitate or revive the Spanish drama, and had he succeeded, the result would have been a set of ignoble pastiches instead of the exuberantly original texts he in fact created.

---

53. We must remember, however, that Mérimée was perfectly capable of writing vigorously within a familiar—and accurate!—urban setting: witness *Les Deux héritages* and a moving tale like *Arsène Guillot,* which takes place in and near the church of Saint-Roch on the rue Saint-Honoré.

54. So Mérimée himself claimed on behalf of Clara Gazul in the facetious Notice to the first part of *Inès Mendo,* as the reader of this volume will see. Not everyone has understood his jokes.

55. Byers 1984, pp. 17, 31 and *passim.* Before Byers, we have Russell King: "He betrayed the Spanish theatre which he endeavoured to imitate" (King 1967, p. 70).

56. In Spanish usage, *comedia* refers to drama in general, comic or tragic.

To be sure, Mérimée made use of a few superficial traits of Siglo de
Oro drama, among them the practice of ending plays with brief epilogues.
Curiously, Byers has nothing to say about these besides remarking that he
"makes fun" of them. She fails to indicate in what the fun consists, and
yet this is the one "willful deformation" which is worth examining,
especially because the epilogues to Mérimée's tragic plays have bedeviled
a number of twentieth-century commentators. While Spanish plays of the
Siglo de Oro do not consistently feature send-offs spoken by one of the
actors, those that do so deliver either a simple farewell to the audience, a
request for applause, forgiveness for faults, or any mixture of these.[57]
Here, for example, are the last lines of Calderón's *Love After Death*, in
Roy Campbell's translation:

> ALVARO. Thus, without further waste of breath,
>   Here ends the play LOVE AFTER DEATH
>   And the famous Alpujarra siege.

And the concluding lines of *Life Is a Dream*:

> SIGISMUND. Thus I came to learn
>   That all our human happiness must pass
>   Away like any dream, and I would here
>   Enjoy it fully ere it glide away,
>   Asking (for noble hearts are prone to pardon)
>   Pardon for faults in the actors or the play.

Mérimée's epilogues are radically different. They do not "make
fun" of the Spanish type; they are just funny. The Spanish and the
Mériméan epilogue both transfer us from the tragic fiction in which we
have lost ourselves to our evening-in-the-playhouse reality. But in the
comedia the transfer is so self-effacing that, as we rise from our seats, the
tragic impression can continue to course unimpeded through our minds.
Mérimée's epilogues, instead, suddenly switch us from hot to cold, that is
to say from the tragic to the comic mode. A surprise laugh quarrels with
our immediate memory of the play. In other words, in the Spanish drama
there is continuity, in Mérimée rupture. As a result, the question arises
whether these epilogues obliterate the tragic impression retroactively and
definitely. Do they inform us in effect that we have been reading or

---

57. Of course, English playwrights wrote such epilogues as well; indeed, the practice goes
back to the Middle Ages and, beyond that, to the Latin comedy.

witnessing parodies of serious drama without, up to that final moment, realizing it?

Biographically speaking, we know why the caustic farewell appealed to Mérimée. Contemporaries and later biographers are unanimous on the subject of the urbane mask he usually wore to conceal the fire within. He was known to be very "English" in his manner—always cool, even when fighting and then reporting on a duel with a husband he had wronged. As he appeared in life, so he often showed himself in plays and stories. After expressing passion at its fiercest, he liked (or, as one now puts it, *needed*) to step back and pretend not to be involved. He practiced, in other words, the "Romantic irony" often discussed by German scholars—immersion and distanciation in rapid alternation.

This was the very strategy Byron had employed repeatedly in *Don Juan* and his other serio-comic poems, and though Mérimée had his doubts about Byron's manner ("he could never stop in time, and, in order not to lose a thought that has come to him, weakens the one he has just expressed")[58] both the man and the writer deeply influenced him. In *Don Juan*, however, the passion/cynicism oscillation occurs *within* the poem, sometimes in neighboring stanzas, and not infrequently within a single stanza:

> Sweet is the vintage when the showering grapes
>   In Bacchanal profusion reel to earth,
> Purple and gushing; sweet are our escapes
>   From civic revelry to rural mirth;
> Sweet to the miser are his glittering heaps,
>   Sweet to the father is his first-born's birth,
> Sweet is revenge—especially to women,
> Pillage to soldiers, prize-money to seamen.
>
> Sweet is a legacy, and passing sweet
>   The unexpected death of some old lady
> Or gentleman of seventy years complete, etc.[59]

In spite of this proximity, critics never brush the humorous part onto the serious one, concluding that Byron is being caustic throughout—that *everything* is a joke to him. Similarly, the special aesthetic of *alternance* of which I am speaking here occurs routinely, as everyone knows, in

---

58. Quoted by Dale 1966, p. 50, together with other passages in the same vein.
59. *Don Juan*, Canto I, Stanzas 124–5.

Shakespeare's plays, as it does in Spanish drama. This alternance is, in fact, one of the defining differences between the classic and romantic literary modes. And again, no one supposes that *Hamlet* is a parody of tragic drama because of its clown.

All the stranger, therefore, that Mérimée's tragic plays, in which mockery occurs strictly and exclusively outside the text of the fictive action either as preface or epilogue, are regularly viewed as jests and parodies. We begin, unsurprisingly, with the *manitou* of Mérimée scholarship, Pierre Trahard: "Mérimée massacres his characters, plays with torture and death and seems to say: 'This has no importance whatsoever.' And in fact, you can be sure that a murder has no importance whatsoever for him: he is having fun with marionettes" (Trahard 1925, Vol. 1, p. 220). And here is a late example: "Let us not believe that [Mérimée] takes himself seriously.... He does not believe in his Inès [Mendo], while Victor Hugo does believe in Doña Sol. Death is a joke" with similar observations even for *L'Occasion* (E. Morel 1988, pp. 35–40).

Half a dozen other quotes of the same kind could be marshalled at this point. But the worst misreadings are those that reduce *Cavajal's Family* to a parodistic joke. Here the epilogue is distinctly less humorous than that of *Inès Mendo*. Instead, we are treated *before* the action starts to two hilarious letters (Mérimée's sense of humor was equal to Byron's); that is to say we are switched, this time, from the comic to the tragic mode rather than from the tragic to the comic, but the effect on twentieth-century critics has been the same. A chorus of voices, listening to one another, intone the mantra that *Carvajal* is altogether a jest. Leading the chorus is Pierre Jourda, whose reflections on *La Jacquerie* I have already noted. In the same volume, Jourda all but guffaws over *Carvajal*. "What was in Mérimée's mind," he asks, "when he joined *La Famille de Carvajal* to *La Jaquerie?*" The answer is clear: "No doubt he yielded, above all, to the desire to mystify the public once more and to present, with a serious mien...a caricature of the sort of melodrama the Parisians delighted in at that time.... Are you fond of exoticism, the worst abominations, incest, rape, torture, poisoning? They are all over the place. Do you like Pixérécourt? *Gaspardo le Pêcheur, Lazare le Pâtre* have not yet appeared, but *Victor ou l'Enfant du mystère, Céline ou l'Enfant de la forêt,* and *Le Solitaire* delight their audiences," and Mérimée is out to debunk such work. How do we know this? The proof (for Jourda speaks of proof) resides above all in the mocking tone ("*le ton railleur*") of the preface, coupled with a mocking passage *about* the play in a private letter which Mérimée wrote to Stendhal—Stendhal, of all men, with whom he habitually exchanged jests, spoofs, and ribaldry.[60] But Jourda takes the letter as critical confession. "Mérimée is having fun at the public's expense" and "We guess that he is having tremendous fun [*il s'amuse follement*] as he cleverly manages his progression of horrors." Startlingly, however, he admits that "very rare are those [of the author's contemporaries] who would have understood.... Stendhal perhaps." (P. Jourda 1931, pp. xxiv–xxvii).

Whether Jourda had actually read Pixérécourt when he wrote his commentary is open to question, since he gets his titles and dates wrong. The first two plays he mentions are not, as far as I can ascertain, by Pixérécourt at all. The true titles of the three plays supposedly delighting audiences at the time Mérimée supposedly decided to satirize them are *Victor ou l'Enfant de la forêt, Coelina ou l'Enfant du mystère,* and *Le Solitaire de la Roche-Noire,* and their respective dates are 1797, 1800, and 1806![61] But let that pass. I have already given a sample of a typical dramatic machine by Pixérécourt. The machinery of the works he exhibited closer in time to *Carvajal* remained unchanged. Mérimée's plays resemble them as little as they do those of Lope de Vega. To believe that Mérimée would have troubled and stooped to debunk them is to manifest a depressing blindness to the nature of the man and writer.

However, Jourda's references to Pixérécourt matter much less than the fact that the "proof" for his thesis is located nowhere in the text of the play; he can find it only in a preface which would seldom if ever be part

---

60. This letter of March 15, 1831, contains a volley of coarse insults aimed at the bureaucrats among whom he was just then working. The relevant passage is brief: "Be so good as to recall that...in the year of the Lord 1829 I edified the public with *Carvajal's Family,* a moral work if there ever was one, inspired by rubbing elbows with bureau chiefs and their wives. In it, sir, one sees a papa who, unable to persuade Mademoiselle his daughter to let him take what he wants, makes her swallow an aphrodisiac." (*Correspondance générale,* I, 90). In fact, Carvajal pours his daughter a sedative and then fails to get her to take it, but a joke in a letter hardly requires the accuracy we expect of scholars and critics.

61. In fact, the career of Guilbert de Pixérécourt or Pixerécourt (1773–1844) was coming to a close. According to the *Tableau Chronologique* he himself drew up for his *Théâtre choisi* (1841–1843), the first of the 120 plays in his list was performed in 1793, the last in 1838, for a total (according to his estimate) of 30,000 performances! Ten of his melodramas were produced in Paris between 1827 and 1829 alone. His name does not appear in Mérimée's correspondence.

of a performance,[62] spoken (unlike the epilogues) by characters who will not even appear in the play, and, worse yet, in a private letter outside the fiction. And to complete the absurdity of the argument, it turns out that almost nobody, in Jourda's own opinion, would have understood that Mérimée had written an hilarious parody.

It would be pointless to dwell on Jourda if his opinion had earned the reception it deserved. Unfortunately, it became the parroted view of nearly every subsequent commentator. A few examples must suffice. "*Carvajal's Family*, melodrama in the Pixérécourt manner, ruthless parody" (Baschet 1958, p. 41). "*Carvajal's Family* is a caricature, a pastiche of melodrama. The reader is warned already in the preface: impossible to take the author seriously.... For what he proposes is a game: to accumulate in the minimum of time the greatest possible number of horrors.... The characters of the play are puppets. But they are handled by a clever writer, and they amuse" (Sigaux 1963, p. xxiii). "*La Famille de Carvajal...* a deliberate and blatant pastiche" (King 1967, p. 67). "The particularly repugnant nature of Don José's obsession brings it closer to the point at which horror is laid on so thickly as to become comic" (Raitt 1970, p. 56). "If one has any doubt about the ironical intention of Mérimée, one need only read the second part of *Inès Mendo*, called *The Triumph of Prejudice*. Here, as later in *Carvajal's Family* (1828) Mérimée takes his inspiration from the melodramas of Pixérécourt only to parody them" (Moss 1980, p. 89). "*Carvajal* is a parody...a buffoonery" (Darcos 1998, p. 81).[63]

I have uncovered but one attempt to look for evidence in the text itself. It occurs in the introduction to the Pléiade edition of Mérimée's works. "*Carvajal's Family* was published within the same covers as *La Jacquerie*. This time the purpose of parody is beyond doubt. It betrays itself in the details of the dialogue, for example, in the question Don Alonso asks of one of his servants: 'Martin, as-tu du cœur?'" (Mallion

---

62. Directors can also omit Mérimée's epilogues, of course—as blamelessly as when they cut out prologues and epilogues when they stage Congreve or Sheridan. My own recommendation to a director would be to keep them in and keep even the brilliant prologue to *Carvajal* with full confidence that the spectators will not be giggling when the tragedy unfolds.

63. A more hesitant voice is that of H. D. Howarth. After noting the view of several critics that Mérimée was writing a parody of Pixérécourt, he finds that "the case does not appear to be proved.... It might be prudent...to keep an open mind about Mérimée's intentions in writing the Clara Gazul plays and *La Famille de Carvajal*" (Howarth 1975, pp. 115–6).

and Salomon 1978, p. xvii). As every French reader knew then and knows today, this "As-tu du cœur" ("Are you brave?" in colorless English) is the famous query of Rodrigue's father in Corneille's *Le Cid*. The parodistic effect of this citation is somewhat attenuated in that, contrary to the editors' statement, it does not occur as direct dialogue but in a *report* by Mugnoz to Carvajal, in the first scene of the play, in which that bandit repeats Don Alonso's words to a servant. Be that as it may, Mallion and Salomon implicitly promise more evidence, for this particular detail, they write, is only an example of Mérimée's humorous intentions. However, no other examples are forthcoming. Paltry evidence indeed! It takes more than one brick to build a house. The obvious verdict must be that Mérimée is guilty here of a minor, inconsequential blemish, a momentary lapse from good taste which occurs, fortunately, at the beginning of the play. Instead, his incompetence would have been monumental if, having decided to write a parody (a low ambition, alien to his spirit), the only jest he had found in his bag was that single "As-tu du cœur?"

Jourda was right in one particular: this naive misinterpretation of Mérimée's most powerful play was unknown to the author's contemporaries. Nor did anyone misread the seriousness of his other non-comedic works, their facetious epilogues notwithstanding. Furthermore, it occurred to no one at the time that *Carvajal* was linked in any way whatever—whether as imitation or as parody—to the egregiously complicated, maudlin, melodramatic, and dimwitted potboilers churned out by Pixérécourt, "who knew how to draw gentle tears from spectators by speaking to them with a strong voice of humanity, forgiveness and virtue."[64] The sheer silliness of this repeated linkage quite takes one's breath away.

La Famille de Carvajal appeared in June 1828. In May 1829 Mérimée published one tale of violence, *Mateo Falcone*, and in October of the same year another, more ferocious yet, *Tamango*. In November he brought out *L'Occasion*. These two plays and two stories form a coherent pattern of creation during what proved to be the most fertile period of Mérimée's life as a writer. They are brief, savage, complex, and all four leave the reader deeply moved though morally perplexed. They are as unambiguously, indeed classically grave as *Le Carrosse du Saint-Sacrement*, published in the same miraculous year, is certifiably comical. Always fearful of appearing "emotional," Mérimée distanced himself from his most passionate works by means of prologues, epilogues,

---

64. J. Janin, quoted in W. G. Hartog 1913, p. 36.

conversations, and letters. Their utter earnestness is in themselves—where, of course, it should be—not in the flippant words with which he presented them. The cover of a book is not to be mistaken for the book itself.

*

The blame for being a playwright largely unperformed, poorly known, and frequently misinterpreted goes in part to Mérimée himself. I have remarked already that his correspondence is modest and reticent. When he alludes to his own plays—ever so rarely—he does so in words of self-deprecation or self-mockery. The reports about the man tell us the same thing. He discourages the actress who has urged him, in 1850, to allow her to perform *Le Carrosse du Saint-Sacrement:* "I have just reread the *Carrosse* and I find, in spite of my paternal entrails, that it doesn't look like a comedy at all. The scenes are stitched together haphazardly [*sont cousues à la diable]* and a thousand defects, which pass muster in a reading, would become tremendous in performance.... I have not the least experience with the stage and feel myself particularly unsuitable to write for the theatre."[65] With letters of this kind, he undercut himself much as he had done in his cold-shower preface and epilogues. Besides, he subtitled his *Carrosse* a a skit (*"saynète"*) and labelled the tragic part of *Inès Mendo* as well as *L'Occasion* "comedies." One need not be a professional therapist to recognize that all these maneuvers are contrivances for psychological self-defence: you remove the target of enemy attacks by getting him to believe that you have demolished it in advance yourself. Is it necessary to say that Mérimée did not wish to be taken at his word? The same year in which he professed that he had no talent for drama, he was publishing a major play, *Les Deux héritages,* and trying to have it produced at the Comédie-Française, the *Carrosse* fiasco there notwithstanding. A year later he brought out *Les Débuts d'un aventurier;* and since these two plays had appeared in periodicals, he went on to publish them together in a book. These facts speak for themselves. The subtle victory he sought consisted in gaining applause for his accomplishments together with plaudits for his modesty. But because the world does not always catch on or comply, modesty can be very dangerous to one's reputation. If Mérimée had issued thumping declarations, bullied directors, newspapers, and censors, attacked the works of others and lauded himself in print and speech, perhaps he would have

---

65. Quoted by P. Trahard 1925, Volume II, p. 114.

imposed his plays at last on directors in his lifetime; perhaps André Antoine would have taken them up in his Théâtre Libre when he founded it in 1887, and perhaps Mérimée's twentieth-century commentators would have changed their tune to his own. Instead, unwilling to press his case, he turned to another literary genre for a quieter kind of success, became a conscientious civil servant, had himself elected to learned academies and decorated with medals, and even turned into a "lackey," some would say, of the Imperial House—another impediment, it may be, to the resurrection of his plays. So they continue to drowse on the shelves of research libraries, a few of them marginally available for purchase, all of them ignored by the world's theatrical profession, and their admirers (all but one of them, by my count) long gone to dust. However, the history of the arts is full of tricks, and there may come a time when Mérimée's best plays will be enrolled in our repertory of classics—at a respectable height in this angelic hierarchy—and people will have forgotten how very forgotten they had been once upon a time.

Selected Bibliography

I list here chiefly the works cited in my critical essay rather than all those I have had occasion to consult. Editions of the plays are included because the introductions to them constitute the main body of criticism of Mérimée as playwright. There is no "complete works" of Mérimée; even the Pléiade edition, now out of print, was a selection. Students of Mérimée can now consult Pierre H. Dubé's comprehensive *Bibliographie de la critique sur Prosper Mérimée, 1825–1993* (Geneva: Librairie Droz, 1997). Its 2,386 entries, most of them annotated, are arranged alphabetically by authors' names and excellently indexed. For computer users, the bibliography can be searched in a variety of other ways as explained in Dubé's Introduction. For later years, the tool of choice remains the annual PMLA bibliography. Also indispensable is H. Talvart et J. Place: *Bibliographie des auteurs modernes de langue française,* vol. 14, Paris: Chronique des lettres françaises, 1959.

Aragon, Louis: *La Lumière de Stendhal*, Paris: Denoël, 1954.

Baschet, Robert: *Du Romantisme au Second Empire: Mérimée*, Paris: Nouvelles Editions Latines, 1958.

Berthier, Patrick, editor of Mérimée's *Théâtre de Clara Gazul*, Paris: Gallimard (Collection Folio), 1985.

Bowman, F. P.: *Prosper Mérimée. Heroism, Pessimism, and Irony.* Berkeley: University of California Press, 1962.

Byers, Jane H.: "The *Théâtre de Clara Gazul* and the Spanish *Comedia*: A Case of Impudent Imitation," in *Hispanofila* (Chapel Hill, North Carolina), Vol. 27 (1984), pp. 17–33.

Combes, Marguerite: *Pauvre et aventureuse bourgeoisie: Roulin et ses amis*, Paris: J. Peyronnet, 1928.

Dale, Robert Charles: *The Poetics of Prosper Mérimée*, The Hague: Mouton, 1966. A thoughtful summation.

Darcos, Xavier: *Mérimée*, Paris: Flammarion, 1998.

Fischer, Walther: "Thornton Wilders *The Bridge of San Luis Rey* und Prosper Mérimées *Le Carrosse du Saint-Sacrement*," in *Anglia: Zeitschrift für englische Philologie*, Vol. 60 (1936), pp. 234–240.

Gautier, Théophile: *Les Maîtres du théâtre français*, edited by A. Britsch, Paris: Payot, 1929.

Gregh, Fernand: *Victor Hugo, sa vie, son oeuvre*, Paris: Flammarion, 1954.

Guth, Paul: *Histoire de la littérature française*, Vol. 2, Paris: Fayard, 1967.

Hartog, Willie G.: *Guilbert de Pixerécourt*, Paris: H. Champion, 1913.

Howarth, William D.: *Sublime and Grotesque: A Study of French Romantic Drama*, London: Harrap, 1975.

Jourda, Pierre, editor of Mérimée's *La Jaquerie, suivie de La Famille de Cravajal*, Paris: H. Champion, 1931.

King, Russell: "Prosper Mérimée: Attempts at Romantic Drama," *Nottingham French Studies*, Vol. 6 (1967), pp. 67–76.

Lanson, Gustave: *Histoire de la littérature française*, Paris: Hachette, 1921.

Levaillant, Maurice, editor of Mérimée's *Mosaïque*, Paris: H. Champion, 1933. This has an excellent account of Mérimée's first journey to Spain.

Mallion, Jean, and Salomon, Pierre, editors of *Mérimée, Théâtre de Clara Gazul, Romans et nouvelles*, Paris: Gallimard (Bibliotèque de la Pléiade), 1978.

Marsan, Eugène, editor of Mérimée's *Mosaïque*, Paris: Le Divan, 1930.

Marsan, Jules: "Le Théâtre historique et le romantisme," in *Revue d'Histoire littéraire de la France*, Vol. 17 (1910), pp. 1–33.

Meier, Harri: "La Carroza del Santo Sacramento de Prospero Mérimée," in *Letras*, Numbers 75–76 (1965), pp. 23–35. An important original contribution (translated from the German).

Milhaud, Gérard: "Un Théâtre sous le masque," in *Europe*, Vol. 53 (1975), pp. 47–58. This particular issue of *Europe* was devoted entirely to Mérimée; unfortunately, nothing of any worth was said about his plays.

Morel, Elisabeth: *Prosper Mérimée: l'amour des pierres*, Paris: Hachette, 1988.

Moss, Jane H.: "Mérimée et Pixérécourt," in *Revue d'Histoire littéraire de la France*, Vol. 80 (1980), pp. 87–89.

Parturier, Maurice, editor (with others) of Mérimée's *Correspondance générale*, Vols. 1–6, Paris: Le Divan, 1941–1947; Vols. 7–17, Toulouse: E. Privat, 1953–1964. For earlier partial editions and for later additions, see Dubé under "Mérimée," but also H. Taine *infra*.

Parturier, Maurice: "Mérimée 'fait de la Résistance' sur la scène du Théâtre-Français," in *Le Figaro Littéraire*, May 8 1948, p. 6.

Raitt, A. W.: *Prosper Mérimée*, New York: Charles Scribner's Sons, 1970. A sound biography—the only one in English.

Sainte-Beuve, C.-A. de: Vol. 2 of *Les Grands écrivains français, XIX siècle, Les Romanciers*, edited by Maurice Allem, Paris: Garnier, 1927.

Salomon, Pierre, editor of *Prosper Mérimée, Théâtre de Clara Gazul, suivi de La Famille de Carvajal*, Paris: Garnier-Flammarion, 1968.

Sigaux, Gilbert, editor of *Mérimée: Théâtre de Clara Gazul, La Jaquerie, La Famille de Carvajal*, Paris: Le club français du livre, 1963.

Stendhal: *Racine et Shakespeare* (1823, 1825).

Taine, Hippolyte, in Mérimée's *Lettres à une Inconnue*, Paris: Calmann-Levy, 1874.

Thieltges, Gerd: *Bürgerlicher Klassizismus und romantisches Theatre: Untersuchungen zu den frühen Dramen Prosper Mérimées*, Geneva: Droz, 1975. A major study, the product of genuinely original research.

Trahard, Pierre: *La Jeunesse de Prosper Mérimée (1803–1834)*, 2 volumes, Paris: E. Champion, 1925.

Trahard, Pierre: *Prosper Mérimée de 1834 à 1853*, Paris: H. Champion, 1928.

Trahard, Pierre: *La Vieillesse de Prosper Mérimée (1854–1870)*, Paris: H. Champion, 1930.

Trahard, Pierre, editor of Mérimée's *Théâtre de Clara Gazul*, Paris: H. Champion, 1927. This is the first volume of what was intended to be a set containing the complete works of Mérimée. Only three volumes were issued, however; this one and the two volumes cited above under Pierre Jourda 1931 and Maurice Levaillant 1933.

Valde, Pierre, editor of Mérimée's *L'Occasion*, Paris: Seuil, 1949.

Carvajal's Family

(La famille de Carvajal)

(1828)

> O malvado,
> Incestuoso, desleal, ingrato,
> Corrompedor de la amistad jurada
> Y ley de parentesco conservada!
>
> *La Araucana*[1]

> 'Twas strange
> How like they look'd! The expression was the same,
> Serenely savage, with a little change
> In the dark eye's mutual-darted flame;
> For she too was one who could avenge,
> If cause should be—a lioness though tame.
> Her father's blood, before her father's face
> Boil'd up and proved her truly of his race.
>
> *Don Juan*, Canto IV, Stanza 44[2]

---

1. In the epic poem by Alonso de Ercilla y Zuñiga (1533–1594) about the resistance of the Araucanian Indians of Chile to Spanish domination, Glaura, daughter of an Indian cacique, rejects the advances of her father's cousin. "Oh wicked, incestuous, perfidious, ungrateful corrupter of sworn friendship and the traditional law of kinship!" (Canto 28). Calling her a tigress, poor Fresolano leaps into battle against the Spaniards and is killed.

2. The fourth Canto of Byron's *Don Juan*, in which Haidée and Juan are discovered by the girl's "piratical papa," appeared in 1821. This epigraph prepares us for the resemblance between daughter and father that Mérimée will bring out in his play.

About the Text

The present translation is based on the 1857 edition of the *Théâtre de Clara Gazul, suivi de la Jacquerie, scènes féodales, et de la Famille de Carvajal*, published by Charpentier in Paris; except for a few passages, duly annotated, which are taken from the first edition—that of 1828, published by Brissot-Thivars in Paris: *La Jaquerie, scènes féodales, suivies de la Famille de Carvajal, drame. Par l'auteur du Théâtre de Clara Gazul.* The Preface is by Mérimée, the Appendix by the translator. Mérimée's own notes to the play are marked [M].

Preface

I found the anecdote upon which the following play is based in the treatise on New Granada written by the unhappy Ustariz.[3] Here is the relevant passage: "Don José Maria de Carvajal was descended from the famous Don Diego, colonel of horse under Gonzalo Pizarro, whose cruelty has become proverbial *(Más fiero y cruel que Carvajal).*[4] And indeed, he lived up to his origins, for there is no plunder, treason and murder he left undone in various places, both in this kingdom and the Gulf of Mexico where he was long a pirate. In addition he practiced magic, and to please the devil who invented it, he committed a number of sacrileges too horrible for me to report here. Nevertheless, he obtained his pardon by means of his hoard of silver, and having settled on *terra firma,* he made the viceroy forget his crimes by subjecting several savage and rebellious Indian tribes to the authority of His Most Christian Majesty. In this expedition he kept his own interests in mind, for he despoiled several innocent Creoles and, accusing them of conniving with the king's enemies, caused them to be executed.

During the time he was plying his trade on the seas, he had kidnapped and married a noble lady, a native of Vizcaya by the name of Agustina Salazar, who bore him a daughter called Catalina. He had allowed the mother to have the girl raised in the convent of Our Lady of the Rosary at Cumana, but once he settled at Yztepa, in the foothills of the Cordillera, he called for the girl, and presently her beauty lit an impure flame in his depraved heart.[5] At first he attempted to seduce her young innocence by giving her evil books and mocking in her presence the mysteries of our holy religion. Seeing, however, that these efforts bore no fruit, he resorted to diabolical guile and tried to persuade her that she was not his daughter and that her mother, Doña Agustina, had violated her conjugal vows. When all these infamous machinations proved ineffectual against Doña Catalina's virtue, Carvajal, whose choleric character could not long consent to the use of wiles, decided to use violence against the innocent creature. First he rid himself of his wife

---

3. See the Appendix.
4. Not Diego but Francisco de Carvajal (1464–1548), "known in the history of America as the *Demon of the Andes.*" Greedy, brutal, and merciless to the Indians, he was at the same time a jolly character by whom it was said to be a pleasure to be hanged. In an intra-Spanish conflict which Gonzalo Pizarro lost, the latter was beheaded and Carvajal, dragged from prison, was butchered by the populace—at the ripe age of 84. Gonzalo Pizarro (1502–1548), brother of the more famous Francisco who conquered Peru, became for a while all but king of that country.
5. Cumana is a town in present-day Venezuela. I have not been able to locate an Iztepa. The Andes form the wild background of Mérimée's play.

by poisoning her, as is generally believed. Then, locking himself up with his daughter and giving her a magical drink (which, however, could have no effect on a Christian), he attempted to ravish her. Driven to the limit, Catalina seized Carvajal's dagger and struck him so hard with it that the scoundrel died almost at once. A few minutes later Captain Don Alonso de Pimentel arrived with a force of Indians and Spaniards, intending to carry her away by force from her father's house. Don Alonso had known her in Cumana and was deeply in love with her, but becoming aware of what had taken place, he abandoned her at once and returned to Spain, where, I have been told, he became a monk. Doña Catalina fled, and her fate has remained unknown. The judge Don Pablo Gomez, who investigated this case, sought in vain to find her. Perhaps she took refuge with the Tamanaqui Indians: perhaps she was devoured by jaguars in punishment for the murder she had committed. It was noticed that on the very night Don José was buried, jaguars dug up his grave and ate the corpse."

(See the history of the proceedings against Beatrice Cenci)

It would have never occurred to me to turn this horrible story into a play if I had not received, almost at the same time, the two letters that follow.

First Letter

Sir:

My name is Diego Rodriguez de Castaneda y Palacios, commander of the Colombian corvette *Regeneration of America*, cruising off the northwestern coast of Spain. We have taken some pretty good prizes for a year now, but this doesn't prevent us from being damnably bored now and then. You can imagine what torture it is for people to be condemned to navigate day after day in view of land without being able to go ashore.

I had read that Captain Parry amused his crew while caught in polar ice by having his officers perform plays.[6] I wanted to imitate him. We had on board a few volumes of plays. We began to read them every evening in my cabin and to look for a suitable work. Sir, you won't believe how they bored us. All the officers were volunteering for watch duty on deck in order to avoid them. Characters, sentiments, adventures, everything felt false to us. Nothing but princes supposedly crazy with love who are scared to touch the finger of their princesses, even when they're holding them a cutlass-length

---

6. Sir William Edward Parry (1790–1855) attempted to reach the North Pole in 1827.

away. Such behavior and love-talk surprised us sailors who are used to brisk work in affairs of the heart.

For me, all these heroes of tragedy are nothing but phlegmatic philosophers, without passion, and with turnip juice in their veins instead of blood—people, in short, whose heads would turn if they grabbed a topsail. If now and then one of these gents kills his rival in a duel or otherwise, right away his remorse chokes him and he becomes soft as a mop. I've been in the service twenty-seven years, I've killed forty-one Spaniards, and I've never felt anything like that. As for my officers, there's few of them that haven't seen thirty boardings and as many storms. You can see why, if you want to impress people like us, you've got to give us stuff different from what the good citizens of Madrid enjoy.

I'd write tragedies myself if I had time, but, between keeping my log and running my ship I haven't got a moment to myself. I've heard that you're a stupendously talented playwright. You'd do me a big favor if you used your talent to write a play that we could perform on board. No need to tell you that we don't want anything vapid; on the contrary, nothing will be too hot or spicy for us. We're not prudes, and the only thing that scares us is pining and moping. If there are lovers in your drama, let them fall to. But why give you more tips? You get my meaning. When your play is finished, we'll agree on payment. If you like Spanish merchandise, no problem.

Aside from that, sir, you needn't fear that you'll be writing for people incapable of appreciating you. All our officers have received the best education, and I myself am not altogether an unworthy member of the republic of letters. I am the author of two works which I'm bold to say are not devoid of merit. The first is *The Perfect Helmsman,* a quarto published in Cartagena in 1810. The second is a treatise of iron cables. I am sending you herewith a complimentary copy of both books, and remain, sir,

Your humble and obedient servant,

DIEGO CASTANEDA

Second Letter

Sir:

I am fifteen and a half years old, and Mother doesn't want me to read romantic novels or plays. In a word, I'm forbidden anything that's horrible and fun. They say it dirties the imagination of a young girl. I don't believe a word of it, and since my dad's library is always open to me, I read as many books of this kind as I can. You can't believe the pleasure a person gets out of reading a forbidden book in bed at midnight. Unfortunately, I've exhausted Dad's library, and I don't know what's to become of me. Couldn't you, sir, you who write such pretty books, write me a very somber, very grisly little drama or novel, with lots of crimes and with love à la Byron? I'd be ever so grateful to you, and I promise to praise you to all my girlfriends.

Yours very truly,

Z.O.

P.S. I would love a bad ending, especially with the heroine dying unhappily.

2nd P.S. If it's all the same to you, could you call the hero Alphonse? It's such a pretty name!

Characters

Don José de Carvajal.
Doña Agustina, his wife.
Doña Catalina, his daughter.
Don Alonso de Pimentel, in love with Catalina.
The cacique Guazimbo.[7]
Ingol, his son.
Don José's chaplain.
Mugnoz, formerly a pirate.
Spaniards, Indians, Negroes, etc,

The action takes place in a sparsely populated province of the kingdom of New Granada, in 16**.[8]

---

7. The cacique was the head of an Indian tribe.
8. This Spanish colony (El Nuevo Reino de Granada) included present-day Venezuela, Colombia, Panama, and Ecuador. New Granada was in the throes of uprising and disintegration at the time Mérimée wrote his play.

Scene 1

(A living room in an isolated dwelling. Downstage, a table and torches, and a serving tray holding the ingredients needed to make maté or Paraguay tea.[9] Present are Don José de Carvajal, Doña Agustina, Catalina, Mugnoz, and Negro slaves)

CARVAJAL *(to Mugnoz)*. And then?
MUGNOZ. And then, sir, seeing as it wasn't enough to make him talk, I gave the rope another three twists.
CATALINA *(stopping her ears)*. Again!
CARVAJAL. And the rascal still wouldn't speak?
MUGNOZ. No matter how much I—
CATALINA. That's enough talk of tortures.... Be still, Mugnoz!
CARVAJAL. Why, is Miss Catalina the head of the household here? Can't I question my people without your consent, wicked little girl?
(He cups her chin in his hand)
CATALINA *(rising)*. You're free to talk about torturing people; I'm leaving.
CARVAJAL. No. I want you to stay.
AGUSTINA. And yet, my dear, Catalina—
CARVAJAL. What! Again stepping between myself and my daughter?—Catalina, stay I tell you. Don't be so sensitive. It's only a Negro.... Wouldn't one think.... *(To the Negroes)* Keep her from leaving. I want you to stay here. What a character! *(Catalina has rushed to the door, but the Negroes have barred her from it; she returns, seats herself with arms crossed. as far as possible from Carvajal) (Aside)* I like to see her that way. What a beauty when she's angry! Look at her bosom heaving! What eyes! Full of rage! She's as beautiful as a young tigress. —All right, Mugnoz, what were we saying?
(While the two men talk, Catalina recites Ave Marias in a loud voice)
MUGNOZ. I kept asking him to name his accomplices, because a man alone can't poison a dozen Negroes, but he gritted his teeth like a dead lizard and wouldn't say a word.
CARVAJAL *(looking at his daughter)*. A head like a goddess.... *(To Mugnoz)* That's because you were soft on him; you're too tender.
MUGNOZ. God strike me! You're unfair to me, sir. I did all I could, but a Negro's hide is tougher than an alligator's.

---

9. "*Ou herbe de Paraguay*" [M]. In a long footnote, Mérimée explains how maté was made, what it was thought to be good for, and how it was drunk.

CARVAJAL *(still looking at his daughter)*. Beautiful girl.... *(To Mugnoz)* So then?

MUGNOZ. So then, as I couldn't draw anything out of him, I returned him to his cell, his leg fastened in a block that weighs a ton.[10] Tomorrow, if you like, we'll burn him alive in front of the house.... It's the custom to burn poisoners, but if you prefer—

CARVAJAL *(absentmindedly)*. No, that's fine.... But, Mugnoz....

MUGNOZ. Sir?

CARVAJAL *(to his wife)*. Go join your daughter, madam; I don't like to be spied on. Leave us. *(To Mugnoz, softly)* You're not telling me anything about Don Alonso de Pimentel. How did he take my refusal? Have your spies found out anything?

MUGNOZ. All I know, sir, is that, for a start, he said to one of his servants: "Martin" (that's the servant's name), "are you brave? I'll be needing you soon." Which, in my opinion, indicates—

CARVAJAL. I don't need your opinion. What next?

MUGNOZ. He told the Jesuit, the one who's in our pay, "Don José de Carvajal refuses to give me his daughter; but she'll be mine by hook or crook."

CARVAJAL. We'll see about that.

MUGNOZ. Since then, Don Alonso has gone more often to see the old chieftain Guazimbo, and he keeps coming closer to our place when he goes hunting with that rascal they call Ingol, the chieftain's son.

CARVAJAL. Closer to us?

MUGNOZ. Yes, sir; close to your house. We find Indians snooping in the neighborhood night and day. They seem to want to know how high our walls are. Yesterday I saw Ingol making a notch on his lance. He was close to the wall; I'm sure he had measured it. This rabble deserves to be met with a volley from our muskets.

CARVAJAL. Good.... Very good.... I'm satisfied.... You can go now. *(Calling him back)* Mugnoz!

MUGNOZ. Sir?

CARVAJAL. We can't let this go on forever.

MUGNOZ. I agree, sir.

CARVAJAL. And I rely on you, Mugnoz.

MUGNOZ. Yes, sir.

CARVAJAL. I'll need to know next time he calls on his friend the chieftain.

---

10. A *"cangue"* in the original. Mérimée explains in a footnote that this consists of two blocks of wood that can be locked around a prisoner's leg; in short, a pillory for the leg.

MUGNOZ. I'll find out.

CARVAJAL. On the mountain path to Tucamba there's a split in the rocks, and heavy brush nearby....

MUGNOZ. I'm familiar with the place, sir, and I was saying—just talking to myself—"A man lying in ambush there one evening armed with a good musket ....."

CARVAJAL. Good.... We'll see tomorrow.... Go now.

(Exit Mugnoz)

CATALINA. At last he's gone!

CARVAJAL. Catalina!

AGUSTINA. Your father calls you.

CARVAJAL. Catalina!

AGUSTINA *(low)*. Go quickly, don't irritate him.

CARVAJAL. Come here, sulky.

CATALINA. What do you want?

CARVAJAL *(imitating her)*. What do you want?... Leave off this tragic air and sit down at this table. Come come, child, peace. Give me your little hand, Catuja. Be fair; shouldn't I punish a scoundrel who poisoned twelve of my Negroes and is costing me over three thousand piasters?

CATALINA. You're the master here.

AGUSTINA *(from the other side of the room)*. May I join you and drink our maté together?

CARVAJAL *(to Catalina)*. Always headstrong; never willing to say "I'm wrong." Come, kiss me, little rebel; it's an order.

CATALINA *(pushing him gently away)*. Let it be. We didn't quarrel, so why do we need to kiss? Mother, father is waiting for you to drink a cup of maté.

CARVAJAL. Catalina. I want a kiss from you.

CATALINA. No, your whiskers and beard would sting me.

CARVAJAL. Yes, I understand you. You don't like my black whiskers....
You'd rather feel the blonde ones of that puppy Alonso on your cheek....
So! She's all blushes now. You could light a match on her cheek.

AGUSTINA. My dear....

CARVAJAL. Who in blazes is asking you? Can't you keep your mouth shut for a second?—And you, Catalina, this sudden blush needs to be explained. What have you got to say?

CATALINA. Nothing.

CARVAJAL. I know you're in love with him.... I know it, ingrate; dare to deny it!

CATALINA. Yes, I love him.

CARVAJAL. You love him and you dare tell me!

CATALINA. Now you know.

AGUSTINA. Daughter!

CARVAJAL. Don Alonso, a miserable infantry captain... low born... a rascal....

CATALINA *(passionately)*. You lie! His family is as noble... nobler than ours!

CARVAJAL. Insolent! Is that how you dare talk to me?

AGUSTINA. Merciful God!...

CARVAJAL. Will you shut up! Hell and damnation!—*(To Catalina)* To dare to contradict your... to dare tell me I lie!

CATALINA. I did wrong, I forgot that I was speaking to my father.... I'm guilty.... But I've been so badly brought up!... I know nothing. I've been kept ignorant on purpose... in the hope I'd always be a child... that I'd be.... Oh my God, come to my rescue! *(She weeps)*

CARVAJAL. You apologize for your insolence by way of another insolence.

CATALINA. I don't know what I'm saying.... I'd better leave.... I'm wrong.... But I can't bear insults against the man I love.

CARVAJAL. The man you love! Your lover! So, you've prostituted yourself to Don Alonso? You confess it?

AGUSTINA. Holy Virgin, what is he saying?

CARVAJAL. Answer me!

CATALINA *(proudly)*. I don't understand you.

CARVAJAL. Oh yes, you're an ignoramus, are you? And yet Miss Innocence already knows how to make love.

CATALINA. I want to be Don Alonso's wife, and I'll never belong to anyone else.

CARVAJAL. I don't know what keeps me!...

AGUSTINA. Dearest Catuja, don't irritate your father.

CARVAJAL *(pacing wildly up and down)*. Very good, young lady, very good!—I see now what a serpent I've nourished.... You're a monster!... But as for your so-called lover... he won't have you, as sure as I live. Let him appear in this house, and try to speak to you and kidnap you....

CATALINA. Don Alonso is a Castilian gentleman.

CARVAJAL. And so?

CATALINA. He doesn't fear death in anything that concerns the woman to whom he is pledged.

CARVAJAL *(drawing his dagger)*. I won't allow you to dishonor my name!

AGUSTINA. Stop, stop him! in the name of our Savior!

CATALINA. Kill me! I'd rather die than live this way.

CARVAJAL. Heartless, unnatural daughter! *(He throws his dagger away)*[11]
Hell is in my heart!... I'm the most miserable man alive!—Everybody hates
me!—You'd like to see me dead, wouldn't you? *(To himself)* Oh Satan,
Satan, give me but one month of happiness, and after that I'm yours. *(He
paces a few more moments in silence; then to a Negro)* Pick up the dagger
and give it to me. *(He goes up to Catalina)* Die, ungrateful daughter! *(He
places the dagger lightly against her throat and then withdraws it with a
great burst of laughter)* Well! Did I scare you?
CATALINA. You've scared me more on other occasions.
CARVAJAL. No... you were scared, admit it, Catuja.... What! Silly girl,
couldn't you see that I only wanted to frighten you a little? It was a joke.
AGUSTINA. A joke! Oh my God! Dear husband, think of the harm you can
do to a woman with what you call a joke.
(Don José shrugs his shoulders. Silence)
CARVAJAL. This maté is vile. My wife must have made it.
CATALINA *(to Doña Agustina)*. This is another joke.
AGUSTINA. And yet, my love, I gave it my best care.
CARVAJAL. The moment you touch something, you spoil it. Now that
you're an old woman, you should at least know how to make a proper cup of
maté. You're good for nothing.
AGUSTINA. You're the only person who's ever said anything like that to
me, my dear. But the maté got cold because you waited so long to drink it.
CARVAJAL. And so on and so on. Enough, you babbler! What a pest to be
married to a woman ten years older than me.
AGUSTINA *(with tears in her eyes)*. It's true that I'm a few years older than
you, Don José, but not as many as you say.
CATALINA. My dear mother! *(She kisses her)*
CARVAJAL. We're all growing older. Maybe you won't need to bear my
sullen moods much longer.... *(Silence)*
AGUSTINA. I hope that we shall keep you yet for many years.
CARVAJAL. Tell me, Catalina, you'd really love me if I allowed you to
marry this Don Alonso? If it's true that he's a nobleman, as you say....
Maybe....
CATALINA. Maybe?

---

11. I have taken the liberty in several places of omitting stage directions which, in my opinion,
are better left to the director. Here, for instance, Mérimée instructs the actor to pace up and
down as if delirious.

CARVAJAL. How she opens her eyes!—That's right, I want you to be happy. Some day, maybe.... However, between now and then, Don Alonso will break his neck while hunting.

CATALINA. You're smiling?

CARVAJAL. I am. You know that Don Alonso loves to hunt.... He spends his life in the mountains, amid the chasms.... He could easily break his neck.

CATALINA. I understand your smile, but I'm hopeful all the same; Our Lady of Chimpaquirá[12] will pity me.

CARVAJAL. Your impertinence increases every day, in spite of your pretended piety.—Well, soon we'll see what happens.

CATALINA. God is my only hope.

CARVAJAL. Right! Pray to him, Catalina, pray to him, and let your mother pray as well that he may bring you deliverance from a tyrant, that he may rid you—

CATALINA. I pray God every day that he may touch my father's heart.

CARVAJAL. God.... Heaven pays no heed to a daughter who asks him for her father's death. I know you... but be careful! Don't push me to the limit!... Those who oppose my will—I'll crush them underfoot, like this! *(He flings a porcelain sugar bowl to the floor).* Have Mugnoz come to me!

(Exit Don José)

AGUSTINA. My beautiful sugar bowl smashed in a thousand pieces! But then, my dear Catalina, why do you talk so provokingly to your father? You know how violent he is, and yet you keep needling him. God, how you both frightened me! Yes, you're the image of your father, just as stubborn, just as irascible.—*(Lowering her voice)* I forgot that we're being overheard. We can't talk while these Blacks are here.

CATALINA *(to the Negroes).* Leave the room.

(The Negroes leave)

AGUSTINA. How she makes them obey her! Never would I have dared to raise my voice the way you did with them. Ah! Catuja, if you were a man, you'd make a mark like one of the conquistadores of this land!

CATALINA. I wish that heaven *had* made me a man!

AGUSTINA. For instance, why tell Don José that you're in love with Captain Pimentel? I know that at your age a girl looks at young men, but one doesn't go and *talk* about it. I noticed that your father always grows irritable

---

12. "This is the most revered image of New Granada" [M]. Mérimée misspelled the name, which was Chiquinquirá. The miracle-mongering image had been described in an extract from Stuart Cochrane's *Journal of Residence and Travels in Colombia during the Years 1823 and 1824,* which appeared in *Le Globe* in 1825. The image is named again in *The Gilded Coach.*

when you talk about getting married. It would grieve him if you left him, because he cares for you so much.

CATALINA. Cares for me so much! Christ!

AGUSTINA. Yes he does. In spite of his rough ways, I see that he loves no one but you. You'd wind him around your little finger if you behaved more gently with him. But you're always taunting him. He's as violent as you are .... You should be more careful. Promise me, my Catalina, to go to his room.

CATALINA. I? Go to his room?

AGUSTINA. And tell him, "Father, it's true that I love Don Alonso, but I love you even more."

CATALINA *(violently)*. I won't utter a falsehood; I don't know how to lie.

AGUSTINA. Oh, my child, a daughter must love her father, Scripture says so. And think how much he loves you, my dear.

CATALINA *(impetuously)*. He loves me more than you think!

AGUSTINA. Don't look at me that way, daughter! It's as if I saw your father!

CATALINA *(taking her hand)*. So this man frightens you?

AGUSTINA. This man!

CATALINA. We can't live anymore under the same roof with him. We must both leave this house. I want to be free, and I want you to be free as well.

AGUSTINA. Leave this house! And my husband, good God! What would he say if we put such a thing into our heads?

CATALINA. Answer me, mother! Can you bear to live here? Is not this house sheer hell for you? And for me!... Mother of God!...

AGUSTINA. I admit that if you were decently married and settled, I'd be happy to enter a convent, one where the rules wouldn't be too strict. Anyway, that's what I would do if Don José granted me permission.

CATALINA. You won't go into a convent; you'll follow me into a family where peace and happiness are waiting for me—something that is impossible here.

AGUSTINA. Dear child, you frighten me. Tell me the truth; do you want to be abducted?

CATALINA. Yes, abducted from shame and infamy. Heaven has given me a friend in my misery, a man who has never been false to his word and who has sworn that soon I will be free. This friend is coming.

AGUSTINA. Don Alonso! This is dreadful! Wretched girl! And your father?...

CATALINA. My father has left me no choice. I must either save myself or be lost. Mother, I beg you to follow me.

AGUSTINA. Where do you want to take refuge?

CATALINA. The cacique Guazimbo will shelter us.

AGUSTINA. Run to the Indians? Sweet Jesus! To the enemies of God?

CATALINA. They are better Christians than your husband, and to escape from this house, I'll run if need be into the savanna and into a tiger's lair.[13] No danger will stop me. And you mustn't remain behind. He'll kill you if I escape.

AGUSTINA *(astonished)*. Who? The cacique?

CATALINA. You'll come with me. You must. Swear that you'll come with me.

AGUSTINA. But—

CATALINA. Do you want to become the accomplice of a horrible crime?

AGUSTINA. Jesus! How you frighten me!

CATALINA. Do you want to thrust your husband into hell? And do you want to damn me to all eternity as well?

AGUSTINA. My poor girl is raving. Oh God, I'm so unhappy!

CATALINA. Are you blind, mother? You must choose.—Should I flee? Or must I become my father's concubine?

AGUSTINA. Holy Mary! Such a word!

CATALINA. Yes, my father is *in love with me*. My father is *in love* with his daughter. Now are you brave enough to run away with me?

AGUSTINA. But—daughter—are you quite sure of this?

CATALINA. Would a mere suspicion be enough to make a daughter believe her father is guilty?

AGUSTINA. God in heaven! I'll never again dare to be alone with him.... And yet... ah! Jesus! Maria! What I have heard!

CATALINA. Raise your hand to this crucifix. Swear to me that neither Don Alonso nor anyone in the whole wide world will ever hear the terrible secret I have just told you.

AGUSTINA. I swear.... Oh, my God!...

CATALINA. So then, mother, this very night, within the hour, Alonso will come for us.

AGUSTINA. Tonight! I'm going to faint.

---

13. If we wink at John Keats for famously confusing Cortez with Balboa, we may allow Mérimée to adorn the Andean landscape of New Granada with savannas and tigers. He could, of course, be twitting us. In any event, the recurrence of the tiger image throughout the play was certainly intended.

CATALINA *(looking out the window)*. The Southern Cross is descending toward the horizon.[14] Midnight approaches. When we hear a tiger's roar, it will mean that our friends have come, and we must go into the garden.

AGUSTINA. All the gates are locked.

CATALINA. They are bringing a rope ladder. I'll throw them a noose from my bedroom window in order to hoist it.

AGUSTINA. We'll have to climb down a ladder?

CATALINA. I'd jump from the top of a tower to be free.

AGUSTINA. Sweet Jesus, give me courage! —Are you sure that your father's asleep?

CATALINA. He must be by now. Come to my room. We've no time to waste.

AGUSTINA. Oh Lord, have pity on us! Saint Agatha, Saint Theresa, pray for me!

(Exeunt)

Scene 2

(A room with alchemical instruments. Mugnoz is raising the heat in a furnace with bellows)

CARVAJAL. Add some quicksilver to the mixture, and if the yellow color that we've been looking for so long appears, you'll call me. *(He walks downstage)* Not that it matters anymore. There was a time when these experiments interested me. Today, if I found the philosopher's stone, I wouldn't be a whit happier than before.—Everything bores me.... She hates me. Even if I weren't her father and were ten years younger... I'd still disgust her.... Alonso will die. Will she love me when he's dead? —Who cares?... She was born to make me miserable... so let her be miserable too. We're two devils that clash; I want to be the stronger one.... Why shouldn't I satisfy the most violent passion I've ever felt, I who know no other law than my desires?—Still.... Oh well! One more crime to complete the list, that's all. Buccaneer since childhood, head of a band of rebels, amnestied for treason, master of a domain got by violence... can I hope that this God whom people call just will forgive me? —Even away from Catalina, my behavior wouldn't change.... Repentance is foreign to me.... I am a *man!* What? I—do penance? Kneel to black-robed imbeciles... recite prayers.... No! Their paradise was

---

14. "This constellation is familiar to all those who have traveled in [South] America. During the night one can tell the time by its inclination over the horizon" [M]. A similar note is found in *The Opportunity*.

not made for me.... And yet... those damned ideas that linger from childhood!...—I believe what they say is true... I believe... but I can't act like them... my blood is hotter than theirs... I belong to a different species .... Which means... this Being created me in his justice so I could be damned.... So be it!... But a man has to look for happiness here below!

MUGNOZ. Sir, everything is evaporating. Another minute and nothing will be left in the retort.

CARVAJAL. Those masters of alchemy are fools,[15] and we the more fools for believing in their formulas for making gold. Put out the fire and go to bed, but first make your nightly round.

MUGNOZ. You can rest easy.

CARVAJAL *(looking off)*. Who is the man in black crossing the great hall?

MUGNOZ *(grinning)*. It's your chaplain, sir, who's been hearing the Negro Friday's confession, since we're throwing him into the fire tomorrow. I'm not surprised that you don't know your own chaplain, seeing as you're too smart to believe all the tales these humbugs tell us.

CARVAJAL. I recognize him now; he came here two months ago.

MUGNOZ. It's your wife that made him come; they're good for women.

CARVAJAL *(after some thought)*. I want to talk to him; go call him.

MUGNOZ *(surprised)*. The chaplain?

CARVAJAL. I don't like to repeat an order. *(Exit Mugnoz)* I've never said a word to him.—Let's see what I ought to do.... Here he is.

(Mugnoz shows in the chaplain, who bows several times to Don José. The latter stares at him)

CARVAJAL *(aside)*. I don't like the looks of him. He's a coward for sure. *(Aloud)* Mugnoz, leave us.... Sit down. What's your name?

CHAPLAIN. Bernal Sacedon, at your lordship's service.

CARVAJAL. You're pious, are you not? You're devout?

CHAPLAIN *(surprised)*. My lord!

CARVAJAL. You've read your Scriptures, haven't you? I read them too when I was in bed with a wound, but the devil take me if I understood a word they say.

CHAPLAIN *(crossing himself)*. My lord!

CARVAJAL. Don't be afraid, I'm not going to eat you. Tell me, have you ever confessed really bad criminals?

CHAPLAIN. Alas, my lord, I have.

CARVAJAL. And given them absolution?

CHAPLAIN. If they repented, my lord.

---

15. In the original: "Raymond Lulle is a fool."

CARVAJAL. Repentance.... It's what you call contrition, is that right?
CHAPLAIN. One needs to distinguish between attrition and contrition, my lord.[16]
CARVAJAL. That's neither here nor there. Listen to me. Repentance opens the doors of heaven, does it?
CHAPLAIN. It does, my lord, provided—
CARVAJAL. Come on, be frank with me. You consider me a great criminal, right?
CHAPLAIN. My lord!
CARVAJAL. Stop my-lording me, and don't have any fear. Talk to me as if I were your equal. Suppose, if you like, that I'd like to confess myself to you. Well?
CHAPLAIN. To begin with, my lord, if you wished to confess—
CARVAJAL. Answer yes or no.
CHAPLAIN. Yes, my lord.... I mean no.... *(Aside)* I'm shaking like a leaf.
CARVAJAL. Idiots who can't understand me! —In a word, what do I have to do to repent so I can be saved? What do I do to show God that I'm repentant? I don't care how harsh the penance may be. What I need is a violent remedy that settles it once and for all.
CHAPLAIN. First... my lord, you know better than anyone... what is fitting. I am sure that everything your lordship will do will be well done... but if it were permissible for an ignorant person like myself to give advice to your lordship... I would dare to point out that nothing pleases God better than endowing new places of worship. If you were willing, my lord, to build a pretty little chapel somewhere on your grounds with a small house for its incumbent, one who could at the same time be useful here... I mean who could—
CARVAJAL *(who has hardly listened to him)*. You monks, aren't you subject to violent, shattering passions? What do you do to drive them away from your minds?
CHAPLAIN. We pray, my lord.
CARVAJAL *(contemptuously)*. We're not made to understand each other. You may leave.
(The chaplain leaves, bowing respectfully)
CARVAJAL. Prayers! Prayers! That's all they know.... If he had told me to fight a tiger with my naked hands, I would have believed him... I would have hugged him... but no, I can't pray like a woman.

---

16. Attrition is horror of sin merely from fear of punishment but without love of God. Contrition occurs when the love of God is present.

(Enter Mugnoz)

MUGNOZ. Sir, there are men in the orange grove. No doubt about it. My dog growls and scratches at the door on that side.

CARVAJAL. He's putting himself in our hands. Let my men pick up their weapons and not make a sound before the enemy enters. Let's go.

(They leave)

Scene 3

(Doña Catalina's bedroom)

CATALINA. They'll be here any moment. A horse was neighing on the mountain. He's coming with his Indian friends.

AGUSTINA. My heart is beating furiously.... I don't know what I've been doing these two hours.... I'd like to take a few dresses along... but I'm not capable of choosing among them.... My poor head is so troubled, I'm dizzy, I don't see anything anymore.

CATALINA. I am taking only this relic, and these pearls for the cacique's wife.

AGUSTINA. What! your beautiful Cumana pearls for a redskin woman! What are you thinking of, daughter? *(A cry is heard)* Jesus!

CATALINA. They're here. Let me raise this light. It's the signal we agreed on.

(A few musket shots are heard)

AGUSTINA. We're lost! We're finished! These red demons are going to kill us!... Don't stay by the window, daughter, a bullet might reach you. Let's hide under the bed.

CATALINA *(at the window)*. What's happening to him? With all these shouts and this tumult, I can't make out who has the upper hand.... I want to be down there, at his side... to support him, to take him in my arms if he's wounded! The window is low enough, I can—

(She places a foot on the window. Doña Agustina runs to her and holds her back)

AGUSTINA. What are you doing? You're going to kill yourself!

CATALINA. Let me go!

AGUSTINA. No, no, you won't jump from that window, or else you'll drag me along. Help! Help!

CATALINA. They retreated.—Ah! That musket shot was fired from the mountain. If they were able to reach their horses, they're safe. *(She sits down)* God willed it so. What's to become of me now? I did my part; I did all I could. I'll wait for the worst with courage.

AGUSTINA. Nobody's firing anymore. God be thanked! But how many people died? I tremble to think of it.

CATALINA *(returning to the window)*. I think they managed to escape. Hush! Isn't this the sound of a distant gallop?

AGUSTINA. Yes, I hear the sound of hooves, farther and farther away.

CATALINA. They are safe!

(Enter Don José, carrying a musket)

CARVAJAL. Awake at this hour? And you, madam, what are you doing here?

AGUSTINA. My dear... sir... I was so frightened... that...

CARVAJAL. Some robbers came near. But thanks be to God, it's all over, they won't return, we killed them all.—Catalina, you're looking at me with your big raging eyes. Do you happen to know who these robbers were? You don't answer me. Would you like to see them? I'll show you their bodies. One of them is quite a handsome lad.

CATALINA *(stepping toward the door)*. Let's go.

CARVAJAL. Yes, let's go. *(But he stops)* It's not a sight for a woman to see. It would upset you too much.—Why are you smiling?

CATALINA *(kissing the relic)*. God be praised; he is safe.

CARVAJAL *(aside)*. She guessed the truth, the little witch. He did escape, but tomorrow Mugnoz will get him. *(Aloud)* Catalina, you musn't sleep here tonight; your bedroom is too exposed.

CATALINA. It's the quietest room in the house... and it can be locked from inside.

CARVAJAL. It will have to be locked from the outside too.[17] In the meantime, you'll sleep in Doña Agustina's bedroom.

CATALINA. Thank you. Good night. Come, mother.

(She leaves with Doña Agustina)

CARVAJAL. She knows everything! —She guessed the truth!... She taunts me.... She'll be mine, or I die!

Scene 4

(The cacique's hut, where we find Don Alonso, his arm in a sling, and the cacique Guazimbo)

---

17. This is how I interpret Mérimée's not entirely clear intention. In the original, Catalina says in a low voice, "there are bolts inside," to which Don José replies, "Bolts? We'll certainly have to put some on your bedroom."

ALONSO. I'm worried to death; I simply must go down to the plain.

GUAZIMBO. Your wound is still bleeding. Stay, and eat the corn of the old cacique.

ALONSO. What will have become of her! Perhaps she's already become a victim of his rage. The scoundrel!

GUAZIMBO. Alonso saved the old cacique's life, and the old cacique has touched his hand. Your enemies are my enemies. Direct my arrow; my hand will send it to its target.

ALONSO. I'm ashamed to expose my friends in a dispute that interests only myself. And yet—

GUAZIMBO. Hasn't the white chief shed the blood of my tribe? And that of my friend?

ALONSO. I shall summon my friends and their people. If you agree to join your warriors to mine I will come to your feast of war within several days.

GUAZIMBO. The red arrow will call up my warriors.[18]

ALONSO. So then, in eight days or less we shall meet here again.

(They take each other's hand. Enter Ingol carrying a dead buck)

INGOL. Where is my brother going?

ALONSO. To the plain, to seek out my friends and take vengeance against the white chief.

INGOL. By what way will my friend go down the mountain?

ALONSO. By the Tucamba path; why do you ask?

INGOL. Along that path a dog is lying in wait who might bite you. A Tamanaco Indian saw him and told me.

ALONSO. What do you mean?

INGOL. Tamanacos have eyes to see; Alonso and Ingol have lances and muskets to kill their enemies.

GUAZIMBO. Crush the serpent's head with a stone, and his venom is no longer dangerous.

ALONSO. So Don José has sent his men out to ambush and murder me.

INGOL. He will never see them again.

ALONSO. Let's go; I can't wait to meet them.

Scene 5

(In Don José's study)

AGUSTINA. You wanted to see me, my dear?

CARVAJAL. I did. Come here.

---

18. "An arrow whose feathers are painted red signifies war for most Indian nations" [M].

AGUSTINA. I'm ready to hear your commands.

CARVAJAL. Come closer. I don't feel like shouting myself hoarse; I know you're hard of hearing.

AGUSTINA. I hear you very well now. What would it please you to have me do?

CARVAJAL. Perhaps you haven't forgotten last night's events, madam?

AGUSTINA. I'm still trembling because of them.

CARVAJAL. Have you no explanations to offer me concerning this episode?

AGUSTINA *(troubled)*. I, sir? What could I tell you?

CARVAJAL. You're turning pale.

AGUSTINA. You have such a rough way... I mean such an imposing way of asking questions... that...

CARVAJAL. Some thieves climbed the walls of my garden last night.

AGUSTINA *(aside)*. I'm breathing again. *(Aloud)* Yes, dear, they were thieves.

CARVAJAL. I don't like to be interrupted when I speak.—Some thieves penetrated my house.... Tell me, are you acquainted with these thieves?

AGUSTINA. I?... Jesus! Maria! I, acquainted with them? Certainly not!

CARVAJAL. You're an impudent liar. I recognized these so-called thieves. You were waiting for them, I know it.—None of this crossing yourself and these grimaces that no longer deceive me.—I thought my honor was safe when I took a wife who was neither young nor good-looking. I was wrong. Old as she is, my wife gives night-time assignations; she waits for young lovers, not caring that they will murder her husband.

AGUSTINA. As true as I am your wife, as true as God—

CARVAJAL. Don't add blasphemy to adultery. I know everything.

AGUSTINA. Heaven is my witness that I never—

CARVAJAL. Silence, traitress! Your accomplices have confessed. Don Alonso came last night to carry you off with him. I know he is your lover. I have proofs.

AGUSTINA. Oh God! Don Alonso? You don't believe it yourself.

CARVAJAL. What gall! To deny the evidence! It's too late for these affectations of virtue. I know what you are at last; I see the blackness of your soul.

AGUSTINA *(clasping her hands)*. Don José, my dear husband!...

CARVAJAL *(fingering his dagger)*. You still dare to call me by that name!

AGUSTINA. Mercy! Mercy! In our Savior's name, I'll tell you the truth.

CARVAJAL. Speak.—So then, it was for you Don Alonso came?

AGUSTINA. No, my dear.... You know very well that he's in love with our daughter, and probably... he came to see her, but without her knowing anything about it.

CARVAJAL. So, vile as you are, it's not enough for you to initiate your daughter in crime, you also want to soil her virgin reputation with your cowardly slander.

AGUSTINA. By God in heaven and this image of Our Lady—

CARVAJAL *(drawing his dagger)*. No more blasphemies! Die!

AGUSTINA. Help! He wants to kill me! Help!

CARVAJAL *(grasping her arm)*. Confess your crime, or I'll kill you.

AGUSTINA. Mercy in the name of God!

CARVAJAL. You refuse to confess?

AGUSTINA. I confess! Yes! Don Alonso came to carry me off... since I have to say it.

CARVAJAL. This confession saved your life. But that's not all. Sit down in that chair, and tell the truth if you want to remain alive.—It is known to me that you have been betraying me for a long time, and that Catalina is not my daughter.

AGUSTINA. Merciful God! Catalina!

CARVAJAL. She is not my daughter, and I want to know who is her father.

AGUSTINA. Oh God, must I bear this cross?

CARVAJAL *(threatening her)*. Answer me! Who is her father?

AGUSTINA. Have pity for me!

CARVAJAL. You refuse to confess?

AGUSTINA. Catalina is your daughter....

CARVAJAL. Ah! You want to die! *(His dagger nicks Doña Agustina's breast)*

AGUSTINA *(crying out)*. Ah! I'm dead! He has killed me!

CARVAJAL. Will you talk?

AGUSTINA. My blood is flowing, I'm sure it is; I'll die.

CARVAJAL. So die!

AGUSTINA *(on her knees)*. Mercy! I'll admit anything you like, but swear that you'll spare my life.

CARVAJAL. I give you my word.

AGUSTINA. Swear by our lady of Chimpaquira.

CARVAJAL. The devil take you! I gave you my word. Go on, talk.... Who is Catalina's father?

AGUSTINA *(aside)*. What name shall I give?

CARVAJAL *(seeing her hesitation)*. Don Diego Ricuarte used to be seen a great deal with you.

AGUSTINA. Yes! It's Don Diego Ricuarte.

CARVAJAL *(playing with his dagger)*. I knew it. Here is a sheet of paper. Come to the table and write.

AGUSTINA. Write?

CARVAJAL. Yes, write what I'm going to dictate, or else this dagger will plunge into your heart.... Here is what I demand of you: that you disclose your crime to your confessor; when that is done, your only punishment will be to leave my house for a convent.

AGUSTINA *(aside)*. Thank God!

CARVAJAL. Write. Put the date. You know what day of the month we are —I never know these things. Now write: "Father... Reverend Father, moved by remorse and resolved to leave the world. I wish to relieve my conscience....."

AGUSTINA. God in heaven! How can I write—?

CARVAJAL. Is it red ink you want in order to write better?—Where are you? "I wish to relieve my conscience of the burden of a crime I have always concealed from you. I have betrayed the conjugal oath I had sworn to Don José, my husband. I have committed adultery with Don Diego Uriarte"—

AGUSTINA. Uriarte?

CARVAJAL *(furious)*. "Ricuarte!" Are you taunting me? I swear to God—

AGUSTINA. I'm only writing what you want me to.

CARVAJAL. Write. "He is the father of a girl named Catalina, who bears unjustly my husband's name. I ask forgiveness of God and men for the scandal I have caused, for which I hope to do penance in the retreat where I shall hide my shame. Help me with your advice, I anxiously await it." Are you done? Now sign.

AGUSTINA. Are you satisfied?

CARVAJAL *(after reading the letter)*. Tomorrow you'll leave this house; you will be taken to a convent. But if you spread the news of my dishonor, or allow in any way my name to be slandered, think twice, because my vengeance will find you even at the foot of the altar.

AGUSTINA. May I go now?

CARVAJAL *(showing her a side door)*. There is your apartment until tomorrow, and kindly do not leave it.

AGUSTINA. What! May I not kiss my poor daughter before I leave?

CARVAJAL. No; the child's innocence must not be sullied by the company of a fallen woman.

AGUSTINA. I want nothing more than to embrace her. I won't speak a single word to her if you don't want me to.

CARVAJAL. I'll consider it. Now go.

(He leads her out. Enter Mugnoz, wounded)

MUGNOZ. Where is he, so I can give him the wonderful news? He'll fly into one of his rages. He'll make my ears ring, but I hope he won't hold me responsible.

(Reenter Carvajal, closing the door behind him)

CARVAJAL. There you are! Well then, Mugnoz, am I avenged?

MUGNOZ. Look at what's happened to me.

CARVAJAL. What about Don Alonso? Is he dead?

MUGNOZ. Dead is it?—I don't know how the scoundrel discovered the ambush I'd laid out for him. Our position was a dream, my lord. All six of us were lying flat on our bellies, wide awake, each one with his musket, listening sharp and counting the minutes for our man to arrive. But those damned Indians had smoked us out. They're a wily lot, as you know. They had slunk like serpents around the bushes and rocks to where we lay without a thought in our heads. Suddenly, paf! a pistol shot from Don Alonso, together with a volley of arrows... and there they were on top of us before we had time to get up. Jack the mulatto, who lay next to me, got nailed to the ground with one of their big arrows; the other four are still lying there, all of them dead or wounded. Myself, after firing my musket without doing any good, I left the battlefield as fast as I could run, but I couldn't outrun Ingol's arrow. The bastard got me in the ribs, as you can see. For all I know, that hellish arrow may have been poisoned.

CARVAJAL. I don't believe it! You saw Don Alonso and you didn't kill him?

MUGNOZ. God almighty, I'd like to have seen you over there! Do you think it's so easy, my lord?... Anyway, his arm was in a sling, which proves that we gave him a present last night.

CARVAJAL *(coldly)*. Another time, then.... Go have your wound bandaged.

MUGNOZ *(aside)*. He doesn't look more stricken than if we'd drunk a glass of wine to his health. *(He leaves)*

CARVAJAL *(after a moment's thought, calls out)*. I want somebody here!

A NEGRO *(entering)*. My lord?

CARVAJAL. Go tell Doña Catalina that I want to see her. *(The servant leaves)* The old woman is locked up... we're free at last.—Catalina has guessed my love.—Let's now declare it. This letter will justify me. Cunning... that's a new part for me to act... and I don't know whether I'll be able to play the fox, I who am used to grasping my prey like a lion. Forward! A last attempt! If I can't win by cunning... all right... I'll win by force.—Here she is.

(Enter Catalina and Dorotea, a Negress)

CATALINA. You asked for me?

CARVAJAL. I need to speak with you. Leave us, Dorotea.

CATALINA. Dorotea, listen. *(She whispers to her)*

DOROTEA. Yes, madam, as soon as ever you call me. *(She leaves)*

CARVAJAL. Sit down. *(He walks up and down for a while in silence)*

CATALINA. I expected to find my mother here.

CARVAJAL *(stopping)*. Alas, Catalina, you see a very unhappy man before you. I asked for you so you can help me bear the griefs that are overwhelming me.

CATALINA. Father....

CARVAJAL *(as if aside)*. Would to God that I were her father!—Catalina, I must impart a painful secret to you... though I am afraid to grieve you.

CATALINA. I am accustomed to grief, but I understand nothing of secrets.

CARVAJAL. Catalina, a dishonored man stands before you.

CATALINA *(rising)*. In affairs of honor a woman is a bad counselor. Excuse me; I am finishing a small embroidery for our Madonna.

CARVAJAL. What! You won't spare a second to pity me... to give your advice to your... to me... to an unhappy man.... Stay, Catalina. I implore you.

CATALINA *(hesitant)*. Speak.

CARVAJAL *(seating himself next to her)*. I married for love, Catalina... but it didn't take me long to find out that I had made a poor choice. I have been most unhappy.

CATALINA. It's my mother you're talking about!

CARVAJAL. Listen to me. *(He draws closer to her)* Perhaps I'm to blame as much as she. I have a violent character, and in my fits of anger I'm apt to be unjust. Indeed, I must have often upset you, my Catalina... and yesterday again. *(He takes her hand)*. Have you forgiven me? *(Silence)*

CATALINA *(making an effort)*. You are my father.

CARVAJAL *(squeezing her hand)*. Hardly were we married when I recognized that we were incompatible; but I was far from suspecting the worst. I stopped loving my wife long ago; and yet.... Look, Catalina, read this letter, and tell me whether an honorable man can help feeling his blood boil when he learns of such infamy. *(He gives her the letter)*

CATALINA *(without opening it)*. Where does this letter come from? What is in it?

CARVAJAL. It's a letter she was sending to her confessor; I caught her writing it. You'll see that she betrayed me; you'll see that her accomplice was Don Diego de Ricuarte... and that he is your father.

CATALINA *(tearing up the letter without reading it)*. I don't believe a word of it.

CARVAJAL. What are you doing?

CATALINA. I know my mother!

CARVAJAL *(picking up a shred of the letter)*. Don't you recognize her handwriting?

CATALINA. I don't want to see anything. I believe nothing dishonorable of my mother.

CARVAJAL. I was like you for a long time, but proof is proof. As God is my witness, this awful discovery has plunged me into despair, and yet... at the same time I felt... I don't know... a kind of voluptuous thrill.... Oh! Catalina, it seemed to me that the affection... this lively tenderness you've always inspired in me acquired a new strength.... A father's love is a great one, no doubt, but there's another love that is greater yet.

CATALINA. Father!

CARVAJAL. Don't call me by that name; I don't like it anymore. It implies an idea of respect that I wish to remove from our intimacy, our love... yes, my Catalina.

CATALINA *(rising in terror)*. What am I hearing?... You frighten me!

CARVAJAL. Stay, stay, my good Catuja, my girl. Doña Agustina has asked me for permission to retire to a convent. I will be alone. How sweet it would be for me to have at my side an angel who would direct my actions, temper the violence of my character, give me an example of virtue.... Yes, my dearest one, only you in the whole world can be that angel... only you can make me happy. Don't reject a love that no one can equal.

CATALINA *(on her knees)*. Father!... kill me, do, I beg you, but don't speak these horrible words!

CARVAJAL. Oh my adorable girl, let me press you to my heart!...

CATALINA *(violently freeing herself)*.[19] Look at this Madonna, she sees you. Are you not afraid that a volcano will open underneath this house to swallow you up?

CARVAJAL. Ah! For you I'd leap into the flames of hell.

CATALINA. Kill me or let me run from this house.

CARVAJAL. Listen to me!

CATALINA *(near the door)*. I can't! You revolt me!

CARVAJAL *(stopping her)*. Do you think I'm your father? No, my Catalina, no, I swear I'm not. If I were your father, would I feel this passion for you? This passion tells me that you're not of my blood.—I see, however, that your

---

19. For the 1842 and subsequent editions, Mérimée toned down this episode. Carvajal merely exclaims, "If you could read my heart!" followed by the stage direction for Catalina: "rising and moving away in horror." The *princeps* is of course preferable and is hereby restored.

heart is full of that feather-light youngster; his embroidered coat has seduced you; you haven't reflected on a young man's superficiality and inconstancy. Ah! If you wanted a love that never changes, more burning than the lava that flows from a volcano.... Where would you find such a love elsewhere than in my heart? I implore you, take pity on me, my love!

CATALINA *(wildly freeing herself)*. Don't hold me back any longer! I must get out! Don't hold me back... or I don't know what I'll do....

CARVAJAL *(still holding her)*. So be it! Leave if you wish; but I have a few more words for you. You know me, and you know that I'm in love with you; never have I felt a more violent passion.... And no law has ever stood in the way of my desires.... Look, look at this arm: it can lift two muskets with the greatest ease. Compare it to yours, so fine and white.... I've said enough. Think it over. You can go now.

CATALINA *(facing him)*. Now is your turn to listen to me. I am your daughter, and you know it. You have given me your energy and your courage. My arm is weak, but I carry a dagger. As long as I have strength enough to hold this dagger and to defend myself with this dagger ... I will not be afraid of you.

(She leaves)

CARVAJAL *(with a savage laugh)*. Fine! Strike your father! I'd rather triumph over a tigress than a lamb. Trump me, do!... By the bones of old Carvajal, I'll be pleased.... And if I'm the winner, we'll give birth to a race of demons.

Scene 6

(Doña Agustina's room. Doña Agustina lies in her bed. Mugnoz and the chaplain stand beside it)

AGUSTINA. Father, do you believe that I am in a state of grace?

CHAPLAIN. I firmly believe it.

AGUSTINA. I hope that your words of consolation will give me the strength to bear this terrible moment.—Oh! when I think of it, I feel a cold sweat all over my body.

CHAPLAIN. My poor lady!

AGUSTINA. Is there no hope? No hope? *(Silence)* —Do you think I have a few hours of life left?

CHAPLAIN. I'm afraid—

MUGNOZ. Look here, I spent twelve years at sea as carpenter and doctor on the *Mombar*, and I've heard the death-rattle of many a brave buccaneer. I'm an expert. And I'll tell you exactly—

AGUSTINA. Oh! Don't tell me anything, Mugnoz. I want death to come to me without my knowing it.—My God, my God! Must one suffer so much before appearing before thee? And all that pain over nothing—because of a glass of lemonade!

MUGNOZ *(aside)*. Yes, but it was well spiced.

CHAPLAIN. The danger of death that accompanies all our actions, even the most trivial ones, must teach us how careful we need to be to walk in the ways of God, since at any moment he can call us to him.

AGUSTINA. Oh! I'm in such pain! My chest is on fire. Mugnoz, can't you give me something to ease this jabbing pain?

MUGNOZ *(handing her a cup)*. Drink this. It will help you. *(Low to the chaplain)* Stop making faces, you. Stick to the spiritual side of things if you please.

AGUSTINA *(feebly)*. Oh God, if my agony must be a long one, give me courage.—Mugnoz, why isn't my husband here? You should ask him to hurry.

MUGNOZ. He'll be coming.

AGUSTINA *(to the chaplain)*. Father... come closer to my bed... closer still.... My daughter... do you know where she is?

MUGNOZ. What is she asking?

CHAPLAIN. She would like to see her daughter.

MUGNOZ. She's gone to the nuns of the Rosary at Cumana. I've told you more than once.

CHAPLAIN *(making a negative sign with his finger)*. Yes, madam, I saw her leave.

AGUSTINA. Alas! My poor daughter!... And my husband who isn't coming!... And yet I need to see him.... I need to talk to him.

MUGNOZ. Look, here he is.

(Enter Carvajal; the chaplain and Mugnoz retire to one side of the room)

AGUSTINA. Thank you, Don José... I thank you with all my heart.

CARVAJAL. I was hoping to find you improved, madam.

AGUSTINA. Ah! I'm in a bad way.... Don José... I am going to appear before God.... I don't want to be damned because of a lie.... But... you know very well... Catalina is your daughter... you never doubted it.

CARVAJAL. Pardon me if, in a fit of bad temper.... Kindly forgive me.

AGUSTINA. Don José!... Give me your hand... if you're not afraid to be infected.... *(Carvajal gives her his hand)* Promise me... it's a dying woman's request, Don José!

CARVAJAL. Any command you wish to leave with me will be faithfully executed.

AGUSTINA *(pulling him down; in a low voice)*. Be a father to Catalina, Don José! Swear to me! Remember that God's judgment is a terrible one.
CARVAJAL *(harshly)*. Your fever has made you delirious. *(He pulls his hand violently away)*
AGUSTINA *(catching at his coat)*. She's your daughter! You're her only protector! You're her *father!*
CARVAJAL. I have to leave you, but I'll return in a while to see how you are.
AGUSTINA. Wait, Don José.... Let me kiss her once, only once.... One kiss, and then she can go.
CARVAJAL. She's gone, she's in a convent.
AGUSTINA *(still holding him)*. To leave her here alone... and die without farewell! Oh my sweet Savior!
CARVAJAL *(aside)*. What a horrible sight! *(Aloud)* Let me go; I have to leave.
AGUSTINA. I beg you!... Ah! Why this dagger?
CARVAJAL. It's my dagger. You know that I always carry it.
AGUSTINA. Throw it away... it's soaked in blood.... Don José... have pity on her! That dagger....
CARVAJAL *(pulling his coat away from her, he joins Mugnoz and the chaplain)*. She's delirious; there's no hope for her.
AGUSTINA. Catalina... my daughter.... Oh! take that dagger away. Blood... knives... Save me! Save me!
CARVAJAL *(aside)*. That clumsy rascal Mugnoz. This woman's agony is horrid.
MUGNOZ *(low)*. If you want me to, I'll pull the pillow from under her, and then it'll be over in a minute.
CARVAJAL. No; let her die easy. *(To the chaplain)* I place her in your care. *(He leaves)*
CHAPLAIN *(presenting a crucifix to Doña Agustina)*. Madam, behold him who suffered so much for you. What is your pain compared to that of Jesus Christ?
AGUSTINA. Take that dagger away!
MUGNOZ. Now she's mistaking the crucifix for a dagger because it's shiny.
CHAPLAIN. Madam....
AGUSTINA. Mercy! Mercy!
CHAPLAIN. Think....
MUGNOZ. Don't torment her anymore; she's done her confession and is ready to set sail for the other world; what else is there for you to do?
CHAPLAIN. She's staring out and her body is stiff.

MUGNOZ. There's a gurgle left... and she's still talking about daggers.
AGUSTINA. Jesus!
MUGNOZ. A spasm... there goes another! It's all over. That's right, her
pulse is dead; she has shipped out for keeps.
CHAPLAIN. May God receive her soul! *(Aside)* The horrors I've had to
witness in this house!
(They leave)

Scene 7

(The same as Scene 5. Carvajal is alone)

CARVAJAL. It was useless.... I was sorry for the woman.... She was no
trouble here.... I don't like to see a weak creature suffer.... Better if I'd put a
good bullet through her head[20]—but what's done is done; let's not think
about it anymore.... A man should never repent.... A woman more or less on
earth, what does it matter?... As for Catalina... what difference is there
between feeling and carrying out this violent desire?... Desiring her, I am
guilty and unhappy; possessing her, I am guilty and happy... so why hesitate?
And yet, I don't know what it is inside me... my courage fails me, and day
after day I postpone the deed I keep planning.... What if nature were going to
betray me? *(With a bitter laugh)* The shame of it![21] They say there are saints
who.... Well, if necessary, I'd drink the same infernal brew I've prepared for
her.... If afterward I die... what of it? I will have been happy. Yes! I'll taste
that diabolic happiness.—And after that, there'll be none left for me on earth.
(Enter Mugnoz)
MUGNOZ. Oh my lord!...
CARVAJAL. What's the matter, Mugnoz? Why this frightened look?
MUGNOZ. Devils in hell! You wouldn't believe me, sir, when I predicted
that this rabble of Indians was going to play you a dirty trick. We could have
saved our skins if you'd called in twenty rascals like myself from the coast,
but your Blacks!... The bastards don't know how to handle either a musket or
a pike.
CARVAJAL. Are you going to tell me what the Indians have done?

---

20. I have again preserved the 1828 reading. Thereafter Mérimée reduced this thought to a
mere "I should have—"
21. This curt but powerful notion, stated in 1828, was prudishly obscured in 1842 to : "What if
nature, the voice of blood, as they call it, performed a miracle?.. I am forty-six years old....
They say there are saints who" etc.

MUGNOZ. Go up to your observatory, by God, and you'll see what they've done. There's more than two hundred of them two musket shots away from your gate, and the worst of it is that I've seen a score of white men among them, obviously brought up by Don Alonso.

CARVAJAL *(aside)*. Yesterday I turned forty-six. My time has come.

MUGNOZ. It's heavy weather for us, and we have to hang tight on the helm; what are your orders?

CARVAJAL. There are only two hundred of them, you said?

MUGNOZ. Christ's gut! That's enough to chop off every head in this house. Do you know how Indians go about cutting off an honest Spaniard's head? They lean on his stomach with their foot and take hold of his hair. Two strokes of their machete, and the head winds up in their hand.

CARVAJAL *(absent-mindedly)*. The Negroes have to be armed.

MUGNOZ. I didn't wait for you to say so, my lord. But the rogues are turning pale under their black skins. If only I had a couple of two-pounders to defend the gate!... Or just the bow-piece we threw overboard when that awful storm hit the *Mombar!*[22]

CARVAJAL *(aside)*. One hour of pleasure.—And then Hell.—Or nothing. *(To Mugnoz)* I'll go encourage my people. *(He rings. A Negro enters)* Bring me a jug of milk. *(The Negro leaves. Mugnoz looks astonished)* Mugnoz, you will lead my slaves. Hold out for an hour, I demand it. When the hour is over, I'll join you and we shall either drive them off or die together.

MUGNOZ. But sir—

CARVAJAL. No reply. Our walls are high. Are you frightened by Indians armed with arrows? Hang you! Ten years ago you wouldn't have flinched if I'd ordered you to board a ship in the face of a cannon loaded to the muzzle.

MUGNOZ. All right! I'll let myself be killed! Let's not talk about it anymore.

(Re-enter the Negro; he places a jug of milk on the table and leaves)

CARVAJAL. Come here. Turn the spoon while I pour this liquid into the milk.

(He produces a flask, from which he pours a few drops into the milk and then carefully hides it again)

MUGNOZ *(aside)*. He's not as steady as he'd like to be....

CARVAJAL. I'm going on a round of inspection.—Take the milk to my daughter. It's her lunchtime. Wait. I don't want a sword. Take it. Let me find it again on my table along with my loaded pistols. Here.

---

22. Mérimée uses more precise naval-artillery terms: falconets *(fauconneaux)* and bow-chaser *(canon de chasse)*.

(He hands his belt, to which both his sword and dagger are attached. The dagger falls from its sheath, Mugnoz picks it up)

MUGNOZ. Here's the dagger that gave such a fright to Doña Agustina. Be careful: it's loose in its sheath.

CARVAJAL. Loose or not, it will do me service before the day is over. *(He hides it inside his vest)*—Mugnoz, are you sure my daughter no longer has her dagger?

MUGNOZ. I am, my lord: have you forgotten that Flora the mulatto woman gave it to you?

CARVAJAL *(striking his forehead)*. I'm turning into a coward!—Go, take the milk while I go talk to the men.

MUGNOZ *(aside)*. Things are turning sour for us.

(They leave)

Scene 8

(The room in which Catalina has been locked)

(Enter Mugnoz; he places a glass of milk on the table)

MUGNOZ *(aside)*. De profundis! That makes two of them.

CATALINA. How is my mother?

MUGNOZ. Very well.

CATALINA. I know that she has been sick. I want the truth.

MUGNOZ. Here is your lunch.

(He leaves)

CATALINA *(alone)*. Miserable scoundrel!... My poor mother! The most horrible thoughts assault me.... No... it can't be.... Don José... he's still incapable of such a crime.... And yet... how fiercely he looked at her.... No... he wouldn't dare... and yet... my poor mother... she's alone, I'm sure... no one cares for her... they will let her... die... and they won't allow me to be near her... the villains! Ah! Don Alonso, you too seem to have abandoned me. But what can he do to save me? Is he alive himself?... My God, will you have no pity for me?... I'd give my life for a single day of freedom!... Ah! *(She hides her head in her hands)* I can't think anymore.... If only I could sleep!... Not a moment of respite for my anguish.... I can't read.... Horrible! To take away my books of devotion and lock me up with these hellish ones instead! Miserable me! I have not enjoyed one moment of happiness since I was born.... *(A confused noise is heard)* What's this I hear? Am I mistaken? Wasn't it the Indians' war-cry?... No. Everything is quiet.... Nothing.... It's the wind blowing.... How my heart beats!... No. I'm mistaken again.... I'm so worn out by my thoughts and my lack of sleep that I'm afraid of running mad.... Often I seem to hear loud voices in my prison.... My head is in a whirl.... *(She sits at the table in despair)* Yes, I feel it... I'm becoming an idiot... here I am again counting the straws in this mat.... *(She rises impetuously)* That is how he wants me, so I can be at his mercy. Oh Jesus, Jesus, have pity, give me courage! *(She falls on her knees, prays, and rises again)* How heavy the air is here! And that little corner of sky that I can see, how brilliantly blue! *(She sits at the table)* My head is on fire. *(She looks at the glass)* They treat me as I treated the animals I used to feed in their cages. If I am ever free again, I'll let them loose, all of them. *(She takes the glass, crosses herself, and suddenly puts it away)* I was about to commit a sin.... Today is a fast day, and I can tell by the sun that it's not yet noon. In the five days I've been imprisoned here I may have forgotten to count which are the days of fast. *(She counts on her fingers)* Yes, I have to go without nourishment today. Another hardship! I was longing for a drink of milk.... In another moment.... Sinner that I am! The sin of gluttony in my situation!... How low one becomes when one is unhappy!... To punish myself I'll pour it out to the last drop. *(She slowly pours the milk into a planter)* I've done something good; I've avoided a sin, and that gives me comfort. *(Noise outside)* Ha! This time I'm not mistaken! A musket shot! He's come to set me free.... Another one!.... Another one! The Indians' war cry! I hear it! Alonso! Alonso!—Ah! *(She flees to the far end of the room as she sees Carvajal come in. He closes the door, throws the key out the window, and looks at the empty glass)*

CARVAJAL. Devils in hell, I'll give you a comedy that's worthy of you! Let heaven, that gave me a father's heart, speak up; my potion will speak louder.

CATALINA. Help! Help!

CARVAJAL. Your cries are useless!

CATALINA. Don't come near me!

(The shouts and musket shots come nearer)

CARVAJAL. They want to break in, but they'll come too late,

(He flings himself on Catalina, who struggles in his arms. She feels the dagger in his bosom, seizes it, and stabs him)

CATALINA. I'm saved!

(She flees to the wall as far as possible from Carvajal, the bloody dagger in her hand, looking white-faced at her father)

CARVAJAL. You've killed your father, miserable girl.... You're my daughter, no mistake... but you've gone me one better.... Go... I curse you... and I'm going there... to prepare hell's torments for you.... Look! Your father's blood!...

(He shakes his bloody hand at her. The tumult increases. Hammering at the door)

ALONSO *(off-stage)*. Hit it! Break down the door!

(The door is beaten down; enter Don Alonso, the cacique, Ingol, armed Spaniards, and Indians)

ALONSO. My angel!... God, what do I see?

CARVAJAL. Spaniards, avenge a father... murdered by his daughter.... There she is... the parricide... avenge me... avenge me!...

(He dies)

ALONSO. What is he saying?

CACIQUE. He is dead.

A SPANIARD. She's covered in blood.

ANOTHER. And still holding the bloody dagger.

ALONSO. Catalina!

CATALINA. Don't come near me!

ALONSO. Who killed him?

CATALINA. I. Run from the parricide....

ALL. She killed her father!

ALONSO. You, Catalina, you!

A SPANIARD. A bullet in the head, that's what she deserves.

(Don Alonso takes a step toward Catalina but stops before the cadaver)

ALONSO *(to the cacique)*. Cacique... farewell... take the unhappy girl wherever she wants to go.... Adieu, you will not see me again.

(He gives his hand to Ingol and leaves, followed by the Spaniards)

CACIQUE. These are the white people, God's children, as the priests call them.

(Ingol grabs Catalina by the hair and raises his machete to cut off her head)

INGOL. Die, you who killed your father.

CACIQUE *(stopping him)*. Our friend wishes her to live. Let her live. The cacique commands it.—Woman, where do you want us to take you?

CATALINA *(after a silence)*. Into the forest.

CACIQUE. Think; the tigers will devour you there before long.

CATALINA. Better tigers than men! Let us go!

(She walks firmly to the door, but, passing before the corpse, she utters a piercing cry and falls to the ground in a swoon)

*

INGOL. So ends this comedy,[23] as does the family of Don José Carvajal. The father has been stabbed to death, the daughter will be eaten. Forgive the author's faults.

The End

---

23. Directors who wish to use this epilogue might want to change "comedy" (typical Mériméan banter, like the Preface) and stick to "drama" as in the original subtitle of the play. The open space I have inserted between the final stage direction and Ingol's farewell does not occur in Mérimée's text, where Ingol's words simply follow the last stage direction without a break. Here the hiatus is intended to suggest two things: that the epilogue can simply be dropped from performance, but that, if kept, a few seconds should elapse before Ingol turns to the audience to speak it. I have introduced the same small breathing space in the other plays of this volume.

Appendix

Naming *"le malheureux Ustariz"* as the inspirer of his play is one of Mérimée's typical literary hoaxes. The Peruvian chemist and naturalist Mariano Eduardo de Rivero y Ustariz (1798–1857) was a student in Paris from 1815 to 1822. Mérimée may have met him, if he met him at all, in the company of Dr. François Désiré Roulin (1796–1874), whom Rivero joined in a French scientific expedition to Colombia and neighboring countries in 1822. Roulin returned to Paris in 1828, the same year in which Mérimée wrote *Carvajal.* The two young men were friends, and Roulin was even at one time the physician of Mérimée's mother. Roulin told many stories—and was to publish some himself—about the worlds he had visited and explored, and thanks to the recent wars of liberation from Spain, Colombia was then in fashion. Rivero y Ustariz, however, remained for many years in South America, where he pursued a distinguished scientific and administrative career. Nothing specifically "unfortunate" is known about him, and all his treatises are purely scientific. Instead, we have a letter from Mérimée in 1832 in which he writes, "Dr. Roulin's whole life has been a series of misfortunes that would be enough for four or five everyday unhappy men *[quatre ou cinq malheureux ordinaires].* " It is quite possible, therefore, that "the unhappy Ustariz" is actually Dr. Roulin in disguise, and Ustariz nothing more than a name Roulin mentioned *en passant,* and perhaps vaguely remembered by Mérimée from half a dozen years before. My own guess—and it is nothing more than a surmise—is that Mérimée's conversations with Roulin interacted in his mind with his reading of *The Cenci,* which he names in parentheses, as if to alert future scholars to his genuine source. It is also possible, of course, that *Carvajal* owes its existence to a story told by Roulin, reinforced in Mérimée's mind by his familiarity with *The Cenci.* French scholars from Pierre Trahard on have suggested a host of other sources, all of them imaginary. The only additional source which does appear to be real is the Marquis de Sade's *Aline et Valcour.*[24] Nevertheless, the critical task that imposes itself is a comparison between Shelley's play of 1819 and Mérimée's drama written less than ten years later. This is not the place to undertake a detailed inquiry, but a few points can be made in brief. Shelley's

---

24. See Gerd Thieltges 1975, p. 237 (note) for this interesting suggestion. Thieltges also names several other works by Sade as possible sources. Thieltges—the most original Mérimée scholar to date—assumes the seriousness of *Carvajal* and Mérimée's other plays. He does, however, make the minor mistake of criticizing Mérimée for having Don Alonso decide to go into a cloister at the end of the play, forgetting that this idea is mentioned only in the play's preface.

villain only hints at incest: Carvajal's intentions are plain from the start. Shelley's heroine allows a third party to murder her father. Less squeamish, Mérimée has Catalina doing her own stabbing. Shelley prolongs the action with garrulous blank verse adjurations, imprecations, and expostulations before Beatrice goes to the scaffold. Mérimée remains succinct, brilliantly so in the conclusion. In this startling and terrifying finale, it is Catalina's lover, of all people, who turns fatally against her. More conventionally, Shelley's Beatrice is condemned by a judge and the pope. Altogether, *The Cenci* shows us a poet who might have developed, had he lived, into a major playwright, as Mary Shelley rightly pointed out. But at this stage in his life he had not freed himself from Shakespeare's nefarious stranglehold on English poets attempting to write tragedies. Mérimée, instead, became a mature writer at an early age and, indifferent to poetry, effortlessly bypassed that *French* menace to creativity, the Cornelian-Racinian model.

The Gilded Coach

(Le Carrosse du Saint-Sacrement)[1]

(1829)

Tu verás que mis finezas
Te desenojan.
Calderón, *Cuál es la mayor perfección.*[2]

---

1. A translation by L. A. Loiseaux (author of *French Prose for Sight Translation* [1935] and several Spanish grammar and composition textbooks) was published under the title *The Coach of the Holy Sacrament* in the *Collection du Vieux-Colombier*, Paris-New York 1917. I have helped myself to this translation wherever it seemed good enough for use. The Holy (or Blessed) Sacrament is the Eucharist which, in the context of Mérimée's play, is carried to the bedside of the sick and dying.
2. From Calderón's *Which Is the Best Perfection?* "You shall see that my delicate attentions will silence your anger."

About the Text

The translation is based entirely on the 1857 text mentioned in the headnote to *Carvajal's Family*. The appendices are by the translator, as are the notes, unless marked [M]

Characters

Don Andres de Ribera, Viceroy of Peru.
Camila Perichole, an actress.[3]
The bishop of Lima.[4]
Tomas d'Esquivel, a cathedral canon.[5]
Martinez, the viceroy's secretary.
Balthasar, the viceroy's valet.

The scene is in Lima in 17–

---

3. The Spanish name, or rather pseudonym, of this very real person was Perricholi. Directors may want to use the latter name instead of the French one. See Appendix B.
4. Mérimée was undoubtedly aware that an *arch*bishop headed the Lima diocese.
5. See Appendix A.

(The viceroy, in a dressing gown, is seated in a large armchair near a table covered with papers. One of his feet is wrapped in flannel and rests on a cushion. Martinez stands near the table with a pen in his hand)

MARTINEZ. The council of Royal Justices[6] await Your Excellency's reply.

VICEROY *(in a fretful tone)*. What time is it?

MARTINEZ. Nearly ten o'clock. Your Excellency has just time to dress for the ceremony.

VICEROY. You say the weather is fine?

MARTINEZ. Yes, my lord. There is a fresh wind from the sea and not a cloud in the sky.

VICEROY. I'd give a thousand good piastres for a good, hard rain. Then I could stay home and coddle myself in my chair, but on a fine day—when all of Lima will be in church—I can't give up the opportunity to be seen, and I won't yield my first place to the council.

MARTINEZ. Then Your Excellency is determined—

VICEROY. Are the mules harnessed?

MARTINEZ. Yes, my lord, they are harnessed to that beautiful coach just sent to you from Spain.

VICEROY. Lima has never seen the likes of it. What a splash it will make! And here I was thinking of giving up that pleasure! Not on my life! My two guards[7] are wearing new uniforms, and I haven't made my appearance yet before the people wearing my robes of state and this new decoration on my chest. This is a splendid occasion that can't be lost. Martinez, I will go; yes, and God willing, I shall walk. Once at the bottom of the main staircase, the worst will be over. What do you say, Martinez?

MARTINEZ. The people will be delighted to see Your Excellency.

VICEROY. I'll go, by Jove! And the Justices who were expecting to play the leading role will burst with envy. Besides, I can't allow myself not to go. The bishop is to refer to my new decoration from the pulpit. One likes to hear such things. Come now! An effort. *(He rings the bell. Enter Balthasar)* Let my robe of state be brought. You, tell the Royal Justices

---

6. Mérimée speaks of "*auditeurs*" here and elsewhere, translating from the Spanish "*oidores*," literally Hearers. The *oidores* constituted the "*audiencia*," a judicial as well as administrative council second in power only to the viceroy. I have chosen to call these magistrates Royal Justices, and their president (as he was titled), the Chief Justice.

7. "A privilege of the viceroys of Peru and Mexico is to have *two* guards." [M]

that they will have to place themselves behind me during the ceremony. Balthasar, give me my shoes and silk stockings. I intend to go to church.

BALTHASAR. To church, my lord! Dr. Pineda has forbidden you to go out!

VICEROY. Dr. Pineda doesn't know what he is talking about. I'm the one who knows whether I'm sick or not. I do not have the gout. Neither my father nor my grandfather ever had it. Pineda wants me to believe that a man of my age has the gout! Martinez, how old would you say I am?

MARTINEZ (*embarrassed*). My lord.... Your Excellency looks so well...surely—

VICEROY. I wager you can't guess, eh?

MARTINEZ. Forty, eh?

VICEROY. No, no, you're way off.... Come Balthasar, let us dress. (*He makes several attempts to rise*) Help me now, you two—more gently!—Aïe! More gently, by Jove! I don't know what it is but I feel as if I had ten thousand needles in my slipper.

BALTHASAR. Do not expose yourself to the air, my lord; it would be dangerous.

VICEROY (*trying to walk*). God almighty, such pain! I'll never be able to put on my shoes. Christ! To hell with shoes and silk stockings! I'd as soon be put on the rack. (*They seat him*) Bring over that stool. Damn! It seems to me I wasn't in so much pain a while ago.

BALTHASAR. Your Excellency should take Dr. Pineda's recommendation to heart. He says that you must avoid the open air. Besides, the ceremony will be very fatiguing. You would have to be on your feet for a long time.

VICEROY. To be sure, it's the fatigue I'm afraid of, because I'm not sick. In fact, I'm quite well now and I could go out if I felt like it. But I don't feel like catching a sickness for the stupid pleasure of holding an Indian chief over the baptismal font.... Basta! Martinez, write to Chief Justice Don Pedro de Hinoyosa and tell him he may hold the child—I mean the chief in my place. Here are the twelve names he is to be given. I hope he enjoys himself. Balthasar, remove these robes from my sight. What a foolish thing it is to show off laces, ribbons and embroideries! And have Pineda sent to me if he's not at this damned baptism. Give me a cigar and some maté.[8] Oh well, since I'm obliged to stay in my room with nothing to do, I'll tend to the affairs of this government. Balthasar, I am not at home to anyone, positively no one. (*To Martinez*) Are you done?

---

8. "A kind of drink common in the New World. It is a kind of tea." [M]

(*He reads the letter Martinez has just written*) Fine.... Good God, you forgot to add my title of Knight of St James, which I've had for six months in Spain and three days in Peru.

MARTINEZ. I beg Your Excellency's pardon for my oversight. (*He adds the title to the letter*)

VICEROY. Balthasar, send a squire with this letter. Come, Martinez, to work. There are a good many dispatches in the portfolio if I'm not mistaken.

MARTINEZ. Yes, my lord. I was going to speak to Your Excellency about them. To begin with the most urgent, here is a letter from Colonel Garci Vasquez reporting that there is great agitation in the province of Chuquisaca, that the Indians hold frequent meetings, and that if he doesn't receive aid soon, they will be in open revolt before the end of the month.

VICEROY. It seems to me, Martinez, that you've already spoken to me about something of that kind. Colonel Garci Vasquez, and the province of—of—those damnable Indian names! Why don't all the Indians speak Spanish?

MARTINEZ. Chuquisaca, my lord. I had the honor of making a report to you about this matter two months ago, the last time you suffered an attack of the gout—I mean the last time you were indisposed.

VICEROY. Well, what did I reply?

MARTINEZ. You said that you would think about it.

VICEROY. So. Well then.... We have hardly any troops. How many leagues from Lima is the province of—you know what?

MARTINEZ. Nearly three hundred Spanish leagues.

VICEROY. Really? I thought it was much nearer. Well, the matter is serious and must not be decided thoughtlessly. I shall consider it. What's this other paper in your hand?

MARTINEZ. It is a petition from Francisco Huayna Tapac, so-called left-hand descendant of the Inca Huayna Capac, who asks to be allowed to add to his name the title of Inca and to carry the arms and enjoy the privileges which the other Incas enjoy.

VICEROY. And—is there nothing to accompany this request?

MARTINEZ. Pardon me, my lord. About an ell and a half of China satin on which is painted the genealogy of the petitioner, from Manco Capac, Titu Capac, Lloque Yupanqui—names that make your hair stand on end.

VICEROY. Never mind, but when a person wants to obtain something of that kind, he should go about it another way. Verifying this sort of genealogy is no small matter. It's usually up to my secretary, and he ought to get some profit from his work. After that, if this secretary has his wits about him—see here, find out from your predecessor how to proceed.

MARTINEZ. I understand. This Inca is very rich.

VICEROY. Let's turn to the next business. Why are you laughing?

MARTINEZ. It's a complaint submitted by the Marquise of Altamirano concerning the parrot belonging to Señora Camila Perichole and against Señora Perichole herself.

VICEROY. Another folly of that wicked girl!

MARTINEZ. "Whereas the aforementioned parrot, at the instigation of the defendant, addresses the Marquise every time that the Marquise passes on the main street in terms which the modesty of the plaintiff forbids her to repeat," she concludes that the Señora Perichole should be strangled—no, my mistake, that the parrot be strangled and that the señora, its mistress, be reprimanded and fined.

VICEROY. What *does* the parrot say?

MARTINEZ. My lord, what it all amounts to is a frolicsome prank on the Señora Perichole's part. When the marquise passes by, the parrot cries out: "How much is an ell of linen?" Now, inasmuch as the marquise, before marrying the marquis, was the daughter of a rich cloth-merchant, she is gravely offended by the allusion.

VICEROY. That girl will turn all the ladies of Lima against me.

MARTINEZ. Here is a letter from the Countess Montemayor, who complains of an attempt by the Señora Perichole to ridicule her on stage in the playlet called *The Old Coquette*.

VICEROY. Again!

MARTINEZ. Your Excellency knows with what perfection this matchless actress catches and imitates everything that's ridiculous.

VICEROY. I do, but she oversteps the boundaries and respects nothing. I will rebuke her severely. Good heavens! I've been interested in the dramatic art all my life, but I will not allow personal insults to women whose families could do me great injury in Madrid.

MARTINEZ. Here is the petition of an invalid captain.

VICEROY. Enough. I'm getting tired. We'll read the rest another time. But while we're on the subject of the Perichole, I want you, my dear Martinez, to speak openly to me about her.

MARTINEZ. I, my lord? What could I tell Your Excellency?

VICEROY. I want you to tell me frankly what is said about her in town, in the circles you frequent.

MARTINEZ. They speak of her everywhere as having a talent of the first rank.

VICEROY. Fine! But that's not what I'm asking you. I want to know what is being said of my connection with this woman, because by now there's no point in making a mystery of things. You haven't been long in my service, but you must have guessed.... What the devil! I'm a man—and just because a person is a viceroy, a person is not obliged to live like a saint.

MARTINEZ. My lord, Your Excellency makes many men envious and, to be quite frank, many women too.

VICEROY. Flatterer! But there is some truth in what you say—perhaps more than you think.

MARTINEZ. Ah, my lord, I speak nothing but the truth.

VICEROY. Since I know that you are entirely devoted to me, I will confide in you, but only on condition that you'll repay my frankness by being equally honest with me. You know I'm not the kind of man who can be shown stars at midday—so take care as to what you tell me.

MARTINEZ. I will speak to your lordship as though I were kneeling before my confessor.

VICEROY. Well, Martinez, let me tell you what bothers me. Perichole is at heart a nice girl, but also a tiny bit irresponsible. She's forever committing indiscretions that may compromise her—and myself as well. Needless to say, I'm not afraid that she'll deceive me. That's not the point at all, not at all, and nothing is farther from the poor girl's mind, but what I fear is that in town it will be imagined that she's cheating on me.

MARTINEZ. Ah, my lord....

VICEROY. Society is malicious and doesn't respect persons of high rank. Besides, appearances are sometimes deceptive.... Even you, Martinez, haven't you observed this or that in her conduct that made you uneasy?

MARTINEZ. How can Your Excellency think—

VICEROY. Come now; to put you at your ease, I'm willing to tell you that Perichole has an aversion to you. She asked me for your post; you'll never guess for whose benefit—for her shoemaker's nephew. I have to admit, however, that this shoemaker produces admirable shoes for her. God almighty, when she dances in *La Gitanilla* in her silk stockings and shoes full of spangles—ah, Martinez, she's a beauty![9]

---

9. Jane H. Byers identifies this as a comedy by the seventeenth-century historian and dramatist Antonio de Solis (Byers 1984, p. 19).

MARTINEZ (*aside*). She`s a bitch!

VICEROY. As I`m fond of you. I sent her on her way. But this business shows you that the girl doesn`t like you. So you`re not obliged to spare her. That`s why I urge you again to speak with total frankness.

MARTINEZ. Ah, my good master!

VICEROY. Speak: but take care not to lie to me.

MARTINEZ. Overcome as I am by Your Excellency`s favors, I don't know how I can ever repay them.... But now especially that Your Excellency has deigned to confide in me, I am deeply at odds with myself... for I dare not say anything... not that I have anything to say... that could harm the Señora Perichole... and perhaps Your Excellency, making a snap judgment, will believe that it is... in some way... a desire for revenge... if one can call something revenge... something that cannot harm... for Your Excellency will surely not hold it against her... since, after all, only trifles are at issue.

VICEROY. What trifles? Do explain.

MARTINEZ. Oh, nothing serious. There is no question that the Señora Perichole loves you.... Your Excellency is so kind! Who could fail to love you? It was perhaps sheer malice that made people say... for, as Your Excellency observed so finely a minute ago, society is malicious.

VICEROY. What did people say?

MARTINEZ. Your Excellency mustn't attach any importance to what has been said, since it was only the first clerk of the silk merchant in Callao Street. And perhaps I shouldn't repeat to Your Excellency the idle talk of people of that class. Your Excellency will perhaps not condescend to listen to such talk, but, after all, Your Excellency ordered me to tell you what I know. and I can only repeat what I heard.

VICEROY. God's body! Tell me what you've heard.

MARTINEZ. This young man, whose name is Luis Lopez, and who comes, incidentally, of a respectable family, this Lopez told me, while we were talking about silks, that the other day he sold eight ells of crimson satin to Captain Hernan Aguirre, who paid ten ducats an ell without bargaining.

VICEROY. To the point!

MARTINEZ. Well, my lord, Luis Lopez claims to have seen this same crimson satin made up into a dress and worn by Señora Perichole. Do you remember the dress she was wearing Sunday night? That is the very one. But my guess is that Lopez was mistaken, especially since the captain said as he was paying, "I won`t haggle over the price, because it`s for my mistress."

VICEROY. For his mistress!

MARTINEZ. Proof, as far as I'm concerned, that he was mistaken. I rebuked him and told him what I thought of his charming story. On the other hand, if I had believed him, he would have told me many more.

VICEROY. Namely?

MARTINEZ. Oh, tales he has picked up God knows where.... For example, that one night a constable caught a man wearing only an overcoat over his shirt in the Avenida del Palacio: in fact, he was holding his underpants in his hand. At first he was taken for a burglar; but once he arrived at the station house, the lieutenant on duty saw that the alleged robber was Captain Aguirre. But what does that prove?

VICEROY. What night was it?

MARTINEZ. He said the night between Friday and Saturday... the night we waited so long for you.... However, several women who are not especially coy live in the Avenida del Palacio. I presume that the captain is courting Señora Beatriz—wait—I'm wrong, because she left for Quito two weeks ago. If it's not she, it's someone else.

VICEROY. Is that all you know?

MARTINEZ. Regrettably, Your Excellency knows that scandal never stops midway, and once the nasty tongues have started wagging against a person, a chorus soon joins in. But what I still have to say is so far-fetched that I'm afraid I'll bore Your Excellency by repeating it.

VICEROY. Not at all. It won't bore me. Go on.

MARTINEZ. At the last bullfight—the fact is that scandal is quite accurate as to details, but at bottom the story is patently absurd. At the last bullfight, your lordship might have noticed a big fellow, well built, lithe as a panther, brave as a lion, a mulatto by the name of Ramon who is one of the most skillful matadors of Lima.

VICEROY. So?

MARTINEZ. They say—you know that scandal-mongers will say anything that comes into their heads—they say it is not unheard-of that some of these fellows have dared to aspire to the favors of certain ladies of quality—and, what is even more extraordinary, that they have seen women distinguished by birth or otherwise lower themselves to the point of favoring the courtship of these wretches.—I'm afraid I'm tiring Your Excellency, who seems to be in pain just now.

VICEROY. Yes, my foot hurts terribly.

MARTINEZ. So then, some idle and wicked persons, of whom praise God there is no shortage in Lima, pretend that they have detected burning looks which the matador aimed at our beautiful actress. It was also noticed that this man, who is a master of his art, instead of drawing the bull toward Your Excellency's box in order to kill him there, as all well-bred matadors always do—well, this Ramon, on the contrary, took his stand under the Señora Perichole's box, thus doing her all the honors of the festival. Alas, there are people who find evil everywhere, even in the most innocent actions! For example, at this very festival—from which Your Excellency, due to your indisposition, was absent[10]—the señora did something which they construed against her, even though at bottom, it was the most natural thing in the world. At the moment when the black and white bull, the fiercest of them all, was killed by Ramon, Señora Perichole's pearl necklace fell into the arena. Ramon picked it up and placed it around his neck after having respectfully kissed it. I am quite sure that this necklace fell by accident, and I daresay that the señora left it in the matador's possession in order to show her generosity. I might add that Ramon didn't sell it as many other bullfighters would have done in order to spend the money at the tavern. He, on the contrary, wears it around his neck throughout the town, proud as a peacock and bragging his head off. Your Excellency can imagine what a morsel this accident provided for scandal! And God knows how people have misinterpreted the affair. According to them, Señora Perichole jumped out of her box, tearing the necklace from her throat, and threw it on purpose to the matador, crying, "Bravo, Ramon!" According to Señora Romer, the actress at the Grand Theater, who occupied the same box—but it's jealousy that maker her say it—Señora Perichole cried, "Bravo, *my* Ramon!" I was placed too far to hear, but I'll wager that she lies, because she's so malicious she had the gall to say that at the last performance of *La hija del aria*[11] the garland that fell at Señora Perichole's feet was thrown by Ramon the mulatto. She goes so far as to assert that Ramon sometimes enters her dressing-room at the theatre and even goes to her house. And it's true that the rascal is bold enough for any mischief. He thinks he's an Adonis in spite of his brown skin; he plays the guitar and would indulge in knife-play if the occasion arose. No one near him would dare to cough or blow his nose when the Perichole sings. He's a valuable man for an actress.—Señora Romer adds that Señora Perichole sometimes locks herself up with him for hours, especially when Your Excellency goes hunting or is unfortunately indisposed.

---

10. That the viceroy was absent is obvious; nevertheless, I have allowed myself to make this even clearer by adding the phrase "due to your indisposition."
11. Title of a two-part play by Calderón (Byers 1984, p. 20).

VICEROY. Is that all you know?

MARTINEZ. Tales of this kind can go on forever, but since I thought little of them and presumed that Your Excellency—

VICEROY. Mr. Martinez, you are a rascal.

MARTINEZ. My lord!

VICEROY. An insolent, shameless liar.

MARTINEZ. My lord, I said nothing to Your Excellency but what I have heard from others.

VICEROY. That is exactly what proves your insolence, sir. What! You dare report to me as gospel truth all the stupid gossip you hear in the theater! What business have you in the theater, sir? Is that your place? Do I pay you a salary so you can spread mischief with the actors? You do nothing; you're a loafer—and a liar. There's not a word of truth in what you've had the audacity to maintain to my face. What! You miserable wretch, you dare to tell me that I'm the rival of a matador! A mulatto!

MARTINEZ. No, my lord... I'm not saying....

VICEROY. I know Perichole. She's a wonderful girl who loves only me. You're a liar, an impudent liar, and there's not a syllable of truth in anyything you've said.

MARTINEZ. Will Your Excellency deign to recall—

VICEROY. Silence!—I took you from the gutter to be in my service. I wanted to make your fortune. But you're unworthy of my kindness. I ought to throw you back into the gutter, but I'm weak enough to be willing to appoint you to another position. I appoint you tax collector in the province of—with Colonel Garci Vasquez. Leave immediately; if you are still in Lima tomorrow, I will have you four dragoons walk you to jail, and you won't get out until I die.

MARTINEZ. Mercy, my lord, have pity! This is worse than jail. Won't Your Excellency remember that I spoke only at your command?

VICEROY. Ha! Still arguing! Who is the master here? By Jove, if I could walk, I'd beat you to death with my cane. Out of here, rascal, or I'll have you thrown out of the window! So! I'm not as good as a mulatto! You scum! Out of here!

(*A loud noise is heard at the door; enter Balthasar, followed by Perichole. Exit Martinez*)

BALTHASAR. My lord, the young lady insists on entering, even though I keep telling her that Your Excellency is busy.

VICEROY. Let her come in, and leave us.

(*Exit Balthasar*)

PERICHOLE. It's very strange that a person can't see you except by storming the door of your study. I hope this is just a mistake on the part of your blockhead of a servant.

VICEROY (*sulky*). I thought you were at the ceremony.

PERICHOLE. I don't know yet whether I'll show myself there; it depends a little on you.—But first of all, how is your gout?

VICEROY (*more sulky*). I don't have the gout.

PERICHOLE. Aha! I see it's nothing but a case of suppressed grouchiness. Too bad; I had something to ask you, and I hoped to find you in a good mood. Farewell; we'll talk about it another time.

VICEROY. Camila, don't leave so quickly. *I* have something to say to you. By Jove! It looks as if you were afraid of a tête-à-tête with me.

PERICHOLE. Oh, I'm seldom afraid of Your Excellency.

VICEROY. Stay. Keep me company when I'm sick. I know you'd rather be chatting with Captain Aguirre, but sometimes one must resign oneself.

PERICHOLE. Aguirre? I just left him.

VICEROY. You just left him.... Excellent, Señora! No need for a preface; we can get to the point at once.

PERICHOLE. My lord, I suspect that you wish to regale me with a little scene of jealousy, inasmuch as you haven't done so in nearly two months. I'm afraid this scene will be a longish one, so if you don't mind, I'll make my request at once. You'll grant it, and we'll postpone rage and reproaches till tomorrow.

VICEROY. I'm in no mood to grant you any favors; you misuse those you have already obtained from me.

PERICHOLE. Fine start! But it's my turn to speak.... All the starched prudes of Lima are in league to mortify me in every way, and why? Because I'm better-looking than they are.—Isn't it true that I'm pretty today?—There's a regular little war between us full of little deviltries and calumnies. I'd give you a few examples if I weren't in such a hurry. In addition, we're straining on both sides to surpass each other in the magnificence of our finery, the good taste of our dresses, and so forth. Naturally we're a godsend to the jewelers and dressmakers.

VICEROY. What in the devil's name have I to do with all this nonsense? If you don't surpass these ladies in the luxury of your dresses, as far as lovers are concerned—

PERICHOLE (*with a deep curtsy*). As far as lovers are concerned, I do exactly the opposite of the ladies. I prefer quality to quantity.

VICEROY. Let me speak, Perichole. I am very serious just now.

PERICHOLE (*speaking at the same time*). Listen to me; I'll be brief and to the point.

VICEROY. I'm very unhappy with you. Your flirtatious ways are talked about from one end of town to the other, and, to speak plainly, you're making me play the role of a fool.

PERICHOLE (*speaking at the same time*). I had a sublime idea today that will make all these women burst with spite, provided you'll show yourself as sweet as when you're at your best.

VICEROY. By Jove! Listen to me!

PERICHOLE. By heaven! Listen to *me*! I'm a woman, you're a Castilian, you owe me respect; so hold your tongue when I speak.

VICEROY. All right, be the first. It'll do you no good once I get my turn.

PERICHOLE. Today, as you know, all the women of Lima are showing off in their finest dresses and spreading out all the luxuries they own. There are five carriages in all of Lima: your two, the bishop's, that of Chief Justice Pedro de Hinoyosa, and finally the coach belonging to the Marquise Altamirano, my mortal enemy—a coach nearly as old as its mistress but still a coach. So then, this morning, having heard that you were going to stay in your room, I put it into my head that you could ensure my triumph over my rival by making me a present of the beautiful carriage you've received from Madrid.

VICEROY. Is that what you wanted to ask of me?

PERICHOLE. You'd make me happier giving me that carriage than if you gave me a gold mine or a province among the Indians.

VICEROY. I must say, a modest request! All she wants is a carriage so she can be lugged to church like a marquise. Unbelievable!

PERICHOLE. You know, Don Andres, that I care little for money. I don't know what this carriage cost you, but you are rich. If it weren't a question of humiliating a set of mortal enemies, you know that I wouldn't ask for such a costly gift. However, if my request shocks you, forget it. I apologize if it was wrong of me to make it. A fault of mine is to act first and reflect afterward.

VICEROY. A carriage! A sight to behold—an actress in a carriage! Are you a bishop, madam, a chief justice, or a marquise, that you must ride in a carriage?

PERICHOLE. Am I not in one person the Infanta of Ireland, the Queen of Sheba, Queen Thomyris, Venus, and Saint Justina, virgin and martyr?[12]

---

12. See Byers 1984, p. 20, for an identification of all these characters in plays by Lope de Vega and Calderón, except for Queen Thomyris. Perhaps, according to Byers, Mérimée

VICEROY. Crazy girl!

PERICHOLE. All these women are surely worth an old marquise, whose father sold woollens in Cordoba to clothe the muleteers.—Come, my little daddy, my Andresillo, I've made you laugh; you're no longer in a bad mood; your nature is to be charming, and you will give me your coach, won't you?

VICEROY. Camila, in the first place your request is extravagant, and secondly, you chose the wrong time, because I have a complaint to make against you.

PERICHOLE. What if I struck you with reprisals?

VICEROY. Listen to me. You're wrong to turn everything into a joke. I assure you that your conduct is no secret to me anymore and that I no longer wish to be your dupe.

PERICHOLE. If you don't give me that coach, I'll go home feeling very low, because I can't see myself walking to this ceremony like a shop-girl, or in a sedan-chair like a matron, after I'd raised my hopes so high! Ah my lord, viceroy of Peru, you are a cruel man! How much did that coach cost you?

VICEROY. Never mind your coach, young Miss, and answer me. I'm perfectly aware of all your actions, and I must tell you that I'm no longer blind to them as I was when I still loved you. Now I don't love you anymore, do you understand? My eyes have been opened; I know who you are.... However, I'd be glad to watch your face trying to justify yourself. Go ahead, try.... Speak, by Jove, speak! What is she thinking about, with her eyes turned to heaven?

PERICHOLE. That beautiful coach!

VICEROY. You'd try the patience of a saint! Damn that coach!—I know that Captain Aguirre is in love with you....

PERICHOLE. I can easily believe that. Give me one of those cigars.

VICEROY.... And that you're in love with him—yes, you are—I know it, I'm sure of it. Deny it—be bold. Deny, for instance, that he gave you a crimson satin dress. Deny it, deny it! I'm not preventing you.

PERICHOLE. He should also have given me a lace mantilla. I tore mine.

VICEROY. And he was surprised half naked under your windows—I know it, I saw it. But go ahead, by Jove, tell me it isn't true. You who are

---

was thinking of an allusion in *I Henry VI*, II, 3 to the queen whose army defeated and killed King Cyrus. We easily imagine Mérimée picking out any humorous range of names from the volumes on his shelf, and, as an *érudit* himself, chuckling at the busy work he might be creating for a future academic.

such a wonderful actress should know how to lie with the same air others assume when they tell the truth.

PERICHOLE. Thanks for the compliment.

VICEROY. You realize, my dear, that this cannot last. Our relationship is going to end. It should have ended long ago—for I'm not the man to subsidize the mistress of Captain Aguirre.—You are very calm. Perhaps you fancy that I mistake your coolness for the tranquillity of innocence.

PERICHOLE (*in a tragic tone*). It is the tranquillity of despair. In all this I see only the lost opportunity of arriving in church in a coach. The clock ticks away, and by the time you ask me to forgive you, it will be too late.

VICEROY. So! I'm to ask for your forgiveness, am I, my sweet? So! You want nothing less! Well, I ask you to forgive me for having discovered yet another intrigue with an illustrious personage.

PERICHOLE. That makes two. When we get to three we'll throw a party.

VICEROY. He is no less than the valiant Ramon, mulatto and matador.—You choose your lovers with discrimination, madam. He is a famous man; all Lima echoes to his name.

PERICHOLE. Perfectly true, and his reputation is not usurped, like that of many others I know. He is the boldest bullfighter in Peru and perhaps the handsomest and strongest as well.

VICEROY. By Jove! You're clearly not a woman who'll leave a viceroy for the first comer. Besides you are clever enough to exchange one lover for two. A fine bargain!

PERICHOLE. A miserable bargain. By my count, it would take three viceroys to make up the price of one captain, and six viceroys for one bullfighter.

VICEROY. Shameless hussy!

PERICHOLE. Don't stop!

VICEROY. A trollop who doesn't even take the trouble and hasn't the human decency to conceal her debauchery.

PERICHOLE. Keep it up! (*Declaiming*) "Cruel imagination! Why do you distress my heart with your sweet illusions?"[13]

VICEROY. To take a matador and mulatto for a lover! You're a Messalina!

PERICHOLE. What does that mean?

VICEROY. You are—

---

13. A note by Mérimée informs the reader that Perichole is quoting from Calderón's *El Magico prodigioso*.

PERICHOLE. Don't hold back, my lord; I imagine that Your Excellency gives way to these fits of fury by his doctor's order. You get all heated up, and that must be beneficial for the gout.

VICEROY. Silence, you wretch! To take a mulatto for a lover!—I've loaded you with favors, by Jove.... For your sake I've nearly compromised myself in the public eye... because it's scandalous that the representative of the king of Spain should look for a mistress in the theater.... I don't know what keeps me from—but I'm a thousand times too kind, otherwise I'd have you locked up.

PERICHOLE. You wouldn't dare!

VICEROY. I wouldn't dare?... Quick, pen and ink, and I sign the order.

PERICHOLE. There would be a revolt in Lima if Perichole were jailed.

VICEROY. A revolt! Ta, ta, ta!

PERICHOLE. Yes, a revolt. Behead or hang all your noble barons, counts, and knights in Lima, not a voice will be raised, not an arm will be lifted on their behalf. Have twelve thousand poor Indians slaughtered, send twenty thousand of them to the mines, and people will applaud you, they will call you another Trajan. But prevent the citizens of Lima from seeing their favorite actress, and they will stone you to death.

VICEROY. Yes, yes.... And suppose I forbid the director to renew your contract, now that it's about to expire?

PERICHOLE. In that case I'll take my guitar, and I'll sing in the street under your windows; my songs will make people laugh at your viceroyalty and your gout.

VICEROY. Very good. And what would you do if I sent you to Spain by the first galleon?

PERICHOLE. You couldn't do me a greater favor. I'm dying to see old Europe, and besides, in Spain I might become the mistress of the prime minister or the king, and then maybe I'll get even with you. I'll have an accusation launched against you; you'll be brought back to Spain in chains, like Christopher Columbus, and you'll thank your stars if I spare you the gallows and just send you to rot in the tower of Segovia.

VICEROY. Until this happens, don't set your foot in the palace again.

PERICHOLE. Never, I assure you, will I obey Your Excellency more willingly.

VICEROY. One moment. As this is the last time we are to see each other, let us settle our accounts. I scorn you too much to oppress you. Andres de Ribera does not stoop to punish an offense when it rises from the gutter.—I have given you considerable sums and valuable presents—keep them. You will be paid three months of your pension, which you can use, I hope, a few weeks from now in the poorhouse.

PERICHOLE. I have listened patiently to your insults and the atrocious slander you've inflicted on me. I attributed it all to the pain that I see you're suffering, but this last outrage cannot be forgiven. I am descended from old Christians[14] and Castilians, my lord, and I hold my head too high to accept gifts from a man I do not love. All your presents shall be returned to you. I will sell my house and my furniture to repay you. In the meantime, take the diamond necklace and the rings you have given me.... By tonight I will have nothing that belongs to you.

(*She takes off her jewels and starts to leave*)

VICEROY. Perichole!.... Perichole! There—don't go—listen to me—must I get up? Aie, aie!

PERICHOLE (*stopping*). Did you hurt yourself?

VICEROY. Did you say it was slander?...

PERICHOLE. I don't remember anymore what I said.

VICEROY. Just tell me that it *is* all untrue, and I'll forget everything.

PERICHOLE. Believe whatever you wish. I kiss Your Excellency's hand.

VICEROY. No, don't go yet.... Perichole.... I was angry... too hasty.... But now let's have a quiet explanation.—So, everything they told me about you was false?

PERICHOLE. Let me leave. Your opinion doesn't matter to me.

VICEROY. Come, come, Camila. So be it! I do think I was mistaken. Are you satisfied?

PERICHOLE. No, no, you were not mistaken.

VICEROY. Wicked headstrong girl! I hate you, but you're so charming.... I love you too much.... I know that everything they told me is false.... But won't you say so?... Just say....

PERICHOLE. No, you insulted me so deeply that I don't very much care what you think of me.

VICEROY. Come now! Well, let's not talk about it anymore.... Please forgive me.... I was wrong. I was in such pain that I no longer knew what I was saying. It's finished now.... Give me your hand.... But tell me....

PERICHOLE. Tell you what?

VICEROY. That you are no longer angry and that you forgive my fit of anger.

---

14. By old Christians was meant Christians who could trace their lineage far back without Jewish or Islamic blood.

PERICHOLE (*giving him her hand*). Yes, I forgive you, because I believe that you truly love me.

VICEROY. But still, out of generosity.... Oh, I trust you!... I'm no longer jealous.... But would it cost you so much to say that you have been slandered?

PERICHOLE. What! Still harping on that?

VICEROY. All right! I've said what I've said.... Let's drop the subject.... I believe you without your defending yourself.... And yet.... See how weak I am!

PERICHOLE. Truly now, my lord, must I point out to you how far jealousy has clouded your reason? Come, let us try to remember your accusations. Oh yes! The crimson satin dress! My God, what an idea!

VICEROY. Yes, it was silly, but—

PERICHOLE. It is perfectly true that I own a crimson satin dress, and it is equally true that I purchased it from a mulatto neighbor of mine who is kept by Captain Aguirre. Whether she got the dress from her lover or from someone else is more than I know.... The bargain was made by my chamber-maid, and you can question her about it.

VICEROY. I certainly won't, my dear. I believe you. (*Aside*) Martinez, you villain, you'll pay for your lies!

PERICHOLE. As for that other tale about Captain Aguirre, I have nothing to tell you except that incidents of this kind are common in Lima, and that I can't prevent them. Besides, I seem to remember that on that day you stayed quite late at supper with me.

VICEROY. Perichole, my sweet, I don't want to hear another word about it. It embarrasses me too much. Thank God I'm no longer jealous. So you were saying about this matador....

PERICHOLE. That your spies were equally accurate about him. It's true that at the last bullfight I was overcome with admiration when I saw Ramon's skill and courage, because as soon as he had plunged his sword into the bull's shoulder, perfectly sure of himself, and without condescending to see if there was some spark of life left in the beast, he wheeled about, turning his back to the bull, and made me a very graceful bow for a man of his profession. Since I knew what that meant, I looked for my purse in order to throw it to him, but I had forgotten it at home, so I took the first valuable object that came to hand. Never would it have occurred to me that anyone could see love in a gesture of this kind. A mulatto! A bullfighter! A man who drinks brandy and eats raw onions! Please!

VICEROY. Yes, yes, I was so wrong, my beauty.... However, if I had been that bull, I would have gathered up my remaining strength and shaken up this Mister Ramon.

PERICHOLE. And I would have cried, "Long live the bull!"

VICEROY. You're adorable! Ask me whatever you like, because I'll never believe that you invite this Ramon who eats raw onions to your house.

PERICHOLE. Excuse me, my lord. You are aware that I will soon be playing the leading role in that comedy by the poet Peransurez. I shall have to sing a song in the dialect of these people; that is why, in order to catch their accent and pronunciation, I have Ramon visit me; the man has a decent bass voice and would sing all day long if you gave him enough to drink.—Let me add one more word. If Your Excellency still nurtures some doubts, you may send the captain to Panama and the bullfighter to Cuzco; though I'm afraid that, in view of all these rumors, exiling them may give rise to some nasty jokes at your expense and mine.

VICEROY. Dear, dear Perichole, how can I make you forget—

PERICHOLE. Love excuses many things, but I warn Your Excellency in the future to guard against servants who pretend great devotion while in fact they are always ready to betray their masters.

VICEROY. What do you mean?

PERICHOLE. I name no names, and the trade of informer will never be mine. I'm young, fairly pretty, and an actress, which means that I'm exposed to any number of insulting propositions. I imagine that a certain little presumptuous fellow whom you honor with your confidence and whom I have had to drive away from my dressing-room has been regaling you with these lovely stories.

VICEROY. The rascal! I always suspected it. The monster! What! He had the cheek to proposition you? You're talking about Martinez, aren't you?

PERICHOLE. I don't want to harm anyone.

VICEROY. You're not going to Garci Vasquez, you villain, but straight to the fortress of Callao,[15] and I'll be damned if you'll be leaving it in the near future!

PERICHOLE. I said nothing against that young man. You can't prove that he's the one I meant.

VICEROY. Leave it to me. I know what I know.—Now, dearest child, you asked me, I believe, for my coach.... Good grief! That's—

---

15. Lima's harbor.

PERICHOLE. Don't mention it anymore; I'm happy enough at this point, not having lost your friendship.

VICEROY. But you really, really wanted it?... The trouble, you see, my dove....

PERICHOLE. Yes, I did want it very much. But after this cruel discussion of ours, I've changed my mind.

VICEROY. You were counting on my giving it to you. But how... devil take it!... that coach... not that I care for it... but what the blazes will people say if—

PERICHOLE. Never mind. Besides, it's almost too late; I wouldn't be in time for the ceremony.

VICEROY. As to that, my mules are quick steppers.... But I'm afraid that those damned justices... and then this Pedro de Hinoyosa... he'll distort the business in his own manner....

PERICHOLE. He hates you because the people love you.... But I'd be sorry to compromise you in his eyes. I understand that he's a gentleman one must treat with kid gloves.

VICEROY. Is he? Well, let him talk! Haven't I the right to give away anything that belongs to me, and to whomever I wish?

PERICHOLE. Don't do it, I beg you. The extravagance of my request suddenly strikes me, and now I blush for having troubled you with it. And then... I made such an effort not to weep a while ago... that I feel more like throwing myself on my bed than going for a drive.

VICEROY. Poor child, how she loves me!... No, my dear, you must have some fresh air, it will do you good. Pineda always orders me to ride in my coach after I've lost my temper. Come, sweet dove, the gilded coach is yours. Ring my people to have it harnessed at once.

PERICHOLE. My lord, I beg you, think it over; now you're too kind, just as earlier you were too unjust.

VICEROY. Ring, I tell you. I want your enemies to die of envy.

PERICHOLE. But—

VICEROY. Enough! If you don't accept this present, I'll believe that you're still angry with me.

PERICHOLE. When you put it that way, I can't refuse you.... But I'm really all blushes.

(*She rings. Enter Balthasar*)

VICEROY. Have the white mules harnessed at once to my new coach, and tell the coachman that the mules, the coach and he himself belong to this lady. (*Exit Balthasar*) Poor little thing! How agitated your pulse is! Come, are you still angry with me?

PERICHOLE. How could I fail to be overcome by Your Excellency's kindness?

VICEROY. Never mind the Excellency; call me by my name, the way you sometimes do.

PERICHOLE. Well, Andres, you have made me very miserable and very happy today.

VICEROY. Kiss me, my angel. I love you like that. I don't want to be viceroy when I'm near my Camila!—Naughty! Do you remember what you said about viceroys and love-making?

PERICHOLE. Silly! You know you're Andres for me, not the viceroy of Peru.—Look at the pretty embroidered shoes Marino made for me; that shoemaker whose nephew I spoke to you about some time ago.

VICEROY. What a darling little foot! I can hide it completely in my hand. About that nephew—you told me he's a bright fellow. I'll have him replace Martinez in my service.

PERICHOLE. No, I don't want to displace anyone. Besides, Martinez is useful to you. He gives you valuable reports.

VICEROY. Vindictive, eh!—Don't worry; he'll sleep in the fortress this very night.

(*Enter Balthasar*)

BALTHASAR. The carriage is ready.

(*Exit*)

VICEROY. Go, my beauty, enjoy yourself, and come back immediately after the ceremony. If anyone gives you offense, don't fail to report it to me. As God is my witness, I'll give the laughers something to cry about.... Don't forget your necklace and your rings. Here, let me attach your necklace.... Ah, you're divine today!

PERICHOLE. I am taking away something more precious that these diamonds; your trust and your love.

VICEROY. You are an angel.

(*Exit Perichole*)

VICEROY. This girl winds me around her little finger. But the truth is, she loves me so much.... I can't refuse her anything.... And yet, giving her my carriage.... What will people think?... An actress in a gilded coach, while I don't know how many noblewomen are only too glad to be carried in a sedan chair.... I guess by now the ceremony must be over.... She'll arrive just in time for the bishop's sermon.... So much the better.... Ah! I hear the wheels in my courtyard. She hasn't wasted any time.... Balthasar!

(*Enter Balthasar*)

VICEROY. Roll my chair to the window and hand me my spy-glass. I want to see what the coach looks like.... By Jove, I'll be able to see her right up to the church-door.... Damn! Look at her go!... Faster than my coachman ever drives me.... Everybody is stopping to look at her.... Some of them are taking their hats off as though it were I driving by!... What a crazy thing!... Now she's on the Plaza.... Good God! She's running into another carriage!... Jesus! Fortunately it's the other one that tipped over.... A crowd is gathering.... What are they going to do? They may insult her.... Balthasar, go see—

BALTHASAR. Yes, my lord.

VICEROY. Good heavens! There's a fight!... You people down there! Run! Arm yourselves! Knock down that rabble!... Perichole! Ha! Very good! She's driving on, thanks to that man who's swinging his stick left and right and opening the way for her.

BALTHASAR. Should I run after Madam's coach?

VICEROY. No, stay here. It's useless now.... However, when she returns.... Tell Sebastian and Dominico to mount their horses, take their muskets, and follow her at a distance... but first let them remove their liveries.... If there's a catastrophe, I'll hold you people responsible.

(*Exit Balthasar*)

VICEROY. The people of Lima are so coarse! They may insult her.... Well! It seems there was no accident after all; the other coach has righted itself and is continuing on its way... and the crowd is entering the church. I hope to heaven that she can come out of all this without more trouble!... I don't care what people say, there's no law against an actress riding in a coach if she owns one.... So much the worse for the countesses if they aren't young or pretty enough for that sort of present.... (*He lights a cigar*) Won't that baptism ever end?... I can't wait for her to come back and tell me the details of this adventure.... Damned leg!... It hurts more, I think, when I'm worried.... Let me see: last time I was sick it lasted five...six days...whatever. This time I hope I'll be rid of it sooner, so I can attend her opening night.... And if I can't go... by Jove, I'll have the performance postponed.

(*Enter Balthasar*)

BALTHASAR. My lord, Doctor Don Tomas D'Esquivel requests the favor of speaking with Your Excellency.

VICEROY. Have him come in.—He's probably coming to deliver a little sermon so he can extract a gift from me. In fact, it's nearly a month since I last saw him.

ESQUIVEL (*entering*). I kiss Your Excellency's hand.

VICEROY. Ah, Esquivel, you have before you a very sick man!

ESQUIVEL. I grieve to hear it. It was, I suppose. this attack of the gout which prevented Your Excellency from attending today's ceremony?

VICEROY. I do not have the gout!... It's a rumor that Pineda is spreading; all I have is a swelling in my foot. I know more about it than he does.

ESQUIVEL. In any event, Your Excellency need not regret your absence from that baptism. You had the good fortune to miss a great scandal.

VICEROY. A scandal? (*Aside*) The devil! Perichole must be in it!

ESQUIVEL. Yes, a shocking scandal, and one, I am quite sure, that would have deeply distressed Your Excellency—especially since it appears that you were its involuntary cause.

VICEROY. Kindly explain.

ESQUIVEL. On a day like this, with such a touching ceremony!... I am truly sorry to trouble Your Excellency... but I must speak, and speak frankly, even at the risk of displeasing you.—My duty and Your Excellency's interest demand it.

VICEROY. I cannot guess....

ESQUIVEL. This famous actress....

VICEROY (*aside*). Here we go!

ESQUIVEL. In whom, it is said, Your Excellency is so very much interested has caused a great disturbance this very day. The protection Your Excellency extends her emboldens her to the point of believing, allow me to say it, that everything is permitted her.

VICEROY. I assure you that I do not protect her.... I merely esteem her talent, which is highly estimable, Dr. Esquivel. But I beg you to give me a full account.

ESQUIVEL. Here are the facts. It appears that she is the proprietor of a coach, and this coach, they say, is a gift from you.

VICEROY. I had no use for it.

ESQUIVEL. Ah, my lord, that coach might have been better employed... but what is done is done, and doubtless Your Excellency had your reasons for giving it away, God grant it!... Enough. I shall report to you what I witnessed. So: she has a coach, and in that coach she drove to church.... On my side, having been delayed by unforeseen circumstances, I accepted a seat in the carriage of the Marquise of Altamirano. We were advancing slowly as is appropriate when one approaches a church. All of a sudden the Señora Perichole arrives at a gallop with her mules, rattling the cobblestones a hundred feet around her. We were about to enter the Plaza;

she wanted to push ahead of us—ahead of the marquise!—in short, she crowded in so close to us that she rammed us with the greatest violence.

VICEROY. Her coachman's clumsiness is to blame.

ESQUIVEL. Your Excellency will pardon me, but I cannot believe that her coachman acted without orders, especially since she put her head out of the window when she saw our carriage and spoke to the man, doubtlessly to order this ugly maneuver.

VICEROY. I hope no accident occurred.

ESQUIVEL. What! It's a miracle that we are still alive! The jolt was frightful: the marquise fell on me and I fell on the marquise's dog, accidentally crushing it.... My wig fell into the gutter... and the marquise received a severe contusion on the hip.

VICEROY. God be praised! I was afraid of something much worse.

ESQUIVEL. It seems to me that this was quite bad enough. Furthermore, the marquise's coach is badly damaged—a superb conveyance which has been admired in Lima for more than twenty years.

VICEROY. I'll pay—I mean, I'll make Perichole pay for the damage.

ESQUIVEL. But what about the scandal, my lord, how will you repair *that*? As far as I am concerned, I see only one way, which is to forbid this lady to drive in a coach, for not only is it a bad example to see an actress in a carriage while so many worthy clergymen have to walk, but in addition her recklessness would endanger the lives of our peaceful inhabitants.... However, I have not yet done, though I regret that I am obliged to vex Your Excellency.—The marquise's servants, indignant at the insult inflicted upon their mistress, remonstrated... manually... with the lady's coachman and valet. Thereupon the rabble which had followed her with yelps of glee took her side, led by a raging rogue, a mulatto, a bullfighter by the name of Ramon, who mauled the marquise's coachman with his stick, broke her squire's sword, and smashed the jaw of one of her lackeys.

VICEROY. The scoundrel! I'll make an example of him!

ESQUIVEL. That is not all. Without paying attention to us, without apologizing, she continued on her way and all but entered the church *in* her carriage. The heads of the mules were under the doorway when she stopped. She descended and made her way noisily through the crowd. Everybody turned around to see her.... The ceremony, which had already begun, was forgotten, and—I tremble to say it, my lord—the bishop himself shared in the general distraction. He forgot to ask the godfather to bring up the new convert, his godson, as a good Christian. As for myself, indignant and distressed to the limit, I left the church in order to apprise you of what occurred and beg you to put an end to the impertinence of a girl who, allow me to tell you, does the greatest injury to Your Excellency.

VICEROY. I expect her shortly, and I shall give her a scolding she'll remember.

ESQUIVEL. I warn you that the marquise will carry her complaint all the way to Madrid if necessary.

VICEROY. My dear Doctor Esquivel, that is something we ought to prevent. You can guess that complaints of this sort can be very harmful to me.

ESQUIVEL. My lord—

VICEROY. You have some influence with the marquise. Persuade her to be satisfied with the damages she will receive. On my side, I pledge myself to give Perichole a thorough dressing-down.

ESQUIVEL. My lord... I don't know whether....

VICEROY. Your church needs a painting for its main altar.... I want Perichole to offer you one as a present to atone for her fault.... Come to think of it, I gave her a Madonna by Murillo that she has been wanting to swap for my Saint Christopher.... You may count on the Madonna.... But do me the favor of appeasing the marquise, will you? Do you promise?

ESQUIVEL. I shall do my best, Your Excellency; however—

VICEROY. And bring your nephew round one of these mornings. We'll try to do something for him.

ESQUIVEL. He is most worthy of Your Excellency's goodness. However, my lord—

VICEROY. I hear a coach entering the courtyard. It must be Perichole. You'll see how I speak to her.

(*Enter Balthasar*)

BALTHASAR. His lordship the Bishop of Lima.

VICEROY. The bishop!

ESQUIVEL. To complain as well, I have no doubt.

(*The bishop and Perichole appear at the door, each trying to give precedence to the other*)

BISHOP. You first, Señora.

PERICHOLE. I beg you, your Grace....

BISHOP (*taking her hand*). Very well, let's enter together.

ESQUIVEL (*aside*). What's this I see? The bishop giving his hand to an actress!

VICEROY. Your Grace, I kiss your hand. I am embarrassed at being unable to rise to receive you, but ailing as I am—

BISHOP. The Señora spoke of your illness to me, and I didn't want to return home without inquiring into your health. This also afforded me the pleasure of bringing her here in my carriage.

PERICHOLE. It is a courtesy that I shall never forget.

VICEROY. What! Did my—your[16]—carriage—break down?

PERICHOLE. It didn't, my lord, but I own it no longer, and I have no regrets, for I have made good use of it, or so I hope.

BISHOP. A good and saintly use.

ESQUIVEL (*aside*). I can't make head or tail of this.

BISHOP. You have given an example of piety exceptional in our age.

VICEROY. Explain....

PERICHOLE. Pardon me, my lord, if I so quickly gave away a present that I had from you, but after I tell you into what hands I have entrusted it, you will forgive and congratulate me.—While I was going from street to street, gently cradled by those soft cushions, a thought entered my mind that instantly dissolved my pleasure. What, thought I, a sinner, a wretched creature like myself... a woman practicing an almost guilty profession—

BISHOP. My daughter, you are too humble, and although I have never seen you on stage, I know that you greatly honor your profession. Saint Genesius was an actor.

PERICHOLE. Yet still—I am carried from one end of town to the other, softly and as quick as lightning; I am sheltered from sun and rain, while persons a thousand times better than I, namely servants of the Lord, carrying spiritual consolation to the sick, are exposed to all the inclemencies of the air, heat, dust, and fatigue. Then I remembered how often I have seen worthy priests, bent with age, walking hastily along the streets of Lima, carrying the Eucharist to the sick, and fearing only to arrive too late at the bedside of the dying. I wept for myself, and the Holy Virgin inspired me, as an expiation for my sins, to render homage to God by means of this coach, which had flattered my pride and which I was not worthy of owning.[17]

BISHOP. The señora made a generous gift of it to our church, along with a pious endowment for its perpetual maintenance. In the future, whenever a sick person asks for the consolation religion gives to the dying, this carriage will be used to carry the Blessed Sacrament, and in that way

---

16. The viceroy catches himself using the intimate "*ta voiture*" before correcting himself to say "*votre voiture.*"

17. See Appendix B.

many souls will be saved, for it happens only too frequently that hardened sinners ask for their Creator only when death is about to grasp them and too late for a poor priest on foot to reach their bedside while they are still alive.

ESQUIVEL. The señora has indeed yielded to a good and saintly inspiration.

VICEROY. I admire you, Perichole, and I should like to be associated with your good deed by taking upon myself—

PERICHOLE. Ah, my lord, leave me the glory of having done it.... I am rewarded enough by this precious gift from my lord bishop. This rosary has been locked for nine days in the shrine of the blessed image of Our Lady of Chimpaquirà.[18]

(*She makes the viceroy and Esquivel kiss it*)

BISHOP. Great indulgences are attached to it.

VICEROY. I'm so happy that I don't feel my leg anymore. Pineda is a fool; I don't have the gout.

PERICHOLE. It's the rosary you just touched that has relieved you, my lord.

BISHOP. Nothing is more likely; I have often seen it to have quite marvelous results.

VICEROY. I believe it, but I'll continue my diet for another two days; after that, your Grace, I should like to do something truly frolicsome and bid you to supper in the señora's apartments so that you two can become better acquainted.

PERICHOLE. I dare not hope that his Grace will condescend to bestow this honor on me. To be sure, our divine Savior broke bread with the Samaritans... and if the deepest secret....

BISHOP. We shall see. Let us wait till his Excellency is well again.

VICEROY. This means he'll accept.

BISHOP. I'm afraid I shall lack the will-power to decline.

PERICHOLE. Would Doctor Don Esquivel care to make up a foursome?

ESQUIVEL. This is too great an honor.

BISHOP. My dear Esquivel, due discretion will be observed.

ESQUIVEL. My lord!

VICEROY. And you will hear Perichole sing... pious songs, of course. Her voice is capable of converting a heathen.

---

18. "An image highly revered in the New World." [M] See the note on this image in *Carvajal's Family.*

BISHOP (*bowing to Perichole and smiling*). I only fear that she may turn one of the faithful *into* a heathen.

ESQUIVEL. Señora, this coach will be for you the chariot of Elijah; it will carry you straight to heaven.[19]

The End

---

19. The allusion is to 2 Kings 2, 11: "Suddenly there appeared chariots of fire and horses of fire...and Elijah was carried up in a whirlwind to heaven." It might not be amiss for an actor to quote this verse and conclude the play with it.

Appendix A

Mérimée calls Esquivel a *"licencié,"* a title translated from the Spanish *"licenciado"*—a person holding a university degree which corresponds roughly to our Master of Arts. Loiseaux, in his English translation of the play, called him "M.A., Professor." It seemed clear to me, however, that when Esquivel speaks, he does so neither as a man holding an advanced degree at a university nor as a professor, but as a priest, whether or not he also holds a Master of Arts and a professorship. Moreover, he speaks as a person directly connected to the cathedral of Lima. Hence I decided that he was likely to be a canon of that cathedral. When I came to the end of the first draft of my translation, using the 1857 edition of *Le Théâtre de Clara Gazul*, I was astonished and quite pleased to discover that Mérimée had slyly substituted *Chanoine* (canon) for *Licencié* as the speaker for Esquivel's very last speech. My hunch was confirmed. Even more surprising was the discovery, through the variants published by Trahard and later in the Pléiade edition, that the original printing of the play, namely in the *Revue de Paris* in 1829, showed Esquivel as a Licencié to the very end. This means that Mérimée deliberately slipped in the man's true title the following year, when he published his second, augmented edition of *Le Théâtre de Clara Gazul*.

The editors who have dutifully entered this alteration as a variant have not commented on it in their notes to the play, and neither, to my knowledge, has anyone else noticed it. And yet this is the only material and interesting variant; all the others are trifling. Two questions arise at this point, however. First, why did Mérimée disguise Esquivel as a *licencié* in 1829? And second: why did he not reveal him fully as a canon in 1830? We can eliminate out of hand the hypothesis that in 1829 Mérimée was afraid, or hesitant, to introduce the figure of a priest into his play, since a priest of a higher order than a canon is a conspicuous character in it. It seems, therefore, that we are looking at another one of Mérimée's literary jokes—one, to be sure, that has lain dormant for some 170 years and remains puzzling as a joke even when it reveals itself.

Appendix B

A note by Mérimée, placed at the end of Perichole's speech "inspired by the Virgin," gives the following information: "A famous actress of Lima called la Perichole, took it into her head one day to go to church in a coach. There were few coaches in Lima at that time, and they all belonged to persons of the highest distinction. La Perichole, who was being kept by the viceroy of Peru, obtained, not without some effort, that her lover make her a present of a magnificent carriage, in which she exhibited herself throughout the city to the astonishment of its inhabitants. After having enjoyed her carriage for an hour or so, she suddenly felt an access of devotion and donated it to the cathedral, wishing it to serve to give rapid conveyance to priests on their way to administer spiritual aid to the sick. She established moreover an endowment for the upkeep of the carriage. Since that day, the Blessed Sacrament is carried by coach in Lima, and the name of the actress is held in great honor." Mérimée provides no source for this note, but thanks to a German scholar, we now know that its source, as well as that of the play itself, is an account of the actress in the first volume of Basil Hall's *Extracts from a Journal Written on the Coasts of Chile, Perú and Mexico*, translated into French and published in 1825 as *Voyage au Chili, Pérou et au Mexique pendant les années 1820, 1821, et 1822* (see H. Meier 1964–5, *passim.*). La Perichole (la Perricholi in Spanish)[20] was the most famous—and notorious—actress of her time in Peru. She was born in Lima in 1748, married a fellow actor in 1775, and died in a convent in 1819. Her real name was Micaela Villegas y Hurtado de Mendoza. Her viceregal lover was Don Manuel de Amat. I do not know why Mérimée changed Micaela to Camila and the viceroy's name to Andres de Ribera, unless he meant to admonish us that he was writing a play and not a history.

Doña Micaela has been the subject of several biographies, among them Luis Alberto Sanchez: *La Perricholi* (4th edition, Lima 1963); Luz Angelica Campana de Hatts: *La Perricholi: mito literario nacional Peruano* (Mexico 1969); and Gustavo Bacacorzo: *Doña Micaela Villegas, La Perricholi* (Lima 1994). A useful work on the theater in Lima, including a few pages on the actress, is *El Arte dramático en Lima durante el Virreinato* by Guillermo Lohmann Villena (Madrid 1945).

---

20. In Spanish, French and several other languages it is customary to precede the name of an actress, singer, etc. by the definite article. Incidentally, Mérimée spelled his heroine's name "Perichole" rather than the expected "Périchole."

The notes in the Pléiade edition of Mérimée's works can be consulted regarding sources which the author could have used for information about Peru in general (Mallion and Salomon 1978. pp. 1200 ff), but to these must be added several other probable sources mentioned by Gerd Thieltges, whose indispensable work was apparently unknown to the Pléiade editors. Thieltges should also be consulted for the allusions in *The Gilded Coach* to French figures (Louis XVIII. for instance) and the politics of the Restoration (Thieltges 1975, pp. 398–404). His work is equally valuable with respect to the socio-political context of Mérimée's other early plays.

The Opportunity

(L'Occasion)

(1829)

Que esa pena, ese dolor
Mas que tristeza es furor
Y mas que furor, es muerte.
Calderón, *El Mayor monstruo, los celos*[1]

---

1. "This grief, this pain is more than sadness, it is fury, and more than fury, it is death."
From *Jealousy, the Greatest Monster*.

About the Text

The French text is again that of the 1857 edition. The footnotes in the translation are all by the translator.

Characters

Pensioners in a convent school:

Doña Maria, or Mariquita.
Doña Francisca, or Paquita, or Francisquita.
Doña Irena.
Doña Ximena.

Others:

Fray Antonio.[2]

Rita, a servant.

The action takes place in the garden of a convent in Havana around the year 1829. To the right we see a small building marked PHARMACY, the door of which opens to the garden, as does its ground-floor window. Upstage, a large orange-tree; downstage, a bower and a bench.

---

2. He is called Eugenio in the original. I have changed this to a name more easily pronounced in English.

(Maria is alone, seated on the bench. She holds an open book but is dreaming instead of reading)[3]

MARIA. He gave me this book and told me to read it....In his opinion I'm to find consolation in it for every human sorrow....I've read and re-read it. but I've found nothing in it to fight against love....Kempis was a great. learned man. gentle. virtuous. and merciful...a saint...but he never knew what it is to be in love....I'm so unhappy! (*She reads*) "Good behavior prize for Doña Maria Colmenares." Good behavior! For him I'm nothing but a well-behaved little girl, in other words a bore...a little girl. in other words an insignificant creature one can't love...or else that one loves like a trained turtle-dove....But—little girls or women. what does it matter? He can't love any of them. He's a priest. he's not of this world. And yet...he's not like the other priests, he makes small-talk, he laughs, and he often speaks to me...speaks to me about what. oh my God!—about the birds I feed. the flowers I grow. Yesterday—how excited he became when he described the palace of the Alhambra! (*Sadly*) He was describing it to Francisca...and I. who have seen the Alhambra. when I tried to put in a word about it. he stopped talking. and the conversation came to an end. Doña Francisca is three years older than I, yet what does she know that I don't?—I sing better. I'm better at the piano and guitar. She can barely keep time when she dances!....Yesterday I noticed Fray Antonio looking brightly at me when I danced with her; his eyes were shining...he was no longer the austere churchman; he looked like a young lover....That's when I should have given him this fatal letter I write and tear up every day. (*She draws a letter from her bosom and quickly reads it*) By now it sounds neither good nor bad. Each time I rewrite it. it becomes colder, but to be sure, the first time round it was improper....And besides, words that move people when you speak them in a low voice make them laugh and feel sorry for you when they read them...I wonder what he'll think of this ending. It was wrong of me to write, "I shall know how to die so as to trouble you no more." I shall know how to die....He'll never believe that little Mariquita "knows how to die." It sounds like a threat, or bluster. " I shall know how to die" sounds like a speech in the theater, when a woman

---

3. If the presence of the pharmacy seems a little too pat, the actress can walk onto the stage at the beginning of the play instead of being discovered seated, and gaze intently at the building before seating herself. Thus she will appear to have *chosen* this place for meditation. By the same token, she will stare at the pharmacy during her opening soliloquy when she speaks of the poison.

is about to stab herself with a wooden dagger....And yet I was perfectly serious while writing these words; I did think of dying. The doctor says that it's very easy; a single spoonful of the poison he was telling us about...sixty seconds of convulsions...and then no more anguish....But one should *do* such things and not talk about them....I'll cross out that sentence when I recopy my letter, and then...(*vexed*) and then what? It will be even flatter and colder than before. Oh, why can't he read my soul?...Shall I give it to him?....What if I spoke to him?...He would interrupt me at once. (*She tears off a small branch*) If this branch has an odd number of leaves, I will hand him the letter....Eleven, twelve, thirteen, fourteen....Even....But—talk to him? Impossible. I *must* give it to him....Let me see; I'll open the book. The first page on the left: " O Satan! I had rather die, and undergo any torment, than consent unto thee."[4] Am I crazy? I must be a fool to allow chance to settle a question that's life or death to me....Yes, I *will* give him the letter; it tells him, at any rate, "I love you," and that's a word I couldn't bring myself to utter aloud.

(*Singing off-stage*).

> The Frenchman when he loves
> Blubbers like a baby in his wine.
> The Spaniard says "I love you —
> But if you're cold, I'm off to dine!"[5]

MARIA. There's the oracle that instructs me what to do. I *will* give him the letter.
(*Enter Rita*)
MARIA. Are you going to sweep the pharmacy?
RITA. Yes, Doña Maria. And dust all those flasks, and open the windows to air the place.
(*She enters the pharmacy. Maria walks up to the window Rita is opening*)

----

4. *The Imitation of Christ* by Thomas à Kempis, III, 6, 4. The section from which Maria reads shows man rejecting the seductions of the "unclean spirit." The "O Satan!" is my addition to Kempis and Mérimée; it simply clarifies the passage.
5. I have taken the liberty of writing this mediocre lyric myself. "Even though I'm not insensitive to poetry, I was never able to write in verse," Mérimée confessed to a correspondent in 1855. Ingrained aversion to composing in rhyme combined, I suppose, with laziness to give Rita a mere piece of prose as follows: "The Frenchman in love cries like a child; the Andalusian, more stoical [plus philosophe] says: I love you; do you want me? otherwise good-bye."

MARIA (*with a forced smile*). Be careful not to break the bottle you were telling me about.

RITA. Jesus! Mary! I'm scared even to come near it. They say you have to swallow some of it in order to die, but still I'd be uneasy if I so much as touched the glass.

MARIA. I can't believe the poison is as violent as you say.

RITA. Ha! Take it from me! Didn't the doctor tell me so himself? Hands off that bottle, Rita! Two or three spoonfulls in a pitcher of water would be enough to kill every one of these young ladies in less than fifteen minutes. It catches you at the throat, you choke, and whissht! it's all over.

MARIA (*pointing within*). Isn't that the bottle, over there?

RITA. No; it's that little flask on the top shelf. Small as it is, it can poison above a thousand persons.

MARIA. That one up there with something white in it?

RITA. That's the one.

MARIA. Good.

RITA. Good? Say rather bad. May the devil twist the heathen's neck who concocted such vile drugs! How is it that these apothecaries, who you expect to carry nothing but remedies for our ailments, how is it they stock the kind of drugs that send you to the other world before you can call a priest?

MARIA (*gravely*). There are sicknesses these drugs can cure.

RITA. God and St James preserve us from those! My own belief is that they're used only for people with rabies, to keep them from biting other folk.

MARIA (*aside*). Think of it, a single moment of suffering!

(*Rita leaves the pharmacy, closing the door but leaving the window open*)

RITA. If I were Mother Superior I'd throw that ugly flask into a hole, because it can do more harm than good.

MARIA. How so?

RITA. Sure....For instance, somebody who wanted to get rid of somebody....Or else, supposing a bad person wanted to end it all....

MARIA. Come now! Who could want to commit suicide?

RITA. Not you, Doña Maria, you who are so well-behaved and so good in school that you put the other girls to shame, but I could name a few hotheads....Listen, I'm sure you won't repeat my words to her—but I wouldn't dare show that bottle to your friend Doña Francisca.

MARIA. Francisca!

RITA. She's always reading English novels; they go to her head. Would you believe that she told me one time that if she were in love with a man, and the man died, she'd kill herself?

MARIA (*with a bitter smile*). You needn't worry.

RITA. I said to her. I said: Doña Francisca. don't say such things: I'm only a poor servant girl, I can't talk like a priest. but I do know that you offend God by destroying yourself. Isn't that right. Doña Maria?

MARIA. "Thou shalt not kill." (*Softly*) On the other hand....

RITA. It's the devil who puts those ideas in people's heads. I knew a girl from Guatemala who. when she came to be eighteen or nineteen years old. got the urge, but really hard, to kill herself. She told me that whenever she looked down into the street from a high window. Satan would tell her to jump. And yet, as time wore on. she got over the idea.

MARIA (*sharply*). How? How did she manage?

RITA. Easy! She kept praying the Lord to deliver her; she went on a pilgrimage. and then a handsome brown-haired mule-driver showed up; he courted her; they got married, and now she thinks as much of killing herself as I do of swinging from a rope.

MARIA (*aside*). I wish....

RITA. Please. Doña Maria, don't repeat anything I said about Doña Francisca.

MARIA. Don't worry...Rita, when you do my room, by my bedside you'll see a little chaplet made of garnets and gold that comes from Mexico. Take it, it's a present for you.

RITA. For me?

MARIA. Yes; I've owed you a present for a long time. You're so considerate to me. And then, sometimes, after I leave the convent, you'll say a special rosary for me.

RITA. Oh my dear sweet young lady! Allow me to kiss your hands; you're too generous...I'll be unhappy when the time comes for you to leave us, even though it will be for your own good. no doubt in order to be married.

MARIA (*sighing*). Who knows?

(*Silence*)

RITA. Should I put fresh flowers in your china vases?

MARIA. Yes, do.

RITA. Thank you, miss.

(*She leaves*)

MARIA (*alone*). Prayers!...I tried them too, but I couldn't drive away the notions that obsess me....What if he were willing to run away with me?...But that's impossible....Then what remains? To flee alone...to flee from the world. (*She looks into the pharmacy through the open window*) One instant of pain!...A pain less sharp than what I've endured day and night for two months. I could—right now—take this treasure and the oblivion it gives....It's so easy to enter through the window; and here's even a stone jutting out that I can step on.

(*She raises herself to the window. Enter Fray Antonio. They do not see each other. Fray Antonio goes up to the orange-tree, extracts a letter from a hollow, and replaces it with his own*)

FRAY ANTONIO. Thank you, my fine orange-tree, loyal as ever. (*He reads*) Anxieties! Reproaches! Ha! You're unfair to me. Ends with kisses! Our two letters are very much alike.

MARIA (*jumping down, aside*). Get thee behind me, Satan!

FRAY ANTONIO (*aside*). Who's the pretty girl? How she jumped! Oh! It's little Mariquita, Francisca's friend. She's quite attractive for her age. What has she been up to in the pharmacy?

MARIA (*seeing Fray Antonio*). Oh!

FRAY ANTONIO. You should have called me to hold your hand, Doña Maria, instead of jumping.

MARIA. It's you....

FRAY ANTONIO. I seem to have startled you.

MARIA. Oh no....It's only....(*aside*) Jesus Maria!

FRAY ANTONIO. I didn't know you were so agile, Doña Maria. May one inquire what prompted you to enter the pharmacy by this peculiar opening?

MARIA. I didn't go in, I swear.

FRAY ANTONIO. To be sure, but you did come out. I bet I can guess what you were looking for.

MARIA. Oh, it's not true!

FRAY ANTONIO. Confess that you've purloined some candy. Take heed, Doña Mariquita! You'll be accounting to me for that sin next time I catch you in the confessional.

MARIA (*aside*). He treats me like a child.[6]

FRAY ANTONIO. I do believe I've scared you....Don't worry, my pretty child, I'm not as mean as you think. Come now! Do you require absolution? *Absolvo te*. But in exchange you must share your loot with me. If you do, I promise not to report you. Hm, how you stare at me!...You surprise me, to tell you the truth. Lately I've observed that you look sad...you've grown pale....What's the matter? You're not ill by any chance, are you?

MARIA. Ill? No, not ill...only unhappy.

---

6. Stage direction: "She covers her eyes with her hand." As in *Carvajal's Family*, I have sometimes omitted stage directions better left to actors and directors.

FRAY ANTONIO. Don't tell me that your parakeet Loretto has given up the ghost!

MARIA. Oh, how little you know me, Fray Antonio; you take me for a child.

FRAY ANTONIO. A child? God forbid! A young lady almost fifteen years old.

MARIA (*gravely*). Can't a person be as much in pain at fifteen as at thirty?

FRAY ANTONIO. Forgive me—my joking is in bad taste, and your seriousness is beginning to alarm me. Perhaps you've had bad news from Spain. I hope the general your uncle is in good health?

MARIA. I think he is. My grief comes from within me. Oh, Fray Antonio, how I wish I were a man!—I wish I were dead.

FRAY ANTONIO. Nonsense! Now I *will* take you for a child. Cure yourself of these ridiculous ideas. You probably got them from books you shouldn't be reading.—What is *that* one?

MARIA. You can see for yourself. The *Imitation of Christ* that you gave me. I don't let a day go by without reading it and hoping it will give me strength, but it doesn't. I've never read a novel, Fray Antonio, but I have a soul, a heart...I live...I ponder things...and...oh! that's why I would like to die.

FRAY ANTONIO (*aside*). The child is in love; that's all they think about in this convent. (*To Maria*) Well, young lady, you'll tell me all about it one of these days. I haven't time right now to preach and scold as you deserve. Yes, as you deserve to be scolded for being so silly. And here I thought that you were more mature than most of the girls. Shame on you, Doña Maria. It's become a kind of fashion to want to die. I hear nothing but complaints about life from children your age.

MARIA. Children! Well, children can wish to die when they're unhappy. *I* have wanted to die, but death didn't want me.

FRAY ANTONIO. What are you saying?

MARIA. You may have heard that I was almost killed by a wild bull two weeks ago. Well—I placed myself in his path on purpose. He came so close to me, I felt the breath of his nostrils on my cheek...and I don't know why he didn't hurt me.

FRAY ANTONIO. If what you say is true —

MARIA (*proudly*). True? Do you think I'm capable of lying?

FRAY ANTONIO. Then what you did was folly and sin. These are the happiest years of a person's life, and especially of *your* life, Doña Maria, you who have everything you can desire. You're an orphan, but you have an uncle who is rich and powerful, and you are wealthy in your own name. A year from now your uncle will come for you and take you back to Spain. You'll be presented at court. You'll make an advantageous marriage.

MARIA. Marriage for me! Oh God!

FRAY ANTONIO. Instead of giving yourself up to this absurd fit of melancholy, you should thank God for the favors He has lavished on you. (*Aside*) I'll speak to the doctor.

MARIA (*vehemently*). Once more, Fray Antonio, I tell you that you don't know me.

(*They stare at each other for a moment, then lower their eyes*)

FRAY ANTONIO (*looking at his watch*). I take it, Doña Maria, that you wish to confide something in me, and I shall be glad to counsel you if you believe I can be helpful. I will be hearing confession tomorrow between noon and two o'clock. Prepare yourself in the meantime by practicing your devotions. I must leave you now. Mother Superior has asked me to share a cup of chocolate with her.

MARIA. You look down on me, I'm afraid, because you're a man and a priest.

FRAY ANTONIO. Doña Mariquita, unless I'm gravely mistaken, your little head has been turned by some fancy of love.

MARIA. You are a priest...but if you could understand —

FRAY ANTONIO. I understand quite well that the regiment of volunteers from Girona arrived a month ago at La Havana, that its officers are wearing brand-new uniforms, and that they hear mass on Sunday at the Church of St James, where you go as well....We shall talk about all that tomorrow.

MARIA. I'll tell you nothing; you wouldn't even hear me, and I'll be miserable to the end.

FRAY ANTONIO. There's a cure for everything, child, except for death. And now good-bye; that cup of chocolate compels me to leave you.

(*He turns to go; Maria holds him back*)

MARIA. I must live or die!...Fray Antonio, listen to me. We're alone....Listen to me, for pity's sake....You *must* listen to me....You can cause me to me live or die...and if you say a word...I swear....Ah, Fray Antonio, you are a priest....I can't speak.

FRAY ANTONIO. Doña Maria, I don't know whether I should laugh at your conduct or get angry with you....No, after all, I do feel sorry for you. Go; go pray, and come to me an hour from now in the convent church. I shall listen there to what you have to say; right now I can't.

MARIA (*taking the letter from her bosom*). The words I can't speak...this letter....

FRAY ANTONIO (*holding out his hand*). What is in this letter? Give it to me.

MARIA (*holding back*). Promise at least that you won't read it while you're in the convent. Read it tonight—not before. Do you promise? And tomorrow....No, don't ever mention it to me....If you return it to me...don't scold me...it wouldn't be any use...just return it....I'll be punishing myself for my folly...but for God's sake don't scold me.

FRAY ANTONIO. Give it. (*He takes the letter*)

MARIA. Have pity on me, I beg you....I resisted as long as I could....No! Don't open it here! (*Fray Antonio has torn the letter open*). Oh God! What are you doing?....Fray Antonio...I beg you...for pity's sake...return it to me, Fray Antonio....You're killing me....Oh, don't read it here!

FRAY ANTONIO. What are you doing?[7] Calm yourself; somebody is coming.

MARIA. Don't read it here...or else give it back to me.

(*Enter Rita*)

RITA. Sir, Mother Superior is waiting for you in her parlor.

FRAY ANTONIO. I'm coming. (*To Maria*) I'll read it presently.

(*He leaves with Rita*)

MARIA (*alone*). So I've given away my secret....Given it away without hope that he'll respond to my love...at the very moment when I saw ever so clearly that he's indifferent to me. But what am I saying? Indifferent!...He's a priest, devout, above reproach; so there's no hope for me. Rather than hear him take me to task, I ought to....And yet...what if he did love me...if he *could* love me....No, he loves only God. Sometimes his voice is so gentle...so tender even....Just now, I felt for an instant as if he were no longer a priest...yet when I was about to speak, he suddenly looked so stern that my courage froze....That evening...when I danced with Francisca, and when I could see him drinking in our pleasure, that's when I should have confessed my love to him. Francisca! She was dancing with me....Oh no, she's not in love with him. If she's in love at all, it's with one of those officers....He does often talk to her...but...no, not about love....Francisca couldn't!...A priest! I'm the only one capable....Such an awful sin, dear God! To be in love with a priest! Only I in the whole wide world am capable of such a horrid, criminal passion...and wretch that I am, that's what reassures me...my crime reassures me! Because at least I won't have a rival....Perhaps he's opened my letter....He might be reading it this very moment....He's probably angry, indignant....That a woman

---

7. Clearly Maria has made a sudden lunge for the letter.

should stoop so low! Or else he's laughing at me, and saying, "That poor crazy child" as he shrugs his shoulders....Almighty God! I'll give them proof that I'm not a child....They will see that I'm braver than a soldier...and that I love as other women can't. I'll die if he won't have me....And what if he won't keep my letter secret? Strange letter...at the end...how did I phrase the end?...I can't remember a single word; my poor head is spinning. "I...if you do not love me...I"....Ah! Why did I give him the letter? Idiot!...Why didn't I *speak* to him? He would have seen my tears, my confusion....While that cold and stiff document, that studied handwriting...with its commas and periods! He'll believe that I'm copying phrases out of novels...he'll call me "child" again....Oh God, make an end of me—because they'll force me to do it myself....Couldn't I send him a note to excuse myself, to explain my letter?...No; that would be even more absurd....Maybe he hasn't read it yet....If he had, he would have come back, or had me summoned....If this anxiety lasts much longer I'll go mad....I asked him not to open the letter till nightfall, and now I dread that he'll obey me....Oh, death is better than this torment of waiting...and tossing and turning in my bed all night! Oh, Fray Antonio, kill me at once. (*She hears talk and laughter off-stage*) Ha! here come my so-called friends, with their laughter and their chatter. More than ever they're odious to me.

(*She tries to get away but is stopped by Irena, Ximena and Francisca*)

IRENA. Maria, Mariquita, where are you going? Why are you running away from us?

XIMENA. What's wrong, Mariquita? Why are your eyes so red? Have you been crying? I know! You've read a novel with an unhappy ending!

MARIA. I have a headache.

FRANCISCA. Poor dear! Yes—your forehead is burning. Stay here in the shade—trust me. Our rooms are stifling. Let's sit on this bench. Rest your head on my shoulder. Besides (*in a low voice*) I've so many things to tell you, Mariquita! You *must* stay and hear me out.

IRENA. Mariquita, we need you to be the judge between Ximena and myself.

XIMENA. A fine judge you're choosing! As if she were an expert in that sort of thing! Francisca, now, could do in a pinch.

IRENA. Who needs an expert? All we want is to hear her preference.

FRANCISCA. Don't trouble her with your ridiculous questions. Poor child! Can't you see that she's sick?

MARIA. What is it all about, Irena?[8]

IRENA. You saw the naval officers who came ashore from the Esmeralda and who attended mass in our church yesterday. Well, Ximena, who is already in love with one of them, comes and tells us that their uniform is handsomer than those of the American dragoons. What do you say to her? Those naval officers dressed as plain as can be, against the dragoons with their green and yellow uniforms, their silver braid, their grey trousers with orange piping, their black helmets with feathers —

XIMENA. Exactly—and looking like canaries, while the sailors, with their blue and red jackets, their white trousers—it's a severe outfit that becomes the military. Besides, I love their gold-bordered hats, and I'm crazy about their daggers.

IRENA. Mule-drivers and dockers also carry daggers; whereas a long sabre that clatters on the pavement—now *that*'s a pretty sight! Not to mention their spurs. They make so much noise entering the church that everybody turns around. Ask sailors to do that!

XIMENA. They don't, because they don't want to act like bullies, the way the dragoons do. All the same, they're daredevils, every one of them. To begin with, think what courage it takes to be a sailor.

IRENA. As if you didn't need courage to be a dragoon! I'd be as scared to mount a horse as to sail on a ship in the open sea.

XIMENA. What about the storms, the shipwrecks, and the naval combats? That's where you need courage! All those cannons that stick out of their gunports and fire chain-shot that kill twenty men at a time.

IRENA. Ladies, take note how familiar Ximena has become with nautical terms ever since she gave her heart away to the captain of a frigate.

XIMENA. I haven't given him a thing, and I haven't even spoken to him, but he came with a letter of recommendation for my aunt. I'll be meeting him at my aunt's house on Sunday. All I know is that he's altogether a gentleman. Besides, you *have* to be a gentleman in order to enter the navy.

IRENA. You may not have spoken to him with your mouth, but you've said a great deal, God be praised, with your fan.

---

8. The original reads as follows: MARIA (*yawning*). What is it all about, Irena? IRENA. Ugh! It's indecent to yawn in people's faces. MARIA. I have a stomach-ache. Mérimée's footnote to the yawn explains: "A fairly common effect of anxiety. It was noted that Ali Pasha, after surrendering to the Turks, yawned continuously during the hour that preceded his death." The reference is to the famous Turkish rebel, described by Byron in *Childe Harold*, whom the Sultan caused to be assassinated in 1822. The passage shows a rare lapse from dramatic virtue under the influence of trivial erudition.

XIMENA. Good heavens! Talk as much as you like—you never stop making little signs and winking at your big captain, Don Rafael Samaniego. What a name! The captain of the *Esmeralda* is called Juan de Garibay, which, let me inform you, is a Basque name, and he wears the cross of Alcantara, and he fought in a splendid naval battle, and he broke an Englishman's arm in a duel, and —

FRANCISCA. How thoroughly you know the story of his life!

IRENA. I don't like pistols, they're stupid. Swords are a lot more graceful. Don Rafael duelled with a sword only a month ago. He's amazingly dexterous.

FRANCISCA. I gather that the military uniform has conquered both of you.

IRENA. Well, it becomes a man. If I were a man, I'd want to be a colonel in the dragoons.

XIMENA. And I, if I were a man, I'd command a ship. Have you noticed the children they call the navy's cadets? How sweet they look in their little blue vests and their white trousers!

FRANCISCA. In short, for you a man is good only if he has stripes on his sleeve and a three-cornered hat or a helmet on his head.

IRENA. There you're wrong. For instance, without travelling far, we can see a very good-looking man every day who *doesn't* wear a uniform.

XIMENA. I know who you mean, and it's true.

FRANCISCA. Who is the man?

IRENA. What a question! Fray Antonio.

FRANCISCA and MARIA. Fray Antonio!

XIMENA. He has the most beautiful hands in the world.

IRENA. And eyes noble and sweet at the same time.

XIMENA. Too bad, though, that he doesn't have a moustache; his mouth is a little too large.

IRENA. Not too large for a man; and his teeth are superb. You should see how he takes care of them. I think they're the reason he recently stopped smoking. Why are you laughing, Paquita?

FRANCISCA. I'm laughing at the profundity of your observations.

XIMENA. What I like best about him is that he's always in a good mood—easy-going and jovial, just the opposite of his predecessor, the late Father Domingo Ojeda, who nagged us over everything and nothing. Fray Antonio allows us to dance among ourselves and sing and laugh, keeps telling us to enjoy ourselves while we're young, and always takes our side against that sour old Mother Superior of ours. He's a lovely man!

IRENA. Do you know what he did for Doña Lucia d'Olmedo?

FRANCISCA. No, I don't.

IRENA. All Havana talks of it; I heard the story at my mother's yesterday.

FRANCISCA. Doña Lucia? The daughter of the magistrate Don Pedro? The girl who eloped with an officer of the dragoons?

IRENA. Exactly. At first her father was fuming fire and brimstone. He was threatening to send his daughter to the Sisters of Penitence,[9] and he had obtained a warrant from the corregidor for the officer's arrest—a lieutenant, a certain Fadrigo Romero, or something of the kind. I hear he's not bad-looking; black moustache, and knows how to strum a guitar. In fact, it's the guitar that seduced that crazy Doña Lucia, because he's a youngest son and hasn't a penny to his name. His pay is all he's got to live on, and you know what *that* is. In short, he had his eyes wide open when he went courting Doña Lucia and her father's riches.

FRANCISCA. Where does Fray Antonio come in?

IRENA. Fray Antonio went to the father, who was spitting mad. He must have preached him one of his touching, eloquent sermons, like his Lenten ones. And then he said: Don't you see that you're going to ruin yourself along with your daughter; you want to punish them for causing a scandal, and you're causing an even greater one, et caetera et caetera. To make a long story short, he preached and preached so hard that the father began to weep. Fray Antonio had placed the ravisher and his victim in an adjacent room. He opens the door, bang! the two fling themselves at the old man's feet, kissing his hands, weeping floods of tears. My father here, my father there....Conclusion: the commissioner's bronze heart turned into soft wax. He raises them, embraces his daughter, holds out his hand to Fadrigo and calls him "my dear son." To top it all, this Don Pedro, who is stingier than a Jew, made such a flip-flop thanks to Fray Antonio that he gave his girl a huge dowry. And do you know why? Fray Antonio convinced him that all Havana would ridicule him if he didn't do things in a grand way.—Hey Paquita! What's the matter? You're crying?

FRANCISCA. I am; his goodness has touched me.

XIMENA. Oh the power of eloquence!

IRENA. And oh the sensitive soul! Ha ha ha!

XIMENA. Here's Paquita in tears. Mariquita looks as if she's ready to cry too. This is all too romantic for me. Come along, Irena; let these girls cry

---

9. "*Filles repenties*" in the original. Cloisters for fallen women, under the patronage of Saint Mary Magdalen, existed in the thirteenth century and probably earlier. Mérimée may have had in mind the "*Fille Pénitentes de la Magdeleine*" in Paris, founded in 1492. The nuns of these orders were pledged to perpetual claustration.

together. I've something to tell you that will make you laugh. Adieu, young ladies; you may have your secrets, but we have ours.

(*They leave*)

FRANCISCA (*hugging Maria*). Dear Maria! My only friend!

MARIA (*looking carefully at Francisca*). I didn't know you were so emotional.

FRANCISCA. Ah, you don't know what goes on inside me. (*A clock strikes, and Maria starts*) You're so nervous today! If your heart were as full as mine, the clock would remind you only of felicities. Is no one watching us? Look, Mariquita; you won't betray me? A letter....(*She goes to the orange-tree and takes Fray Antonio's letter. Maria watches her without interest. Francisca quickly reads the letter and kisses it*) Dearest little Maria! Let me kiss you too. But tell me why you have to be sick today. When I'm happy, I want everyone I love to be happy too.

MARIA. I'm in pain.

FRANCISCA. It's true; we've noticed how you've changed recently, but it's because you've grown, you've become a woman so fast!...Let time take care of things, and one day you'll be as happy as I, and then you'll be fit again.

MARIA. You're so very happy, are you?

FRANCISCA. Oh, I am, and I've no other desire than to continue as I am for a long, long time. But my happiness is choking me, Mariquita, and I simply must confide in you, even though, looking at your pretty scowl, I realize that you're in no mood to hear my story. You're my best friend, and one of the burdens of friendship is to listen to the joys and griefs of one's friends. People here take you for a child because you're the youngest of the older girls; but you're so good, so reasonable, so....(*she kisses her*) You're so dear to me that I want to reveal myself only to you.

MARIA (*sighing*). I'll listen, since you want me to. (*Aside*) It'll make time pass more quickly for me.

FRANCISCA. Well! (*She stops*) Do you realize that you look so grave that I'm intimidated?...Don't stare at me like that. And...no reproaches, young miss. Respect your elders!...Mariquita, I'm in love, and someone is in love with me. (*Maria squeezes her hand*) Look at you! Now it's *your* turn to have tears in your eyes. So, young lady, I've caught you out! What! You too! Who would have believed it? "There are no children anymore," as Mother Superior says. These tears are all the proof I need that your little heart has spoken. Come, tell me. Is he a captain in the dragoons? A naval officer?

MARIA. Nobody, I assure you. I cry easily because I'm not well, so there's no reason....(*Francisca wags her finger at her*) No, I swear to you....But they say that love makes one so unhappy....I'm scared for you, Paquita.

FRANCISCA (*smiling*). And who told you all this?

MARIA. Who? Everybody....Mother Superior, our confessor....

FRANCISCA. Fray Antonio! And do you believe him?

MARIA. They talk to me about matters I know nothing of...so I believe them.

FRANCISCA. Child! Let me inform you, my dear, that they're deceiving you, that love is the supreme good, and that without love one lives in hell. Doña Mariquita, you look to me like a little hypocrite. But it's up to me to be the first to speak; we'll confess you afterward.

MARIA. Well then, with whom are you in love?

FRANCISCA. Oh Mariquita, if you were in love, you'd probably pick a boy your own age, a young officer fresh from the military academy, and you'd be dreaming only of the joy of being married and of walking along the harbor arm in arm with your husband. Yes, that would be very pleasant. But there's another love...as strong, even stronger than marriage...where marriage (*she lowers her voice*) is impossible.

MARIA. How so?

FRANCISCA. Yes, Mariquita. For instance, one can be in love with...a married man. If a man has married in this or that circumstance...whichever...enough that he was never in love with his wife...she's old and ugly, mean...or else, let's suppose the woman is young and inexperienced and married to an old man...or else....However, you are so virtuous, all this must sound wicked to you.

MARIA. Oh no! I believe, Paquita, that love is sometimes stronger than all laws, human and divine....They say that love arrives one doesn't know how, and when you realize you're in love, it's too late to weigh whether it's right or wrong.

FRANCISCA. So you say, my little angel! For being so sweet you get another hug. Tell me though, where did you learn this doctrine?

MARIA. I don't know....I've heard it....So you're in love with a married man?

FRANCISCA. You know that I'm not a model of religious fervor. And the two years I spent in England have taught me not to take too seriously everything our sanctimonious preachers tell us about heretics. In England I saw excellent priests who have wives and children.

MARIA. So?

FRANCISCA. So? So you still haven't guessed?...Never mind. With you I needn't beat around the bush. You said that love is above human and divine conventions, so you'll understand and forgive. In a word, my dear, I'm in love with a priest, and the priest is Fray Antonio.

MARIA. Fray Antonio! Oh God!

FRANCISCA. Himself. I struggled for a while, but now, when I think of the time I've wasted by not loving him, I'm tempted to weep for the days I've sacrificed to virtue, or rather to prejudice. Dearest, you're acquainted only with friendship, or at most a fever in the head that you mistake for love....But true love, forbidden love....Oh Mariquita, I love you better than any woman I know....I can think of nothing I wouldn't do for you. And yet—if in order to save Fray Antonio I had to....But how stupid to think of what can't happen. No, my angel, a lover doesn't prevent me from having a friend, and I'll be the happiest of women, because I have at once the most tender of lovers and the most loyal of friends.

MARIA (*stupefied*). Fray Antonio!...loves you!

FRANCISCA. I can see that your philosophy is a little shaken. Your scruples or prejudices are so deeply rooted in your heart that you can't excuse me. For you a priest is not a man. Sacrilege and profanation come to your mind. Well, I shared your ideas before I yielded to my passion, and now that I live for nothing else, I'm glad that I sacrificed something for my Antonio. Yes, I wish I'd been far more devout than I was, so I could have made him an offering of my fear of hell and given up my soul for him, because to renounce everything, to suffer everything for one's beloved is heavenly bliss.

MARIA. And he loves you?

FRANCISCA. Does he love me! Love me! Can you ask? Every drop of blood in his heart is mine; every moment of his life is filled with my image. And yet I tell him from morning to night that he doesn't love me, and he, on his side...oh! we outdo each other flying into rages....But these fights are delicious, they keep one alive. You don't know, my dear girl; because of me, he refused to go to Spain, where he might have had a bishopric on the day he landed.

MARIA. And you've loved each other for a long time?

FRANCISCA. To tell you the truth, I don't know. Right now I feel I loved him at first sight, and yet it's only six weeks ago that we declared our love to each other. At first I thought him the brightest man I'd even seen. I admired every word he spoke. Whatever he said, however insignificant, stuck in my mind. No other man seemed clever next to him, and I couldn't enjoy myself anywhere if he wasn't present. Presently I noticed that he had singled me out among the girls. He spoke to me more often than to the others. He asked me a hundred questions, and I was so flustered every time he talked to me that my answers came out all topsy-turvy. Evenings, when Mother Superior had us in her room for music, he always stood behind my chair, and when I was seated at the piano I always saw his head in the mirror above the instrument. How many times I lost my place in the middle of a piece! Fascinated, abashed, ready to faint, I thought the score and the mirror were swaying before my eyes. And then, again and again, my good Mariquita, you'd come to the rescue; you'd point to the right place on the sheet; you'd encourage me. And as you leaned over my chair, I could see your head in the mirror next to his. Both of you seemed to love me. Both looked so sweetly at me! And you, when you sang, my poor Maria, you who have ten times my talent, Fray Antonio didn't listen, he was impatient for the music to end so he could approach me again and resume our conversation. I discovered that I was in love with him, and at first my mind was deeply troubled. In love with a priest! A man who cannot marry! But then I remembered the wives of priests I'd seen in London, and I called to mind all the women who've made miserable marriages....I have never known a happily married couple. Yet all this time I avoided being alone with Fray Antonio; I no longer talked to him; I looked at him only out of the corner of my eyes, and I saw how depressed he'd become, how his eyes were moist and entreating when he looked at me....We were pitiable, both of us. Then I heard that Fray Antonio had not felt a true calling when he took orders and that some unhappy circumstances had impelled him to take this step. You can't imagine my grief, Maria, at the thought that he had renounced the world because of despair over a woman. I couldn't bear the idea that Fray Antonio had loved somebody else. I wasn't even sure yet of being in love myself, and already I was jealous....Oh Mariquita, jealousy is so cruel!...May you never feel this ugly emotion! How many sleepless nights I spent, my pillow drenched in tears, biting my sheets with rage!...Finally I heard the true motive that had driven him to wear that ugly cassock.

MARIA. Was it love again?

FRANCISCA. His mother was very sick....The doctors had given her up....She was a very pious woman....Antonio was seventeen years old or less. His dying mother said to him, "If you pledged yourself to God, I am sure that heaven would grant you your mother's recovery." He didn't hesitate, and even though he was studying to be a doctor, he gave it all up, became a priest, and his mother recovered.

MARIA (*as if to herself*). At any rate he's generous.

FRANCISCA. Everything I heard about him increased my love. I was sure of his, but he hesitated to confess his passion because of his age and his profession; so I decided to be the first to speak and force him to declare himself. I tried starting circuitous conversations with him that would bring in the word "love" from far afield, and yet when the moment came to utter the magic word, my courage always failed me. Finally one evening, we were all dancing in this very garden under a bright moon, and he, leaning against that orange-tree, was gazing at us. When I swung in front of him, a flower fell from my hair. At first he pretended not to see it, but then he let his handkerchief *happen* to drop over it; he stooped to pick it up together with my flower. When we stopped, I drew near to him and whispered with a laugh—yet I was trembling and I could distinctly hear my heartbeat— "Fray Antonio, you took my flower; return it to me...." I could tell that he was startled. He returned it to me just as a little cloud was veiling the moon. "Why," he asked, "do you deprive me of the thing you threw away as a trifle, but I picked up as a treasure?" He was smiling and trying to sound light-hearted, but it was all so very serious for both of us! "Take it," I said, "it's yours since it means so much to you." I stretched out my hand; the flower fell, and my hand found itself in Antonio's. At that point I began to tremble so violently that I would have dropped to the ground if he hadn't held me. I don't know what he said to me, or what I said to him, or how long we remained under that orange-tree, but by the time we separated we knew we were both in love, and we had found a way of meeting again. Shall I tell you how? You're going to scold me. I pretended that I wanted to be confessed. I went to church, I knelt in the box, and there God heard vows of love instead of confessions and admonitions. Only our fingertips could touch, but I felt the fire of his breath caressing my mouth...and we kissed the grill in a frenzy....Oh! If I could have thrown myself into his arms then and there, I would gladly have perished in exchange for an hour of bliss.

MARIA. So you're both happy!...But what if you're found out?

FRANCISCA. Oh, that's impossible. Antonio is so prudent! He enters this garden only at night,[10] and only once did he reluctantly consent to come up into my room. It was crazy of me, because, as you know, my cell is next door to that of Mother Superior, and one can hear every word. Fortunately, Señora Monica was sleeping noisily enough to reassure us. However, our usual rendez-vous is over there, you see, among the flowers....That's where we were last night. I was holding his hand; his head rested on my breast; I felt the artery of his temple throb; we were both so weary, so overcome with bliss, that we couldn't speak. We watched

---

10. A puzzling statement since we have seen him in the garden in broad daylight and will see him there again shortly. Accordingly, in production the actress should say, "We meet here only at night."

the stars, we saw the Southern Cross slowly descending through the sky,[11] and now and then a light sea-breeze shed blossoms from the orange-tree over our heads. Oh Mariquita, we were in heaven! If you knew what delight there is in loving! How, I ask, does one not die of it? (*She hides her head on Maria's neck*) Ah, Maria, Maria....However, young lady, these mysteries are not for you to know as yet....You are too young, my little friend. I who am three years older have only become wise in the past few weeks; so be patient, your time will come. The only point that worries me is that he and I have no shelter; we camp out! What shall we do in the rainy season? The garden will be impossible. Perhaps we'll use the gardener's hut.

MARIA (*with a bitter smile*). That's all you see ahead of you....Rash girl! You'll be caught before the month is over. They'll see Fray Antonio climbing the convent walls. He'll be arrested; your intrigue will become public; they'll lock him up in some Trappist monastery, and you'll be sent to the Sisters of Penitence. Why don't you run away with him? Believe me, it's the most prudent solution...your only chance of salvation.

FRANCISCA. You frighten me, my dear girl! You forget that Fray Antonio is poor, and that *I* am dependent on the allowance I get from my grandfather. An elopement takes more than love. Our romances don't mention it, but one needs money, lots of it. I blush to tell you, my dear, how sometimes, when I look at the little Virgin in our chapel adorned with heaps of precious stones, I long to grab them so Antonio and I can vanish together. It's an idea that has earned me some lofty moralizing from Antonio.

MARIA. You should have turned to me. You know I'm rich; I have plenty of money in the bank that I'm free to dispose of, and valuable jewels besides.

FRANCISCA. Generous friend! This is the Maria I know! But I couldn't accept such an enormous sacrifice.

MARIA. A sacrifice? Mere money!

FRANCISCA. Antonio would never accept money from a woman. I know him too well; he's proud and even a little haughty. But here's our plan. Antonio is hard at work on a book about the Church Fathers, and the income he will draw from it —

---

11. Mérimée's note, as in *Carvajal's Family*: "Constellation whose position over the horizon allows one to tell the time at night." The editors of the Pléiade edition point out that this constellation cannot be seen in the northern hemisphere.

MARIA. Nonsense! My diamond earrings alone will sell for more than all the books he'll ever write.

FRANCISCA (*somewhat piqued*). I don't doubt that your earrings are very costly, but Antonio's book is first-rate, and it fills a gap in scholarship. He'll be able to name his own price for it...at least enough to take us to Jamaica, where we intend to settle.[12] He'll teach Spanish and Latin; I'll do needlework and cook. It will be ever so much fun!

MARIA. Yes, but what if you're caught before the book is finished?...Accept my diamonds and leave; and after that, live happily...if you can.

FRANCISCA. We simply can't accept such an expensive present, my dear, but if you insist, I'll ask Antonio for permission to borrow just enough so we can charter a small boat to Jamaica.

MARIA. I don't need my diamonds; I'll never wear them; accept them; I insist. Here. Here's the key to my jewel-box; take the diamonds and leave this very night.

FRANCISCA. But —

MARIA. Take it, I say, and leave me.

FRANCISCA. I understand, Maria. I've scandalized you; you despise me and want to get rid of me. I stand condemned by your austere virtue or your piety. You still care enough for me so you don't want to see me ruined. But if you don't love me as before, I refuse your gift.

MARIA. You're very much mistaken if you think I'm being pious or worried by scruples. If you truly love Fray Antonio, if you're truly happy with him...then you've acted right.

FRANCISCA. Your voice trembles, and you can't hide your anger. Mariquita, tell me, what's the matter with you? Is it me you're angry with? Answer me.

MARIA. I told you I'm sick....I have a horrible migraine, and for an hour you've been talking to me about your Fray Antonio and about....Look, I need to be alone, so take my key.

FRANCISCA. No, not before consulting Antonio.

MARIA. Fine! Do as you like, but leave me to myself for the love of God! Every word you speak shatters my head.

FRANCISCA. I'll leave you alone, Mariquita, since that's what you want, but give me a hug at least to show you still care for me.

MARIA (*offering her cheek*). Are you satisfied?

---

12. An English colony, therefore a safe haven where they can marry.

FRANCISCA. I'm holding you as I hold Antonio. His breath is as sweet as yours. But you're angry. I'm going.

(*She leaves*)

MARIA (*alone*). Who could have thought it?...I had no hope, but I didn't expect this final blow....Fray Antonio loves another woman! He loves Francisca.[13] Well, she's pretty, and what else do men want?...Doña Francisca my rival! My preferred rival! Could I ever have suspected it?—They want me dead; I'll satisfy them. Thank God, that window is still open, and the precious vial will soon be mine. Let my destiny be fulfilled. (*She enters the pharmacy through the window and emerges shortly afterward looking at the vial in her hand*) It's nothing much; death has an aspect here that doesn't frighten me much. A minute of pain and it's all over.—I wish I had waited before giving him that letter; I would have died holding on to my secret. How they would have tormented themselves trying to guess why I killed myself!—They say it's shameful for a girl to throw herself at a man. (*With disgust*) That's what Francisca does....He'll show her my letter and discuss it with her. My letter is stupid and ridiculous, but my death will redeem it. What will they say about it?—Would Francisca have killed herself in my place? She? With that low mind of hers! She would have cried, and then, with her handkerchief still wet, she would have cheered up again, while *I*....They will be forced to admire my courage; they'll say, "That little Maria, whom we took for a child, died with the bravery of a soldier, of a Roman." They will be forced to cry over me, and my glory will be to have made them happy. To have made Francisca happy, Francisca whom I detest, whom I would have stabbed with the greatest pleasure while she entertained herself by slowly tearing out my heart....Let it torment her that she'll owe her happiness to her rival; perhaps the day will come when Antonio will make the comparison between us....No, no one would have loved you as I did. And you, when I am dead, you'll take your pleasure with her in the bed you bought with my money.[14] So be it! Let the sacrifice be complete; let him

---

13. One is inescapably reminded of Racine's *Phèdre*. Racine's heroine is in love with a man supposedly bound to chastity. After a powerful inward struggle, she confesses her love to him and is rebuffed. Her last consolation—the belief that she can have no rival—crumbles when she discovers that the apparently cold object of her desire is in fact very warmly in love. These and other hints of an influence that may have been subconscious by no means detract from the high originality of Mérimée's handling of similar materials.

14. "*Tu te holgarás con ella en la cama comprada de mi dinero.*" Explicit when he described scenes of violence but always averting his writer's eyes when it came to erotics, Mérimée placed this ravaging thought in a Spanish footnote, adding "I know not how to translate"

know me at last for what I am. (*She writes on a pad*) "I bequeath to my friend (*with a bitter laugh*)—my friend!—Francisca Gomez all my diamonds and the money on deposit with the firm of Arias y Candado, which my uncle has allowed me to dispose of as I please." (*She hears a noise*) Ah! It's Rita. Time to shut the window. Death has flown out of it, and I hold it prisoner.

(*Enter Rita*)

RITA. It's me again. I've come to close that window. (*She does so*) What's the matter, miss? You look so sad.

MARIA. It's only a bad headache.

RITA. Why not lie down in your bed? Would you like to take some medication?

MARIA. Nothing, thank you. Ah! Rita, would you press some lemons for me in a glass of water?

RITA. Right away.

MARIA. Wait, don't bother. A glass of water will do.

RITA. It will only take a minute.

(*Exit Rita*)

MARIA (*alone*). This little fresh garden is the only thing in the world that I leave with regret. No, I don't, since Fray Antonio and Francisca use it as the theater for their loves. (*Looking at her hands*) I'm trembling...and yet I'm not afraid. A woman may not be as strong as a man, and yet there was a brave Castilian general who also trembled before the fight. Who's coming? Fray Antonio!

(*Enter Fray Antonio*)

FRAY ANTONIO (*aside*). The poor child is trembling; I feel sorry for her.

MARIA (*aside*). He's hesitating.

FRAY ANTONIO. Donã Maria, here is your letter. I have read it.

MARIA. Spare me your reproaches, Fray Antonio; they are no use.

FRAY ANTONIO. No, Doña Maria, I do not intend to reproach you, because I imagine that your conscience has already spoken and that you repent from the bottom of your heart having written me this strange letter. The shame I see in your face proves to me that your heart is not corrupt. It was your head, still young and foolish, that made you heedless. I *could* impress upon you how wicked it is, I might even say impious, to speak in so...worldly a manner to a minister of the Lord who is bound by the most

---

as a typical jest. Needless to say, a modern director will transplant the footnote into the script itself, as I do here.

solemn vows. My conduct must have been reprehensively easy-going if it caused you to cast doubts on my piety. I believe that I am as guilty as you, and therefore I have no right to complain. But I do wish to show you, my poor child, the extent of your folly. Let us suppose for a moment that I had been capable of forgetting the oath I have sworn at the altar and that I had been guilty of an action that is criminal for all men, but sacrilegious and abominable for a priest; to what a train of calamities would you have condemned yourself! A layman who seduces a young girl can always repair his fault; a priest cannot. For a while the crime can be hidden from the world, but sooner or later the secret is known, and a dreadful scandal results. Your reputation—a woman's most precious treasure—would be lost forever. Thus, in exchange for a few days of deceptive pleasure, you would face years of regret and remorse.

MARIA. Fray Antonio, why didn't you remember these fine observations while you were making love to Francisca?

FRAY ANTONIO. Francisca? What do you mean?

MARIA. Francisca has told me everything, Fray Antonio. I have the right to be angry with you. I was honest with you, too honest, and you're a hypocrite with me.

FRAY ANTONIO. I beg you not to believe —

MARIA. And it's here, in this garden, under this orange-tree, that you talk to me as a priest! Why don't you tell me, "I'm in love with Francisca"? *That* would have been the gentlemanly thing to do.

FRAY ANTONIO. I'm speechless! So, young lady, you are the mistress of our secret, and you can destroy us if you wish.

MARIA. And what have I done, Fray Antonio, to make you believe that I'd stoop so low?

FRAY ANTONIO. I confess I'm mistaken; but I must appear so very guilty in your eyes....I *am* so very guilty!...I knew I was exposing your friend to terrible dangers. Believe me, I struggled long and hard to overcome this fatal passion, and if I gave in at last —

MARIA. You needn't justify yourself to me; I understand and I approve of what you did. You can avoid all those dangers; so I told Francisca....You must escape together to a country where you can be married.

FRAY ANTONIO. Ah! I want nothing better, but —

MARIA. It's easy with money. I can lend money to Francisca. Live happily with her.

FRAY ANTONIO. So much generosity confounds and humbles me....

MARIA. Adieu, Fray Antonio. You understand that conversing with you has lost some of its charms for me; so let us part.

FRAY ANTONIO. My gratitude —

MARIA. Adieu.

FRAY ANTONIO. Allow me (*he tries to kiss her hand*) —

MARIA. I'm no longer a woman for you, Fray Antonio; at best I'm...a *friend*....

FRAY ANTONIO. May you find someone who will be worthy of you!
(*He leaves*)

MARIA (*alone*). The end is near. I see Rita coming slowly with the drink that will deliver me from all the griefs of this world.—She's afraid to spill some of it.—She looks as if she were walking in a procession. Mine will be a strange one. She who caused my death will probably hold one of the corners of the cloth over my coffin....And he will sing the funeral mass. (*She laughs*) But I'm mistaken. As a suicide destined to be damned I won't be carried into church. They'll bury me in some remote corner. Who cares? As long as, in my hole, the ideas that torment me will be gone.
(*Enter Rita*)

RITA. Here's a tall glass of lemon-water; I cooled it with snow. Drink before it heats up.

MARIA. Dearest Rita, I'm sorry to keep bothering you, but, if you please, return this book to my room.

RITA. Yes, Doña Maria.

MARIA. I'll be leaving the convent soon, Rita. I won't take my pet birds with me, so I'm giving them to you to take care of.

RITA. You're leaving the convent?

MARIA (*after writing something on her pad and tearing off the page*). Yes, I am. Here; if you give this note to the firm of Arias y Candido, the bank on the Plaza del Mar, they will give you 300 piasters.

RITA (*dumbfounded*). Doña Maria....

MARIA. It's also to buy seed for my birds.[15] You'll take good care of them, won't you?

RITA. Good heavens! There's no need for money; it's enough for me that they come from you.

MARIA. No, take it, and carry the book to my room.

RITA. You're crying....

MARIA. It's nothing; go.

RITA. I was waiting for you to drink —

---

15. The "also" is added, namely on the assumption that its absence in the original is due to a slip of the pen. Since Rita expresses her gratitude a few moments later, it is clear that much or most of the money is for her.

MARIA. I'll return the glass and saucer myself; leave me....

RITA. My good young lady, how strange you are today! (*Maria waves her away*) You load me down with presents, and you cry....

MARIA. Adieu, Rita. (*Rita wants to kiss her hand; Maria embraces her*).[16] Leave me; go, please go.

RITA (*aside*). Leaving the convent makes her cry instead of dancing with joy like the others.

(*Exit Rita*)

MARIA (*alone*). This girl is the only creature who cares for me here. When I said adieu to her, I felt my strength slipping away....Courage! In a few moments it will be all over. (*She pours part of the vial's contents into the glass*) No change of color. I don't know, but I'd be more horrified by a black poison than by a transparent drink like this. (*She places the glass on the bench*) It takes courage to die....If I drop the glass, I save my life that's about to escape....Shame on me! I would despise myself. Now then!

(*As she is about to lift the glass, enter Francisca*)

FRANCISCA. Mariquita, I've come to torment you again. So! Are you in better spirits?

MARIA. Better, and in a while I'll be better still.

FRANCISCA. Dearest, do me another favor, a big, big favor. If you'll grant it to me, I *will* accept the money you offered me.

MARIA. Speak.

FRANCISCA. The gardener has just bought a large dog; he says it's to guard his oranges. This is most inconvenient for us! Let me have your room for tonight. It opens onto the small courtyard with its low wall, easy to climb over. We've got a rope ladder. You'll take my room, and you'll have my books to keep you company.

MARIA. You need my room?

FRANCISCA. Yes, my dear friend.

MARIA. It will be yours tonight.

FRANCISCA. You're so good, Mariquita! Instead of camping outdoors as we do every night, we'll be snug in your room with its beautiful alcove!

MARIA. Is that all you want?

FRANCISCA. You're an angel!—Oh, here's a lemon drink! Are you going to drink it all?

MARIA. You want that too?

---

16. "Rita wants to kiss her hand" does not occur in the first version of the play published in *La Revue de Paris* in 1929. It is one of Mérimée's rare interesting and significant

FRANCISCA. It's huge! Let me drink half of it. The heat is killing me.[17]

MARIA. Drink, and may it do you good.[18]

FRANCISCA. I'll drink first, and then, as folk say, you'll be able to read my mind.

(*She drinks*)

MARIA (*aside*). And you'll be able to read mine.

FRANCISCA (*throwing what remains in the glass to the ground*). Pah! What a horrible taste!...What was in that glass?...Horrible! My throat's on fire....What's the matter with you? Why are you looking at me and crying?...You're trembling....Heaven help me, I'm on fire....My God!....What did you make me drink?...Answer me!...Maria!...I'm choking, I'm burning....Water! Give me water!

MARIA. Miserable me! What have I done? Help! Help!

FRANCISCA. Ah, I'm dying!

MARIA. Paquita! Paquita! Don't die!...Help!...Forgive me! Forgive me!

(*Enter Fray Antonio, Irena, Ximena and Rita*)[19]

MARIA. Help her! She's poisoned; *I* poisoned her! I'll be my own judge! I'll drown myself in the well!

(*She runs away*)

*

FRAY ANTONIO (*to the public*). Don't be too angry with me for having caused the death of these two amiable young ladies, and be good enough to excuse the author's faults.[20]

The End

---

revisions, for it catches him paying close attention indeed to a psychologically authentic detail.

17. The heat of the day has been mentioned only once before; hence, in performance, a torrid afternoon can be suggested now and then by non-verbal means.

18. Mérimée must have weighed the obvious alternative of having Maria impulsively *offer* the glass to Francisca. Instead, he slightly decriminalized her impulse by implying that if Francisca had not demanded the drink, it would not have occurred to Maria to offer it. There is, I believe, merit in both alternatives.

19. I doubt that Mérimée would grumble in his grave if, in production, Fray Antonio appeared at Maria's call alone, unaccompanied by a chorus of distraught mute women.

20. See my note to the epilogue of *Carvajal's Family*.

Inès Mendo

[A play in two parts]

(1825)

About the Text

The French texts for both Inès Mendo plays are taken from the 1857 edition used throughout this volume. The Notice which precedes the first play is by Mérimée. His own notes are again marked [M].

Part One

Inès Mendo or the Defeat of Prejudice

(Inès Mendo, ou le Préjugé vaincu)

Sease ella señoria, y venga lo que viniere.
Don Quixote, Part II, Chapter 5[1]

---

1. Sancho Panza, ambitious to marry his daughter into high society, tells his wife: "Let her be *her ladyship*, come what may." (Translation by J. M. Cohen, Penguin Classics, p. 499) For Teresa Panza's reply, see the epigraph for Part II of the play.

Characters

Inès Mendo.[2]
The king and his guards.
Don Luis de Mendoza.
Don Esteban, his son.
Don Carlos.
The priest of Monclar.
Juan Mendo.
A notary and two witnesses.
The jail warden.
A constable.
A servant at the scaffold.
A maid.
Peasants and other citizens of Monclar.[3]

The action takes place is in the village of Monclar in Galicia (1640).[4]

---

2. "Clara Gazul makes Inès speak in a Galician patois; one feels it is impossible, in a translation, to convey the slight linguistic differences that distinguish the inhabitants of several Spanish provinces. We shall observe only that, in the second part of *Inès Mendo*, the language Inès speaks is much more correct, and it is only from time to time that one hears in it some vulgar expressions and dialect words" [M]. This note is, of course, part of Mérimée's elaborate pretense that the plays are a translation from the Spanish by one Joseph L'Estrange. In actuality, Inès speaks perfectly limpid French in both plays; Mérimée either could not or would not allow his heroine to lapse into dialectal vulgarisms. The same is true of her father.
3. My list of characters is somewhat more accurate than the one Mérimée himself provided.
4. "A few months before the Portuguese revolution" [M]. Galicia is in the northwestern corner of Spain, just north of Portugal. Spain occupied Portugal from 1580 to 1640. In that year the Spanish yoke was thrown off, and John of Braganza became king as John IV. There is no Monclar in Galicia.

Notice

This strange comedy was composed by Clara Gazul at the request of a friend of hers, a lady passionately fond of improbable, tearful novels. The author, who has studiously imitated the old Spanish comic writers, made no attempt to avoid their common defects, like too much rapidity in the action, the lack of development, etc. We should be grateful to her as well for not copying their *culto* style, so wearisome to readers of our century. For the rest, Clara Gazul's intention in writing this comedy was only to make of it a kind of prologue to the second part, *The Triumph of Prejudice.*[5]

---

5. This Merimean Notice is a mixture of jest and truth, not to mention the illogical "We should be grateful to her *as well*" instead of "*however.*" The *culto* manner was the elaborate and often far-fetched language many Spanish poets and playwrights adopted in the seventeenth century.

Scene 1

(In Mendo's house. Mendo in conversation with the priest)

MENDO. When I hear talk about a burglary or murder, I can't help growing pale, as if I myself were the guilty party. Up to now I've had no blood on my hands... but if some day....

PRIEST. Thank heaven, our villagers are simple, good folk. It's been ten years since anyone has heard of a crime here in Monclar.

MENDO. And yet this horrible idea never gives me peace. Every night the same dream startles me awake. I see myself in the market place, at my feet a young man, blindfolded, hands clasped in prayer. The alcalde hands me the ax and says to me: Strike!...

PRIEST. Prayers will deliver you from this vision, Mendo. At the time I took holy orders, the picture of my cousin would come to me in my dreams at night, telling me to throw off my habit and run away with her to America. Fasting and prayers have rid me forever of these unpleasant phantoms.

MENDO. I'll never be rid of mine!

PRIEST. Remember that things could be worse for you, Mendo. When an inquisitor condemns a man on shaky grounds, do you think he has greater peace of mind than you? When a judge signs a death warrant, do you think his conscience lets him sleep? And yet they've tried their best to seek out the truth. But what a hard task that is! Who else but God can boast that he knows who is guilty? People's opinion torments you... but living in isolation as you do, few of them know you. Not a single villager is old enough to have known your father's profession....

MENDO. My father!

PRIEST. I believe that the alcalde and I are the only persons who know that an unjust law compels you to take up your father's work. But even if the profession men call infamous were engraved on your forehead, even then, Mendo, you should offer your suffering to God, glorify his name, and wait patiently for the time when he shall deign to call you to him. Today you are excommunicated, but one day you will stand among the elect.—Do you think there are distinctions of rank in heaven?

MENDO. My only hope is in God!

PRIEST. You have no son who will inherit your unhappiness. Thank God for that blessing.

MENDO. But what about my daughter, my poor Inès? My shame will follow her!... She doesn't know my horrible secret yet. I don't know whether I'll ever be able to reveal it to her.... I ought to place her in a convent... but will she find a refuge there?

PRIEST. I believe she will, Mendo.—She'll find a husband there to whom a pure heart matters more than an unblotted escutcheon. Good-bye, Mendo; I must visit a poor sick man whom I can help thanks to Count Mendoza.

MENDO. The noblest and best of men!—Great lord that he is, he condescends to call on me—a favor he doesn't bestow on the alcalde. If ever he finds out!...

PRIEST. Don't be anxious, but be cautious all the same and don't become too familiar with him. Adieu.

(*Mendo kneels and the priest leaves*)

MENDO. Cursed, exiled from mankind!... No one who sees my name on my tombstone will say a "*Requiescat in pace.*" A prayer a murderer would obtain!... And what have I done to deserve my fate?... Doesn't Scripture tell us that "the son shall not bear the sins of his father?"[6]

(*Enter Inès*)

INES. Good morning, Papa.

MENDO. Good morning, Daughter. You look embarrassed, as though you wanted to ask something of me.

INES. Well—

MENDO. Go on, let me hear what it is.

INES. It's... dear Father... since I've tidied the whole house... I'd like to take a walk to Moor's Hill... if you'll let me....

MENDO. Do you meant to walk by yourself?

INES. Dearest Papa.... Don Esteban....

MENDO. Listen to me, Inès. Go if you wish. I'll speak to you simply as a friend, though I *could* address you as your father. We are poor and of no account.... The man you're going to see is rich and noble. Remember the fable of the pot of clay that went travelling with the iron pot and came away all in pieces.

INES. And yet, Esteban's father—I mean Don Esteban's father—Don Luis, is so good to everybody!... He visits you all the time.... You know how much he cares for you.

MENDO. Don Luis settled here only three months ago; he lives like us far from the village, and I'm the only human being nearby; that's why he comes to us. As for Don Esteban, since you're the only woman in the

---

6. "Ezekiel, xviii, 20" [M].

vicinity whose skin is soft and white,[7] it's not surprising that he likes you. But beware. Even if nothing more than the difference in rank stood between us, even then Inès Mendo could never be the wife of Esteban de Mendoza.... You wouldn't wish to be his mistress... so avoid anything beyond politeness with the Mendoza family.

INES. And yet Don Luis is always saying that though he is a lord, he doesn't care about nobility and has as much regard for a peasant who is the son of honest folk as for a grandee of Spain.

MENDO. It's all fine talk, but when the time comes to put it into practice, these beautiful paradoxes are quickly forgotten.

INES. And Don Esteban... he's a baron and an officer in the guards... well, he says that a nobleman can marry a commoner, because he ennobles her, and then no harm is done to his blue blood. He knows all about it, he does. Besides, we all descend from Adam, as the priest tells us. It's only one's calling that makes the difference. His grandfather was only a knight, and mine—what did Grandfather do?

MENDO (*troubled*). My father!... He did... the same work I do.

INES. I can see I've given you pain with my talk. If you truly, truly don't want me to, I won't see Esteban anymore.... But, dear little Papa... please, let me bring him to you just today; he will have something to say to you.

MENDO. I'm speaking to you for your own good; stop seeing him.

INES. And yet he loves me so much.

MENDO. Do you believe it, my poor Inès?

INES. I'm sure of it. Father dear?

MENDO. What?

INES. What if he wanted to marry me?

MENDO (*shrugging his shoulders*). Nonsense!

INES. And if he told you so?

MENDO. Let me be.

INES. Here comes Don Luis.

(*Enter Don Luis de Mendoza*)

DON LUIS. Greetings, neighbor, greetings my child. Leave us alone for a minute and go into the garden where you'll find company.

MENDO. Inès!

DON LUIS. Silence; it's I who order her to leave. You, stay. I have something surprising to talk to you about. (*Inès exits*) But first I must reprimand you. You're a strange fellow, Mendo, and worthy of blame.

---

7. "*La seule femme des environs qui ne soit pas absolument noire*" [M]. A literal translation would be imprudent.

You are the only friend we have in this part of the world, and yet you never pay us a visit.

MENDO. Forgive me, my Lord. A poor farmer like myself can't be a companion to a man of your rank.

DON LUIS. Fiddlesticks! Noble rank doesn't mean more to me than my old boots. What's your objection if I prefer your company to that of a grandee? Besides, aren't we a bit indebted to you? When our mules were about to throw us over a cliff, wasn't it you who leaped, grabbed their bridles and stopped them?

MENDO. Anyone else would have done the same thing.

DON LUIS. So be it. But listen to me. I'm not proud. I'm a philosopher. I've read the ancients. Look here, my friend, people are fools, what with their prejudices about nobility. The house of Mendoza is one of the oldest in Spain, and if you please, I belong to its oldest branch. And yet, I'd just as soon be called Juan Mendo as Don Luis de Mendoza.

MENDO. What! To be Juan Mendo?

DON LUIS. I admit that Mendo hasn't as fine a ring as Mendoza. Mendo, Mendoza.... Ah, that *za* has its value! But let's drop our names and talk business. You know my son—lovely boy, isn't he? Loaded with courage, intelligence, and talent, officer in the guards, about to be named to a brilliant post. Ten duchesses have been making eyes at him. He could have married the daughter of the Duke of Bivar if he'd wanted.... The duke of Bivar—you've heard me. The Bivar weren't born last year!

MENDO. One would have to be blind not to admire the Baron of Mendoza.

DON LUIS. But I'm a philosopher, I am. What, said I to myself, is high birth? What did I do for Providence that it made me Count of Mendoza, grandee of Spain, first class, and commander of the Order of Alcantara?[8] All this doesn't raise me in my own esteem. The ancients have taught me how to think. Ah, Seneca!...[9]

MENDO. I don't see—

DON LUIS. Let me get to the point. Guess what. My son is in love with your daughter and wants to marry her.

MENDO. Marry my daughter!

DON LUIS. At first I objected, but he had lost his head, and since a misalliance on the man's side is not overly consequential, and the Mendoza, thank God, have enough nobility to dignify two families, I gave

8. The grandee first class had the right to keep his head covered while speaking and listening to the king. The military-religious Order of Alcantara, headed by a grand commander, existed since 1156.

9. Born in Cordoba, Seneca was particularly prized in Spain.

my consent, and I've come to settle on a date for the wedding. So? What do you say to that?

MENDO. My Lord—what a stain on your coat of arms!

DON LUIS. Fiddle-faddle! Doesn't the male ennoble? Besides, I've taken a liking to you.... And I have other reasons, too. First of all, I'm a philosopher.... And then, one day, the Duke of Medina Sidonia, who was arguing with me, defied me to give my son to a commoner. I want to show him that I practice my philosophy.... Furthermore, the king recently gave a governorship to Don Rodrigo Pacheco, who had done the same thing as my son.

MENDO. My Lord... it cannot be.... Do you know who I am?

DON LUIS. The most stubborn man alive, God help me!

MENDO. A Mendoza allied to—

DON LUIS. A peasant? That's between you and me and nobody else. How do you answer *that*?

MENDO. Don Luis, I respect you... I even make bold to love you... but we mustn't see each other anymore....

DON LUIS. The man is crazy!

MENDO. I can't give you my reasons, but believe me, they are just.

DON LUIS. Devils in hell, you peasant! What! My son loves your daughter, your daughter loves my son, Esteban is willing to marry her, I consent, and you, instead of thanking me for the high honor, your wits begin to stray.... Is it that your highness deems us too poor or not noble enough for him?

MENDO. Inès herself feels—

DON LUIS. Very good! I'll let her decide. If she accepts, so will you, agreed? Who ever saw the likes of this fellow declining to rise in the world!

MENDO (*after some thought*). In that case, I'll tell her what she needs to know. She's my daughter, and has more right than a stranger to know my secrets.

DON LUIS. Aha! Your secrets! So you have secrets. Some terrible secret, no doubt. Are you a Jew? How many men have you murdered?

MENDO. I?

DON LUIS. Forgive me, my good friend; don't be angry with me. I know that you're a good man and a good father. Your calling is one that I honor; farmers are the people who allow us noblemen to live.... And besides, aren't we all descended from Adam, as Seneca tells us?

MENDO. My Lord, the thing is impossible....

DON LUIS. Come now! You've had a bad night. I'm on my way now, but I'll be back before long. Remember that you promised to allow your daughter to decide freely.

MENDO. She will be free.

DON LUIS. Then you're caught. Good-bye for now. (*He goes and then returns*) No threats now! Don't try to scare the poor girl. Tell her.... Never mind, I'll warn her myself. You and your ideas—you should be locked up in the madhouse.

MENDO. She won't hesitate.

DON LUIS. We'll see. Good-bye, Juan Mendo. I've never seen the likes of you!

MENDO. My Lord, I am at your feet.

DON LUIS. Don't say "I am at your feet." It's too servile. Speak like the ancients: "I kiss your hands." That's quite enough.—Come to think of it, Mendo, I'll find some post for you that will wash you clean of farmer's mud.

MENDO. Ah! Can I ever be washed clean?

DON LUIS. Still harping on that! I'm off!

(*He leaves*)

MENDO. Who would ever have thought—?

Scene 2

(*In a valley. Don Esteban and Don Carlos meet*)

DON ESTEBAN. Don Carlos, what brings you here?

DON CARLOS. Is it possible? Lord Mendoza in this wilderness?

DON ESTEBAN. What the devil are you doing here? How could you leave the pleasures of Madrid?

DON CARLOS. I'm shooting game in the countryside. The army has given me a six-month leave, and I'm staying with my father who's the alcalde of that hole they call Monclar. And you?

DON ESTEBAN. Same story. My father has just purchased some land here. Any luck so far?

DON CARLOS. No; I haven't fired a single shot. Just now I had my horse and hounds taken home. (*With a mysterious air*) I was glad to take a walk in these parts.

DON ESTEBAN (*worried*). Oh? Can you tell me why?

DON CARLOS. I'm in pursuit of another quarry... the kind, my dear fellow *you*'re famous for hunting. I'll wager that it's a pair of fiery eyes that have brought you to that newly acquired property.

DON ESTEBAN. Oh no! What a strange idea!

DON CARLOS. Then listen to me. In the three days since I've arrived in this miserable hole, I've noticed a charming little peasant girl who lives nearby. Look! Can you see that house in the distance? That's where she lives.

DON ESTEBAN (*aside*). Mendo's house!

DON CARLOS. A delicious morsel, my dear baron. Though her father's a farmer from what I hear, she has a body! Lustrous hair, dark eyes, and hands—well, tolerable hands, though that's her weak point. All things considered, I intend to enjoy her.

DON ESTEBAN (*angrily*). Captain, the person you mention is not going to be one of your conquests.

DON CARLOS. A peasant girl!

DON ESTEBAN. Peasant or otherwise, you will kindly direct your hunt in another direction.

DON CARLOS. Aha! You're claiming priority, are you? So be it, but two hunters may well go after the same hare.

DON ESTEBAN. Enough jokes! Let me inform you, sir, that this peasant lass you're laughing over will be my wife tomorrow.

DON CARLOS. Your wife?

DON ESTEBAN. Exactly.

DON CARLOS. Ha! Ha! Ha! The joke is excellent! Oh, I admire your serious intentions. But have you forgotten that conquests are passed from friend to friend after two weeks of possession?

DON ESTEBAN. Once more, sir, I am speaking in all seriousness. From now on, be so kind as to look upon Inès Mendo as the baroness of Mendoza.

DON CARLOS. A peasant girl the baroness of Mendoza! Splendid! Played like a master, you hypocrite! Come, look more serious yet.

DON ESTEBAN. Enough!

DON CARLOS. After your honeymoon you'll become more tractable and allow *me* to marry her a little, ha! ha! ha!

DON ESTEBAN (*slapping his face*). This will prove to you that I'm serious.

DON CARLOS (*drawing his sword*). And this will punish your insolence. (*They fight. Esteban kills Carlos*)

DON ESTEBAN. So—no more jests from you. Now I'd better take care of myself. In our provinces they're devilish hard on affairs like these. Off to Madrid... but first I must take leave of Inès; my father will bring her to Madrid, and our marriage will be delayed for no more than a few days. (*Exit Don Esteban. Enter two peasants*)

FIRST PEASANT. It's like an infestation of vermin—all the discharged soldiers have turned into thieves. But I'm not afraid of them. The other day I sent two of them running for their lives. I was cutting wood near Navaja at nightfall when one of them, who was lying flat on the ground—(*he stumbles over the corpse and falls to the ground*) Ay! Gentlemen! Take my money but don't kill me!

SECOND PEASANT. Dummy! Here's a man who'll never kill another one again. Holy Jesus! It's the captain, the alcalde's son!

FIRST PEASANT. With a hole in the middle of his belly!

SECOND PEASANT. Look over there! A man running away. It's the murderer for sure. If we catch him, the alcalde will give us a good reward.

FIRST PEASANT. I'll go look for help in the village.

SECOND PEASANT. No; stay here by the corpse; I'll go run after the murderer.

FIRST PEASANT. Hurry up; I don't like to spend too much time with a dead body.

Scene 3

(*In Mendo's house*)

MENDO (*alone*). I needed this walk to refresh my blood... and prepare myself for the final sacrifice.... I must speak at last.... It was madness to believe that I could conceal from her who she is.... Her head is full of illusions that will make her miserable forever.... It's my fault.... The education I gave her fed these illusions.... I should have placed her in a convent when she was still a child. She wouldn't have known me. She would have become a nun without dreaming of a sweeter life in the world.... Now she's passionately and crazily in love—a love I can't tear from her without also tearing out her heart.... Oh, I am much to blame! But my daughter—the only friend I could have in this world.... I didn't have the courage to part from her.... Poor child! I must tell her the truth at last.... I'll break her heart... but waiting any longer would be too dangerous.... She'll realize that her only refuge will be in a cloister. Here she is. Courage!

INES (*entering*). Dear Papa, I've been a disobedient girl. I went for a walk with Esteban, and then Don Luis joined us, and he spoke so kindly to me that I was overjoyed. Esteban said that he wanted me for his wife, and Don Luis said that you told him I would be free to decide. Is it true, dearest Father? Or were you only joking? I love him so much! Can I tell you a secret? He made me accept an engagement ring.... I refused it at first, because it's too beautiful... but Don Luis insisted.... Here it is.... See how it shines.

MENDO. Inès, listen to me; this may be the last time I speak to you.

INES (*smiling*). Pooh!

MENDO. Inès.... A man who would kill his fellow-man—such a man is odious to all mankind.

INES. Yes, Papa.

MENDO. But what if he were compelled to kill his fellow-man?

INES. How could he be compelled? He can always choose to die instead of killing a man. But what are you trying to say?

MENDO (*after a silence*). So you agreed to become Don Esteban's wife?... You know that his family is one of the most illustrious of Spain. It goes back to the days of King Pelayo nine hundred years ago. He is connected to all the nobility of Castile; all the grandees of Spain are his friends.... Don't you think he will suffer when his relations and friends mock him because of this misalliance? You love him.... Would you want him to be endlessly taunted because of his wife?

INES. It was up to him to think of this beforehand.... I come from a line of honest farmers and old Christians.... Many a duchess, says Esteban, was nothing but a poor Morisco a hundred years ago.... And then, when he began to court me, I told him to make his fine speeches to ladies and leave us country-girls in peace.... But he showed me so much love... so much love! that I'm sure he'll be happier with me than with an Infanta of Aragon.

MENDO. This marriage will deprive him of a fortune; have you thought of that, Inès?[10]

INES. He's rich, and then he feels as I do that a little love is worth a great deal of gold.

MENDO. An Inès Mendo the wife of a Mendoza! A peasant's daughter and a grandee of Spain!

INES. The prince Don Pedro married a peasant girl, didn't he, and her name was also Inès. So the story tells us.[11]

MENDO. And the story ends in bloodshed, as you know. Besides, Inès' father was a farmer.... Did Don Pedro.... Do you know whether I'm even a farmer?

INES (*smiling*). I can see well enough what you are.

---

10. The fortune in question is probably a dowry, and this could be spelled out in production.

11. This is the famous story of Inès de Castro, the illegitimate daughter of a nobleman, not a peasant's child. The son of the king of Portugal married her in secret, but the king had her murdered in 1355.

MENDO. No, Inès, you don't know!

INES. Father, what's the matter with you? How you look at me! I'm distressing you. Maybe you're trying to tell me that there's a blot somewhere on our name.... Maybe one of our grandfathers did something wrong.

MENDO. And what if it was your father?

INES (*frightened*). It can't be!

MENDO (*beside himself*). I am telling you!

INES. Jesus, Maria!... But it isn't true.... You're saying this only to scare me... to make me give up this marriage. And even if it's true, what crime can it be that you haven't expiated by the penitent's life you've led in this house? You're harder on yourself than a monk.

MENDO. My poor Inès! The stain that's in me will be wiped from you only when I die. Forgive me for having passed it on to you! Inès... I'm not guilty of any crime, and yet there's not a man who would be my friend.... Poor Inès!... They forced on me the horrible profession of my father.... I am the executioner of Monclar.

(*He leaves and closes the door behind him*)

INES (*alone*). I've lost Esteban! (*She remains silent for a few moments in deep gloom*) But you, my poor father, how I pity you!... Where is he? He stood here a few moments ago... because it wasn't a dream... he spoke to me; how could it have been my imagination? And yet this door is closed. Ah! Now I remember.... (*She runs to the door*) Father! Father! Come back! I'm still your daughter! Hold me in your arms! Come to me; I want to be your consolation as long as I live.... He doesn't hear me! (*She knocks at the door*) Father! Father! You're driving me to despair. Are you too going to abandon me?... Oh Esteban, Esteban, I've lost you.... And just when I was so happy! In one second I've become the most wretched woman in the world. Instead of marrying, all that's left for me is to hide in a hole.... I'll have to tell him everything... because it would be wrong to hide such a thing from him.... If only he hadn't proposed, I would have been less sorry to lose him. I must confess the truth to him.... Yet how will I go about it, to say to his face, "Esteban, I am the daughter of—" Oh! I'll never have the courage. And yet he must be told.... Otherwise he'd come to the house, and that would hurt me even more.... Well then, I'll write to him.... He won't see me again.... I'll enter a nunnery and think of him always.... I'll pray to God for him... and I won't dishonor his noble name: so it must be. Let me summon all my courage.... I think that my tears have brought me some relief. Yes; now I think I can write him that letter.... Oh, if only I'd known before whose daughter I am!

(*Enter Mendo holding a money-bag*)

INES. Father!

MENDO. Here, Inès, is what belongs to you. This money is yours; it comes from your mother. It will help you to be admitted to the convent of your choice.

INES. Oh my Father! Don't order me to leave. I have lost my Esteban; don't deprive me of my father. Let me dedicate my life to consoling you and to being your friend.

MENDO (*weeping in Inès' arms*). God! Why didn't you give her another father?

INES. God! Let me sustain him for many years to come!

MENDO. Now you see why you have to give up the man you love. Will you find the courage to release him from his promise?

INES. Yes Father.... I feel that I have to.

MENDO. Sooner or later they'll learn the truth, whether from the alcalde or someone else. Don Esteban is a noble young man. You can speak frankly to him. Tell him... who you are. Tell him that only the father who raised you is to blame, because he kept you in the dark. Better that he learn the truth from us rather than from other people.

INES. Very well. If it must me, I'll do it.

MENDO. Write at once. I'll leave you.

(*Exit Mendo*)

INES (*alone*). How shall I go about it?... Yes—speak the truth without preamble.... Alas! It was he who gave me this inkstand. (*She writes*) Perhaps he will pity me a little.... "Adieu, Inès...." And you, my dear ring, which I hoped to keep all my life. We must part so soon.... I am no longer fit to wear you. Adieu! Adieu! (*She kisses the ring repeatedly*).

(*Enter Don Esteban*)

DON ESTEBAN. Let me return those kisses, dearest Inès.

INES (*running to a corner of the room*). Ah!

DON ESTEBAN. Did I frighten you, Inesilla darling? Don't be afraid, it's your lover.

INES. I have no lover anymore.... I'm an unhappy girl who has to be flung aside.

DON ESTEBAN. You, flung aside, Inès!... Don't you recognize me?

INES. In heaven's name, leave me, leave me, you must!

DON ESTEBAN (*moving toward her*). What's the matter with you? You're driving me to distraction! Why so frightened?

INES. Don't touch me! You'll dirty yourself!

DON ESTEBAN. This miserable Mendo must have troubled your mind. That's all I needed! Inès, stop this childishness.... Don't you love me anymore?

INES. Oh, I do!... It's something I can't help.... Here... take the letter, there, on the table, and leave me.

DON ESTEBAN. Come now! Why are you afraid of me?

INES. I may no longer love you.

DON ESTEBAN. Those scruples again! You like to make me angry. Here's your punishment. (*He takes her by force into his arms*)

INES. It's not my fault; you forced me; I couldn't warn you away in time.... Here, this will enlighten you....

(*She gives him the letter. Don Esteban, still holding her, reads it. He is overcome. Inès falls at his knees, weeping. Don Esteban remains stunned for a few moments. Then, suddenly, he tears up the letter, and causes Inès to fall to the floor*)

INES. Ah!

DON ESTEBAN (*raising her*). Inès? Did I hurt you?

INES. Oh, you still call me Inès! Allow me to kiss your feet.

DON ESTEBAN. Unhappy child! What crime have you committed to make you kneel at my feet!

INES. I found out just now. If I'd known sooner, I wouldn't have allowed you to care for me.

DON ESTEBAN. Poor Inès! Did you think I'd stop loving you? Aren't you the same Inès who has enchanted me?

INES. I'll never be able to keep from loving you.

DON ESTEBAN. Foolish prejudices! Shall I allow you to destroy my happiness? Shades of my ancestors! I'll renounce you before I give up this girl!

INES. You don't despise me then? I'll die of joy!

DON ESTEBAN. I love you; I love you as much as before.

INES (*weeping*). Esteban... no, you can't love me, you're a Mendoza.

DON ESTEBAN. I am your lover... and I prefer being your lover to being a lord.

INES. If I could die now, I wouldn't dishonor the man I love.

DON ESTEBAN. I care nothing for the opinion of men. What is it next to your love? But you're bleeding, my dearest, I was so violent, I hurt you. My best Inès, let me stanch the blood with my kisses.

INES. Ah! I'm too happy. (*She flings herself in his arms*)

(*Enter a constable, accompanied by armed peasants*)

CONSTABLE (*touching Don Esteban with his staff*). In the king's name, you're under arrest. Give me your sword.

DON ESTEBAN. Wait, you scoundrels!

CONSTABLE. Help me, men.

INES. Help! Father! Help!

(*Don Esteban is disarmed*)

DON ESTEBAN. Don't be afraid, Inès; it's nothing.

(*The peasants drag him away*)

INES. Help! Help!

(*She faints. Enter Mendo with drawn sword*)

MENDO. What's going on here?

CONSTABLE. Nothing except a murderer we've caught.

MENDO. My daughter!

CONSTABLE. The young lady was embracing this gentleman when we entered.... It's only natural....[12]

MENDO (*threatening him*). Rascal!

CONSTABLE. If you strike me, I'll report you to the alcalde.—And while we're on the subject, Mendo, you've been hiding the fact that—

MENDO. Get out!

CONSTABLE. You'll be exercising your skill in the near future, Juan Mendo. Sharpen your axe, and get him at the first blow—remember, he's a gentleman.

(*Exit, laughing*)

MENDO. Mary! Help me!

(*Enter a woman who helps him carry Inès out of the room*)

Scene 4

(*Interior of the prison of Monclar. Don Esteban is sitting at a table, in deep thought as he reads his death warrant*)

DON ESTEBAN. So this is the end. (*He throws the warrant down*) I'm glad, after all, that I kept Inès away. Her tears would have shaken my courage. And today I need it. Many times I've heard the whistle of enemy bullets at my ear and remained calm, but the block and the axe are somehow more horrible to contemplate.—I wish I could find it in myself to be as brave right now as the soldier I once saw who whistled as he walked to the gallows. (*He whistles*) No, no swaggering. Just firmness, resignation; and besides, whistling a false note just at that moment would

---

12. "This gentleman" implies that Don Esteban is still in the room, but the stage direction a few lines earlier has him being led out, and besides, if he were still in the room, he would hardly remain silent. So we must imagine the constable turning Mendo to an open window and pointing at the men marching away outside. Incidentally, Mérimée's arresting officer is a *greffier*, that is to say a court clerk. This strikes me as odd, and it must have had the same effect on the anonymous English translator whose *The Theatre of Clara Gazul* was published in 1825, for he (or she) changed the man's title to peace officer.

be damaging to a man's reputation. Dear God! Grant me the favor of dying like a gentleman, like a soldier!—Who is at the door?

(*Enter a notary and two witnesses*)

NOTARY. My lord, I am the notary you asked for, and here are two fully qualified witnesses.

DON ESTEBAN. Thank you. No news from my father?

NOTARY. No, my lord. However, I hope that he will find the king in time. His Majesty is thought to be at no great distance from Monclar.

DON ESTEBAN. Come what may! Are you ready to set down my testament? It won't be a long one.

NOTARY. Let us hope that it won't be needed. Your name?

DON ESTEBAN. I, Esteban Sandoval, Baron Mendoza, captain of the guards.

NOTARY (*writing*).... Of the guards, hereby give and bequeath my soul to God.

DON ESTEBAN. Is that the formula?

NOTARY. Exactly; it's the protocol required by law.

DON ESTEBAN. Observe it with utter precision; I wouldn't want my will to be broken some day.

NOTARY. You can rest easy with a professional like me. A man who has been a notary for thirty years doesn't leave holes in an authentic document.

DON ESTEBAN. Fine. Continue. I bequeath all my property to Inès Mendoza, formerly Inès Mendo.

NOTARY. Who is....

DON ESTEBAN. My wife, daughter of Juan Mendo, executioner of Monclar.

NOTARY. Good God! Do you really want me to write this?

DON ESTEBAN. I demand it.

NOTARY. Legally wedded wife?

DON ESTEBAN. Yes, though our marriage has been secret. (*Aside*) I won't go to hell for that lie.

NOTARY. If, as you say, the marriage was secret, I would advise you to avoid lawsuits by inserting a signed act of recognizance.

DON ESTEBAN. Do as you see fit.

NOTARY. I am inserting it.

DON ESTEBAN. Ready? Furthermore, I desire that it be engraved on my tombstone, which will be erected in the cemetery of the village of Monclar, that a Mendoza, in defiance of prejudice, married the daughter of an executioner.

NOTARY. Good grief! If I were you, I would drop this engraving.

DON ESTEBAN. I demand it.

NOTARY. So be it. It's what the Romans called *Poenae nomine legatum....*[13] Kindly read and sign.

(*Don Esteban reads the will and signs along with the two witnesses*)

DON ESTEBAN. Thank you. My father will settle your honorarium; but I should like you to take this purse and distribute its contents to the poor so that they may commend my soul to God in their prayers, as well as this ring, which I beg you to accept as a memento of the unhappy Don Esteban.

NOTARY. Oh, my lord, how I wish that I could—

(*Enter the jail warden*)

JAIL WARDEN. My lord, it is with the deepest regret—

DON ESTEBAN. I understand you.—Adieu, gentlemen. Remember me in your prayers.

NOTARY (*to the clerk*). Gently, my friend; it is contrary to custom to proceed to execution so promptly after the sentence has been pronounced. The case is not urgent. This gentleman's father is appealing to the king. His Majesty will be arriving in a few hours. Wait for his decision.

JAIL WARDEN. The alcalde's orders are to proceed at once.

DON ESTEBAN (*smiling*). It appears to me, Don Melchior, that this gentleman is not so deeply attached to the forms as you are.

NOTARY. This is illegal. I protest.

JAIL WARDEN. My lord?

(*They leave*)

Scene 5

(*A scaffold in the middle of the marketplace. Enter Don Esteban, constables, Mendo, a servant carrying the axe, the priest, the jail warden, and inhabitants of Monclar*)

PRIEST. Farewell, my son. God will be merciful to you. Soon you will escape from the sorrows of this world.

(*He embraces Don Esteban*)

---

13. The formula speaks of a legacy that cannot be voided by an heir. Like the 1825 English translator, I have made deep cuts in this chapter of legalisms, especially a lengthy reading by the notary of the testament in all its details. Patrick Berthier, in his edition of *Le Théâtre de Clara Gazul*, reminds us that Mérimée had taken a law degree at the time he wrote the play—probably in 1823, when he was twenty years old. It is, I think, unnecessary to underline at every turn of the play that it is the work of a beginner. As for the two witnesses, a director can obviously dispense with them without harming anyone.

JAIL WARDEN. My lord, allow us to blindfold you.

DON ESTEBAN. No, I shall look death in the face. And you, Mendo... do your duty; do it well if you can. (*He kneels and places his head on the block*) Is this as I should be?

SERVANT. Yes, my lord. May God have mercy on you.

ALL (*except Mendo*). Amen!

DON ESTEBAN (*to the priest*). Adieu, father.

SERVANT (*to Mendo*). You're taking the axe in your left hand?

MENDO. I'm no longer the executioner!

(*He hacks off his right hand. Huge tumult. Enter Inès. She climbs onto the scaffold*)

INES. Stop! We'll die together! You'll kill your daughter and him together!

MENDO (*showing his mutilated hand*). Can I hurt him anymore?

INES. Father!—Esteban!

JAIL WARDEN. What's the meaning of this?

PRIEST. Let us wait for the king!

PEASANTS. Mendo, you're a good fellow, and so is this gentleman. Don't be afraid; we won't allow the alcalde to have you killed.

(*Several climb onto the scaffold and chase the constables; others crowd around Mendo. Enter Don Luis on horseback*)

DON LUIS. Pardoned! Pardoned! Stop! God be praised! I arrived on time. (He alights from his horse and embraces his son)

DON ESTEBAN. Embrace my savior. He cut off his hand rather than strike me.

DON LUIS (*embracing Mendo*). Ah, Mendo! What are my titles compared to an action like yours? You're a Roman, like Seneca.

(*Drumroll. Enter the king with his guards*)[14]

ALL. Long live the king!

KING. Why this tumult? Where is the alcalde? Don Luis, kindly explain. I can hear nothing in this confusion of voices, all saying the same thing.

(*Don Luis speaks in his ear*)

ALL. Mercy! Mercy!

KING. Admirable generosity! Juan Mendo, on your knees. And now rise again, Don Juan Mendo; I hereby knight you.

MENDO. Sire, I kiss your feet, but—

KING. Don Esteban, I grant you my pardon, but on condition that you marry Mendo's daughter.

---

14. "The sudden intervention of the king which ends the comedy is not rare in the old Spanish plays (see *The Alcalde de Zalamea* and a hundred other plays)." [M]

DON ESTEBAN. Such is my dearest wish.

INES. At last I am allowed to love you!

KING. I will sign the contract myself. Call a surgeon. And may God grant that **prejudice be conquered** throughout Spain.

*

INES. Thus ends the comedy of Inès Mendo. Forgive the author's faults. If this first part has had the good fortune of pleasing you, the author hopes that you will welcome the second part, whose title is THE TRIUMPH OF PREJUDICE.

The End

Appendix

For a producer who wishes to forego Part One of *Inès Mendo*, I would suggest that the following speech, or one like it, be spoken by one of the actors as a prologue to *The Triumph of Prejudice*:

In the year 1640, Don Esteban de Mendoza, a young Spanish nobleman, fell in love with a poor country girl whose name was Inès Mendo. Not only were the two lovers separated by a deep social gulf, but, to make matters worse, Inès was the daughter of the village executioner, an infamous occupation that made him practically a pariah. Juan Mendo, conscious of the dangers of a misalliance, opposed the union of the two lovers, but Don Esteban was determined to marry Inès in bold defiance of the prejudices of society, and in this he enjoyed the full approval of his father, who held the same advanced views of social equality. One day, however, Don Esteban ran into an officer friend of his who was spending a few weeks in the countryside. This friend had seen Inès and was planning to seduce her for his amusement. When Don Esteban revealed that he was about to marry the girl, his friend roared with laughter at what sounded to him like a joke. A duel ensued; Esteban killed his friend, was apprehended, and turned over to Juan Mendo for execution. When the fatal moment came, Mendo raised the axe in his left hand and hacked off his own right one rather than behead Don Esteban. Just then Esteban's father arrived, followed by the king of Spain. Don Esteban was pardoned, heroic Juan Mendo was knighted by the king, and the lovers were reunited. After they were married, the couple moved to the Mendoza estate in the province of Estremadura in the west of Spain on the Portuguese border, in part because Don Esteban had been assigned the post of governor of that province. His jurisdiction included the fortress of Aviz, which stood inside Portuguese territory. It was a difficult assignment, because Portugal, occupied by the Spaniards for eighty years, had risen in revolt against its conquerors. Soon its own John of Braganza would become king of a newly independent Portugal....

Part Two

Inès Mendo or the Triumph of Prejudice

(Inès Mendo, ou le Triomphe du préjugé)

> Que si de los zuecos la sacais a chapines,
> no se ha de hallar la mochacha,
> y a cada paso ha de caer en mil faltas.
> *Don Quixote*, Part II, Chapter 5[1]

---

1. Teresa Panza's voluble replies to her husband's social ambitions for the family include the passage of the epigraph: "If you raise [our daughter] from clogs to high-heeled shoes... the girl won't know herself. Then she'll come a thousand croppers at every step." (Translation by J. M. Cohen, p. 499). The savory discussion between Sancho and Teresa could well have given Mérimée his impulse for writing the two *Inès Mendo* plays.

Characters[2]

Doña Inès de Mendoza.
Doña Serafina, Duchess of Montalvan.
The abbess of the Ursulines at Badajoz.
Don Esteban de Mendoza.
Juan Mendo.
Don Cesar Belmonte, a Portuguese nobleman.
The corregidor of Badajoz.
Pedro, servant to Don Esteban.
A Portuguese innkeeper.
Portuguese soldiers and citizens.
Servants.
Constables.

The setting is on the estate of the Mendoza in Estremadura, then at Elvas, and finally in Badajoz.[3]

---

2. Incomplete in the original, as in the first play. I have filled in the gaps.
3. Estremadura is a province in western Spain, bordering on Portugal; Badajoz is an important Spanish town on the Portuguese border, while Elvas is nearby in Portugal.

Act One[4]

(*An apartment in the ancestral hall of the Mendoza in Estremadura*)

DON ESTEBAN. Aren't you ever going to speak correctly? Will you stick to your village vocabulary for the rest of your life?
INES. What do you want? Rioja wine comes in goatskins and will always smell of goat.
DON ESTEBAN. A pretty proverb in the mouth of the Baroness of Mendoza! Disgusting!
INES. Day and night you nag me for a yes or a no. Not a moment's peace!
DON ESTEBAN (*pacing the floor in a rage*). Ha!
INES. Is it my fault that you're in a bad mood? Because our neighbors give us trouble, am I to be the one who suffers?
DON ESTEBAN. Insolent rabble! I'll get even with them!
INES. Why did you unearth them from their run-down mansions and invite them here? Poor as churchmice and vain as peacocks—they think they'd be lowering themselves by showing us some respect. And all this because of my poor father! He paid a high price enough for the title the king gave him. I hope you haven't forgotten, Esteban.
DON ESTEBAN (*grasping her hand*). My love, I'll never forget. Tell me though, wouldn't the coolest of men become wild when he hears these starving hidalgos come along one after the other with the same story: "My wife, Countess so and so, is indisposed; Doña this and that is unwell...." And that studied insolence toward your father, and this affectation of never calling you Doña Inès, never addressing a single word to you!...My blood was boiling!
INES. Bah! You should have laughed.
DON ESTEBAN. It's not a laughing matter to me. And while we're on the subject, *you* gave them plenty to laugh about, what with your naive remarks and your village talk. Besides, why inform them that you had prepared the dish of chickpeas yourself? Should a baroness know how to cook?
INES. You used to say that you loved the way I made them.
DON ESTEBAN. They will be laughing over this for a month. The Baroness de Mendoza was shelling peas in the kitchen!
INES. Peas or beans, they ate what I gave them like people who often go hungry when they're at home.

---

4. Still pretending to be the translator of Clara Gazul, Mérimée uses, instead of "act," the Spanish term *jornada,* translating it as "*journée.*"

DON ESTEBAN. And then, in spite of thousands and thousands of warnings, you kept calling me "sweetheart." Can anything be more ridiculous? Country-bumpkin talk.

INES. Wicked man! Who'd believe there was a time when you upbraided me if I called you my lord? During our honeymoon you kissed me every time I called you "sweetheart."

DON ESTEBAN (*kissing her*). It's a name that reminds me of the sweetest moments of my life. But don't you see, my own Inès, before the world, before those threadbare and impertinent hidalgos, we have to put on our grandest airs.

INES. I'll do my best, sweet—my dear. But don't frown anymore, let's hug and make peace.

DON ESTEBAN. My Inesilla, can I ever bear you a grudge? It's for you and only for you that I was in hell yesterday. God! When I think of it, I begin to fume again. These prudes who refuse to dine with you!

(*Enter a servant*)

SERVANT. My lord, two letters for you.

(He leaves)

DON ESTEBAN. What's this handwriting? I don't recognize it. (*He reads*) "Don Gil Lampurdo y Mello de Porra kisses the hand of Don Esteban Sandoval, Baron Mendoza, and begs the honor of his presence at the ball he is giving at the manor of La Porra, Tusday next, for the ladies and lords of the province." And he does not invite you! God's body! (*He tears up the letter*) He'll pay dearly for this insolence! God in heaven! I'll make an example of him that will teach politeness to all the Porra to come![5]

INES. Gently, gently, my dear Esteban; I'm so unhappy when you fly off the handle. Calm yourself for my sake.

DON ESTEBAN. You don't know how a gentleman suffers when he is insulted.

INES. Sweetest heart!

DON ESTEBAN. Don Gil or Don Devil, I'll show you!...

INES. He's too much beneath you....Look; read the other letter. Reading letters is fun.

DON ESTEBAN. I want the rascal to—(*looking at the letter*) Oh!

INES. Why are you surprised?

DON ESTEBAN. It's from the Duchess of Montalvan.

INES. Are you so familiar with her handwriting that just by reading the address you know who it's from?

---

5. "Here is an untranslatable pun. *Porra* in Spanish means ridiculous pride" [M].

DON ESTEBAN. Oh! It's because....That's right, I knew her well...long ago.

INES. An old flame?

DON ESTEBAN. Something like that, before I met you....Here, read it yourself. (*He gives her the letter*)

INES. This is generous of you. (*She opens the letter and returns it to him without reading it*) And here is how I respond.

DON ESTEBAN (*reading aloud*). "My very dear Esteban...."

INES (*laughing*). "My very dear Esteban!" Better read to yourself.

DON ESTEBAN (*aloud*). "My very dear Esteban, I am leaving Madrid, or rather escaping from the city. I am crossing into Portugal for reasons that I shall explain to you in detail, provided you are not afraid of compromising yourself by granting hospitality for a few hours to a banished woman.— So, you have made a fool of yourself by getting married, and if rumor—" (*he reads silently*).

INES. Louder now, my dear.

DON ESTEBAN (*pretending to read*). Brr...brr..."and if rumor doesn't err, you have taken a wife. All the best, Serafina."

INES. Oh, you're not yet sharp enough, Esteban. "You have made a fool of yourself by getting married, and if rumor doesn't err, you have taken a wife." Is that how a duchess writes? I trust I could do better.

DON ESTEBAN (*pocketing the letter*). She's a silly woman. However, she's arriving today, Inès, indeed at any moment. Go dress. I wouldn't mind it if you dazzled her. She's a coquette who has seen better years. We'll make her bite her lips when she sees you. Come to think of it, you're a little pale today; a bit of rouge might not look bad on you.

INES. Why do you want me to cheat? If you love me when I'm pale, why should I try to please anyone else?

DON ESTEBAN. Dearest Inès!—Still, it would please me to have her admire my choice.

INES. Very well! I'll put on a little rouge to please you, sweetheart. But as for adorning myself with gewgaws—

DON ESTEBAN (*impatiently*). Don't go saying "gewgaws" before the Duchess! Go dress, my angel. A beauty like you can never look awkward. (*He kisses her*)

INES. How can a girl resist such compliments? I'll tell my maid to make me beautiful.

(*Exit*)

DON ESTEBAN (*alone*). So the Duchess of Montalvan is coming here....—Why should I feel any emotion?...—Yes, I once loved her...like many others...neither more nor less. Let her say anything she likes about my marriage—what does it matter to me? I love Inès...will her criticisms prevent me from loving her? I'm sure I won't even feel her mockery....She has a wicked tongue, that much I know....What upsets me is that she's arriving today, just when Inès is not looking her best...pale...almost yellow...rings around her eyes...damn it, that woman will notice and grin!...Poor Inès!...But let her dare to taunt me about this marriage!...She'll see how I take her joshing, by God....—She was a fine woman once upon a time...this Duchess. Once upon a time, that is to say five years ago. I owe her my reputation among the women. I fought my first duel over her....I was wounded in this arm, I remember, and I went to her, bleeding and ever so proud, in order to have it bandaged. She dressed the wound herself; she wouldn't allow anyone else to come near. And before laying on the bandage, she kissed the wound over and over...and sucked the blood....I was young; her kisses felt like a hot iron....Whenever I remember that moment my heart gives a leap....Ah, Don Juan Ramirez, how grateful I was for the sword-cut I received from you!

(*Enter Juan Mendo, a stump for his right hand*)

MENDO. God bless you, Don Esteban! Delighted to see you so merry today.

DON ESTEBAN. Mendo, you'll hurt me if you don't call me son.

MENDO (*embarrassed*). I've come...to take my leave of you. I'm going away....

DON ESTEBAN. Going away? Where?

MENDO. Back to where I came from....I've a relative in Galicia—a brother I haven't seen in many years.

DON ESTEBAN. Ha! This brother of yours is a mighty recent acquisition! How is it you've never mentioned him before?

MENDO. I...I don't know....

DON ESTEBAN. Something bothers you in this house and makes you want to leave it.

MENDO. Nothing, my dear Don Esteban...but I need to leave...I must go....

DON ESTEBAN. But again, for what reason?

MENDO. I have business in Galicia....

DON ESTEBAN. You're a man of secrets, but I think I've guessed what this one is. The impertinence of these rustic gentlemen offended you yesterday, and you wish to leave a place where you're exposed to this kind of unpleasantness. But I ask you to remain with us; Father, stay and you will be satisfied with my vengeance. I'll vex them every which way. I own almost all the land around here. I'll prevent them from fishing, from hunting; I'll sue them right and left. As governor of the town of Aviz[6] and military commander of our province, I'll billet our soldiers in their houses when our troops march into Portugal.

MENDO. But why should you bring troubles on your head for a trifle? Leave these people to their prejudices; I forgive them, and I yield the battlefield to them. Victory belongs to the greatest number.

DON ESTEBAN. No, by all the devils in hell! You won't leave us, now that I know your real reason. Never will it be said that a Mendoza submitted to anybody's whims. You'll remain with me, even if all Estremadura marches against this castle in order to drive you from it.

MENDO. Listen to me, Don Esteban. You saw how I objected to this marriage from the start. People should marry their equals. I'm untouched by prejudices, I mean by the usual opinions concerning noblemen and commoners, but when fate has given us birth in a given class of mankind, we find our attachments, our friendships within that class. They are based on similar tastes, customs, and ideas. We ought to remain where God has placed us. Heaven disposed otherwise in our family. You have connected yourself to a poor man who, even though His Majesty made him a gentleman, will never be respected as such. You'll earn nothing but grief trying to force this respect on the gentry. A man—an old man, not a very amusing one, nor useful to you in any way, and with nothing to do here, must not lightly condemn a gentleman like you to endless slights. I owe you so much already—

DON ESTEBAN. And I?

MENDO. No, Esteban, let me go....As far as my daughter is concerned, she lost her name when she married you. She acquired the name of Mendoza, which is capable of erasing any hereditary blot. Besides, if you feel that someone has insulted you on her account, you are her husband, and you are bound to defend and avenge her. But I, as long as I remain with you, I'll be like a leper who will turn everybody away from your house and prevent you from enjoying all the pleasures and prerogatives which are yours by right.

DON ESTEBAN. Your noble speech is useless, Mendo; you'll stay. Don't you see that I prefer your company a thousandfold to that of the little hidalgos of Estremadura? Let them go the devil a thousand times!

MENDO. I don't know what to say, My Lord. I am so used to receiving favors from the Mendozas that I am no longer know how to refuse them. But I fear that some day you'll repent having kept at your side an ignorant, invalid peasant....

---

6. Aviz is nearby in Portugal. The name should be pronounced close to "Ahvith."

DON ESTEBAN (*embracing him*). Invalid for my sake! Can I ever forget what you did for me, Father? Can I ever repay this debt?

MENDO. What I did—

DON ESTEBAN. We'll get even with them, I assure you.—And while we're on the subject, a fine lady is arriving here today—the Duchess Serafina de Montalvan. She comes to us from Madrid. We're all putting on our best Sunday finery to receive her....It's a silly whim of mine...but for my sake, take off this dark suit and put on something more gallant.

MENDO. You are making a mistake keeping me here.

(*He leaves*)

DON ESTEBAN (*alone*). Well well well! I've done a good deed; it will give me more strength to resist Serafina's seductions....—Seductions! Bravo for modesty! When a man has a poor little conquest to his credit, how easily he persuades himself that every woman craves the honor of becoming his slave!...But wouldn't it be correct for me to ride out to meet the duchess?...Doing so might grieve Inès, however.—Still, it's simply a courtesy which one owes to any woman....Why should I be less of a gentleman with a duchess than I would be with a merchant's wife? I'll have my horse saddled. Too late, I think.

(*Enter a servant*)

SERVANT. My Lord, a lady in a coach drawn by six mules has just entered the courtyard.

(*He leaves*)

DON ESTEBAN. I'll go downstairs to greet her.—Strange agitation! As if five years hadn't gone by since I saw her last, and five years are hard on a pretty woman.

(*He leaves. Enter Inès, badly made up and covered with diamonds*)

INES (*alone*). How eagerly he ran to meet her!...And when he received her letter, he looked blissful!...He wouldn't read it all to me....—I don't dare show him that it hurts me, because, of course, he doesn't do it on purpose. He loves me, and I'd be ungrateful if I were jealous. And yet I'm only a simple village girl without refined manners; maybe he'll grow sick of me when he compares me with a witty and charming lady from Madrid. No; Esteban is too kind to stop loving me. (*She sees the duchess*). Oh God! She's beautiful!

(*Enter Don Esteban, hand in hand with the duchess*)

DON ESTEBAN. My dear Inès—the Duchess Serafina de Montalvan. Lady Montalvan, allow me to introduce the Baroness de Mendoza.

DUCHESS. I am delighted to make your acquaintance.

INES (*awkwardly*). So am—I am too.

DUCHESS. What horrible roads! I am bone-tired—ah!

INES. And yet, you were riding in a carriage.

DUCHESS (*smiling*). That was the very reason.

DON ESTEBAN (*to the duchess*). May I offer you a chair, Lady Montalvan? (*Low to Inès*) Inès, what's the matter? Sit down.

DUCHESS. The baroness seems unwell. Are you indisposed, madam?

INES. I, madam?

DON ESTEBAN. She is somewhat pale because she tired herself yesterday; she is usually quite rosy-cheeked.[7]

DUCHESS. When a person's skin is as lovely as that of the baroness, pallor is not a flaw. (*Don Esteban bows*) Indeed, it looks more distinguished.

INES. My lady is very kind, but....

DUCHESS. The baroness is extremely young. I should guess her to be no more than twenty-four or twenty-five years old.

INES. I'll be five—what am I saying? I'll be twenty come Michaelmas.

DUCHESS. You have not been long in this chateau?

DON ESTEBAN. Not long at all. I took up this residence because of our proximity to Aviz, which I command as governor. I never expected to entertain you here. But tell me, madam, what is this banishment, as you call it, that has driven you so far away from our court. I hope that the cause for your presence in Estremadura, at the very confines of Spain, is not a very serious one.

DUCHESS. Not very serious! Do you realize, Don Esteban, that I am a fugitive in the literal meaning of the word? Here is my story. The king was my friend until Duke Olivares[8] became his minister. I tried by every means to be friends with the duke. He repelled me with contempt. This led to open war. I tried to get him dismissed by placing my own man as the king's confessor. Olivares, instead, gave him a mistress. The mistress succeeded, and Mercury became the king's confidant.

INES. The duke's first name is Mercury? What a funny name![9]

DUCHESS. Be that as it may, Olivarès wanted revenge. He was now all-powerful. He accused me of meddling in I don't know what Portuguese conspiracy—that wretched business of John of Braganza who wants to

---

7. This has to be reconciled somehow with the earlier stage direction which informs us that Ines is wearing make-up ("*rouge*" in the original), however poorly applied.

8. The Conde-duque Olivares (1587-1645), chief minister of Spain from 1621 to his fall in 1643. He proved unable to halt Portugal's secession from Spain in 1640.

9. A director who doesn't trust his audience to catch the joke (Mercury sometimes acted as go-between in Jupiter's love affairs) could substitute the following exchange:
DUCHESS. ...Olivares, instead, gave him a mistress. Aphrodite succeeded, and the duke became the king's confidant. INES. The mistress is called Aphrodite? What a funny name!

throw off our yoke and make himself king of Portugal. Such nonsense! It's I who am stealing Portugal from his most Catholic majesty! They were going to lock me up in some convent, perhaps even in the Tower of Segovia. I found out in time, and without waiting to be arrested, I took to my heels—so fast that they've probably just discovered that I'm gone from Madrid. I'm crossing into Portugal...where I'll be a conspirator, since that's what they're determined I shall be.

DON ESTEBAN. The cowards! Sending a lady to the Tower!

INES. But—that confessor?...

DON ESTEBAN (*low*). Inès, lady Montalvan needs some refreshments. Go take a look, will you?

(*Inès leaves. Silence*)

DON ESTEBAN. I didn't ask you whether you had a pleasant journey.

DUCHESS. Very pleasant....By the way, you are in touch with the commanding officer in Aviz?

DON ESTEBAN. I am. He keeps writing me. But we have so few soldiers here in Estremadura that I'm unable to send him reinforcements. Why do you ask?

DUCHESS. No reason.

(*Silence*)

DON ESTEBAN. The weather has been—

DUCHESS. Why this embarrassed look? Have you something to tell me?

DON ESTEBAN (*affecting indifference*). No.—Do you think my wife is pretty?

DUCHESS. Very pretty.

DON ESTEBAN. Unfortunately she's very shy, and that's what made her appear awkward to you. You quite disconcerted her.—Was it in Madrid that you heard of my marriage?

DUCHESS. Yes.

DON ESTEBAN. Would you tell me frankly what people are saying about it?

DUCHESS. Frankly?

DON ESTEBAN. Yes.

DUCHESS. It's generally criticized, since you want to hear the truth. On the other hand, our court philosophers say that it provides a good example. There have been songs, sonnets, barbs...what shall I tell you? In short, the opinion is that you've been a fool....But in Madrid everything is so quickly forgotten! Your marriage hasn't been mentioned in months.

DON ESTEBAN. And you, madam? Dare I ask for your opinion?

DUCHESS (*with dignity*). It is somewhat peculiar, Don Esteban, that you should address that question to *me*—especially since my advice would be useless to you and come too late.

DON ESTEBAN. I ask for your forgiveness. I was joking. What is done is done. I have no regrets.

(*Silence*)

DUCHESS. Don Esteban, my...friendship for you is the same as it was. We have been going our separate ways for a long time, but if one of us is to blame, that one is certainly not myself.—I have had no word from you since you left for the army.

DON ESTEBAN. Your reproaches overwhelm me; I deserve them.

DUCHESS. I, Don Esteban, have kept alive the memory of our old friendship, and, in my disgrace, it is to you that I have turned for asylum. Perhaps—

DON ESTEBAN. I am proud to accept this flattering mark of confidence....

DUCHESS. As your friend, I was pained by your marriage. As your...but I dare not now utter the sweeter name you once gave me...I suffered, yes I suffered deeply to see my Esteban misled by his generosity into committing an extravance—forgive the word, it is that of a friend. One day, surely, you will regret it. Not the misalliance. A spirit like yours rises above vulgar prejudices.—I won't mention what may be shocking with regard to the father....[10] On the contrary, it's the romantic and appealing side of this affair....But alas, I see you paired for life with an uneducated peasant-girl. After her first child, her beauty will disappear, and that is when one feels the value of an educated woman....However, I hope I'm mistaken. I have only caught a glimpse of Doña Inès...perhaps I'm biased...jealous...you think that a jealous woman is speaking. Yes, I am jealous, Esteban, I was in love with you, I was....If I had seen you matched with a woman who is graceful and intelligent, a woman, in a word, made for you—I still would have suffered at the loss of a heart that had been mine...but at least it would have consoled me a tiny bit to know that you were happy, happy in your inner self and in public opinion. I would have said: he could not be mine, but he found a companion worthy of him.

(*She turns aside, weeping*)

DON ESTEBAN. Madam...I feel, as I must...how flattering....

(*Enter Inès and a servant*)

---

10. The Duchess must be referring to Mendo's infamous profession of old. This could be made explicit in production; the Duchess could say: "I won't mention the fact that the father was the village executioner."

SERVANT. Dinner is served, my lord.
INES. We're having a beefstew with chickpeas, just the way you like it.[11]
(*The Duchess sighs. Exeunt omnes*)

Act Two

(*The setting is the same as in Act One*)

INES. My dear?...
DON ESTEBAN (*absent-mindedly*). Hum?
INES. You're angry with me?
DON ESTEBAN. I? Why should I be?
INES. I said so many dumb things to that beautiful lady; the harder I tried, the worse it went.
DON ESTEBAN. Basta!—Is she still in her room?
INES. Yes.—It's funny how one feels ill at ease before certain persons. I've never seen such a grand lady.
DON ESTEBAN. She's taking a long siesta.
INES. Did you notice how beautiful her hands are? I wish I could ask her with what she washes them to get them so white.
DON ESTEBAN (*smiling*). Not everybody can have white hands, Inès. One has to be born a duchess for that.[12]
INES. Still....
DON ESTEBAN. She went up to her room ages ago....
INES. My father is acting strangely today. How he stared at dinner when he looked at the duchess!
DON ESTEBAN. Did you notice how kindly and gracefully she—Doña Serafina spoke to him?
INES. I did, but still he looked anxious....
DON ESTEBAN. It's his customary look.—She must be awake by now, Inès. Go up to her room...go...one can't be too attentive to one's guests....
INES (*low, sadly*). Especially to beautiful ladies.
(*She leaves*)
DON ESTEBAN (*alone*). Stupid ideas of one's childhood! Stupid prejudices! You drive them out, you think you're free of them, and then they return as strong and as dangerous as ever! I shook off their yoke; I trampled on them, but I pay the cost of this victory. I almost

---

11. Mérimée uses the word *puchero*, and provides a note: "A stew with chickpeas. This dish is a little vulgar."
12. "This idea seems to have been borrowed from Lord Byron." [M]

regret...no...but I'm punished for having tamed the enemies I despise....They return to the attack....Since the arrival of the duchess, my wife, my good Inès...seems to have lost some of her beauty....—Her naivete no longer delights me....There was a time!...I blush to be ignorant of the fashions of the day in this remote manor-house....The demon of worldliness wants to chain me to Serafina's chariot...but I have the strength to overcome this feeble challenge, since I've already recognized the traps the enemy is setting out for me. Haven't I been victorious in more strenuous battles? Spain will not soon forget the example I have given, and after that, I have the right, I think, to count on my strength of mind.... She showed off her grandest airs. But I'll torture her as well. After what has passed between us, I didn't expect to be treated like a puppy fresh out of college. She behaves as if she pitied me!...The coquette!...She's still as beautiful as an angel....Ah! Marital fidelity!...Luckily it applies only to the ladies.

(*Enter a servant*)

SERVANT. My lord!...

DON ESTEBAN. What is it?...You look scared.

SERVANT. My lord...it's the corregidor of Badajoz.[13]

DON ESTEBAN. The corregidor?...

SERVANT. He has his men with him....He wants to talk to you.

DON ESTEBAN. Fine. Let him come in.

(*Enter the corregidor*)

CORREGIDOR. I kiss your lordship's hand.

DON ESTEBAN. To what do I owe the honor of your visit?

CORREGIDOR. My Lord, I am deeply sorry to be obliged to execute an order I have just received from Madrid. The Duchess of Montalvan is in this house and is preparing to cross into Portugal.

DON ESTEBAN. Who told you that she's here?

CORREGIDOR. Gently, if you please, and without raising our voices. I recognized her carriage in your coach-house.

DON ESTEBAN. So you know one coat of arms on a vehicle from another!

CORREGIDOR. As well as the next man, my Lord. As it happens, there's no coat of arms on the duchess' carriage...but the servants talked.

DON ESTEBAN. Looking at your beard, I should have thought you too sensible to listen to servants.

---

13. The audience will quickly catch on that this is a royal official; however, the servant's line could be changed to "it's the magistrate—the corregidor of Badajoz." The corregidor should be on in years and unarmed.

CORREGIDOR. I am aware that giving up your guest is painful to you, but you would hardly wish to give asylum to an enemy of the king.

DON ESTEBAN. Sir, I have neither duchess nor enemy of the king in my house. Take yourself to the devil and leave us in peace, or I shall have you punished for your insolence.

CORREGIDOR. No insults, my lord, if you please. You will not have me punished, because you are no longer governor of this province.

DON ESTEBAN. What is the rascal saying?

CORREGIDOR. It would distress me to offend your lordship by ordering a judicial search of your dwelling.

DON ESTEBAN. If you were insolent enough, by God! you'd see what happens to a low-born rogue ennobled a week ago when he meddles with a grandee of Spain.

CORREGIDOR. And you, my lord, might learn to treat the laws with more respect. One last time, tell me where is the duchess.

DON ESTEBAN. Get out, or else my men will kick you out.

CORREGIDOR. You force my hand. Men, come in!

(*Enter a couple of armed constables*)

DON ESTEBAN (*ringing a bell*). Ruffians! Is that how you treat a Mendoza! You villain, you'll pay for your audacity!

(*Enter Don Esteban's servants*)

CORREGIDOR. In the king's name! Don Esteban de Mendoza, you are under arrest. (*He touches him with his staff*)

DON ESTEBAN. Drive out these rascals! What's this? The staff in this peasant's hand paralyzes you? Come, I'll teach you your duty. (*He draws his sword*) Let this do the talking. Out, rabble, out.

(*He drives them out before him. Enter Inès and the Duchess*)

INES. They're going to kill him! Help! Help!

(*Reenter Don Esteban, returning his sword to its scabbard*)

DUCHESS. Well done, my Lord Baron. Impossible to strike harder with the flat of one's sword!

INES. Sweetheart, you're not wounded, are you?

DON ESTEBAN. No.

DUCHESS. May one inquire of your Excellency what reason of state made you exercise your arm on the backs of these poor devils?

DON ESTEBAN. Madam, I need to tell you something in private....Inès, leave us for a few minutes.

INES. I, sweetheart?

DON ESTEBAN. Yes.

INES. Will you be long?

DON ESTEBAN. No, no; but leave us.

(*Exit Inès*)

DUCHESS. Very mysterious, all this. If you weren't married, I'd be alarmed.

DON ESTEBAN. Lady Montalvan, it pains me to mar your high spirits. Let me inform you that the corregidor of Badajoz was here to arrest you.

DUCHESS. Is that so?

DON ESTEBAN (*fatuously*). Yes, Doña Serafina. I exposed myself to the wrath of the law, which is trying to bury your loveliness from the world in the Tower of Segovia.

DUCHESS. O valiant knight errant! Tristan, Lancelot, Amadis...receive the thanks of an unfortunate and persecuted damsel! Ha, ha, ha!

DON ESTEBAN (*with forced laughter*). You haven't changed—always the same.

DUCHESS. Dear me! I'd better drop this untimely merriment. Dear Don Esteban, complete your task. Give me four sturdy horses. Tonight I must reach Portugal.

DON ESTEBAN. Command me. Everything here is yours.

DUCHESS. Alas! hardly have I arrived that I must be leaving you....I shall probably never see you again. But I have no choice.

DON ESTEBAN. Madam, I—

DUCHESS. Let's waste no time. Do you have a reliable, brave, determined man who can accompany me? I left my squire in Caceres, where he had broken his arm.

DON ESTEBAN. Doña Serafina, do you not know a person in this place who would be proud to serve you?

DUCHESS. What do you mean?

DON ESTEBAN. Serafina! Once upon a time you would have insisted that I accompany you...to protect your flight.—Why do you refuse me now?

DUCHESS. My dear, dear Esteban!

DON ESTEBAN. Serafina!...Speak!...Tell me that you choose me as your knight.

DUCHESS. No, Esteban, I can't. You have already done too much by exposing yourself to the anger of a cruel minister. If you accompanied me into Portugal, you'd become my accomplice in their uprising, and Spain would be forever closed to you....No, my dear, I can't so lightheartedly ruin you. Remember that as governor of Estremadura, anything you do, however innocent—

DON ESTEBAN. Let Olivarès rage to his heart's content! I could wish for greater dangers in your defence. Besides, if I go with you, I avoid pursuit from the Badajoz authorities, which I handled rather roughly just now....Doña Serafina, do not deny me, I conjure you. (*He takes her hand*)

DUCHESS. Impossible!...You cannot abandon your family...your beloved Inès....Oh! That name ought to make you forget poor Serafina and the dangers she will face.—Adieu, Esteban, remember me from time to time.

DON ESTEBAN. I will not leave you! Your freedom, perhaps your life, is menaced. How could I live, knowing you are exposed to a thousand dangers? What! I, a soldier, I am to live at peace in my home, mouthing sterile good wishes for my—my guest—my own Serafina. (*He falls to his knees*)

DUCHESS. Oh, my God! Was I not unhappy enough? Must I drag my only friend into ruin with me?

DON ESTEBAN. Serafina, say yes, I implore you in the name of the wound I received for you.

DUCHESS. Is it not cruel of you to remind me of those times?

DON ESTEBAN. You consent! God be praised! I will follow you to the dankest dungeon of Segovia!

DUCHESS (*feebly*). And...your Inès?

DON ESTEBAN. I think only of you...of the dangers that threaten you on all sides....Inès...she will remain here to weather the storm.

DUCHESS. Ah, if she knew what you intend to do!

DON ESTEBAN. I'll find a pretext....

DUCHESS. Very well, I consent. But take me only as far as—

DON ESTEBAN. Don't mention the place where we shall part.

DUCHESS. Cruel Olivarès! Have you enough victims now?

DON ESTEBAN. Fear nothing for me. I have powerful friends at court. But your generosity exaggerates the poor service I render you.

DUCHESS. God! Grant that I be the only victim!

DON ESTEBAN. I am familiar with the back-roads. Our enemies will have to be infernally sharp to catch up with us. You couldn't take a better guide.

DUCHESS. Why, why did I come here of all places?

DON ESTEBAN. God be praised that you did!

(*Enter a servant*)

SERVANT. Two letters for you, my lord.

(*He leaves*)

DUCHESS (*looking at one of the letters*). The minister's seal!

DON ESTEBAN. What does he want? (*He reads the letter and then hands it to the duchess*) You see, they don't trust me either at court. I am recalled. They want me to return at once to Madrid.

DUCHESS. Obey, Esteban, or else you are ruined. You see that you are already compromised.

DON ESTEBAN. All the more reason for avoiding the tiger's claws. So: I am an outlaw too. Good!

DUCHESS. Oh, my God....

DON ESTEBAN (*after reading the other letter*). This one is from your friend and mine, Don Rodrigo de Yriarte. He informs me that I'm thought to be no stranger to the troubles in Portugal, and that I had my reasons for settling so near to the heart of the rebellion....Wonderful! Considering it was *they* who sent me here![14]

DUCHESS. I am so unhappy! I don't know what advice to give you....

DON ESTEBAN. We'll put our heads together once we're safe.—Hush! Here's Inès.

(*Inès half-opens the door*)

INES. Can a person come in?

DUCHESS. Good heavens, baroness! I'm truly angry at my Lord Don Esteban. The news from Madrid he imparted to me in secret didn't deserve to be a mystery—and especially not for you, madam.

DON ESTEBAN. My dear Inès, the duchess insists on leaving us. I will have the horses harnessed at once. (*Low to Inès*) I'll escort her up to the orange-grove.

INES (*low*). Do you want me to go with you?

DON ESTEBAN. No; the dew is rising; you'll catch cold.

INES. You're travelling by night, madam? Aren't you scared?

DUCHESS. The countless misfortunes I've suffered have toughened me somewhat.

INES (*low to Esteban*). Why did you beat up these constables?

DON ESTEBAN. They were rascals....They dared....A stupid business about...about poachers, you see....Nothing you'd understand.

INES. And yet, the servants are saying—

DON ESTEBAN. They're a set of chatterboxes who don't know what they're saying, and you're a fool to listen to them. I have orders to

---

14. In the third act we will find conclusive proof that Serafina has been plotting from the start to implicate Esteban in the conspiracy. Tips in the second act: her disingenuously casual inquiry about the fortress of Aviz and—more subtly on Mérimée's part—the fact that Don Rodrigo de Yriarte is a friend of Serafina as well as of Esteban. The latter has never been a suspect—indeed, he was deliberately despatched to Estremadura. Why then is he suddenly under a cloud? It can only be because he has been slandered and denounced in Madrid by Serafina and her friends as a first move in their plot. On the other hand, the corregidor's irruption is clearly an unplanned event—an accident Serafina quickly exploits. But we need to assume that the plot to implicate Esteban was originally a general one, involving the understanding that further moves would have to made on the spur of the moment.

give.—Show Doña Serafina the flowers you've been growing with your own hands.

INES. Oh yes! Lady Montalvan, come see my Arabian jasmines.

DUCHESS (*to Esteban*). As soon as possible, yes?

(*Exeunt omnes. After a while, enter Mendo*)[15]

MENDO (*alone*). There's something impertinent in rich folk even when they're being polite. This duchess was mocking us, and Don Esteban was looking at her more than at his wife. I'm afraid that Inès will be sorry she married a great lord.

(*Enter Inès*)

INES. She's gone at last, and to tell you the truth, I'm glad of it.

MENDO. Is your husband escorting her?

INES. As far as the orange-grove. He wouldn't let me come along on my little white mare.—I must tell you I'm quite worried.

MENDO. Why?

INES. He took his pistols, even though there are no robbers in these parts.

MENDO. He may have taken them...to reassure the duchess.

INES. What dangers are there on the road?

MENDO. None, I hope.

INES. What if the king's men catch up with Doña Serafina?

MENDO. It takes time for them to reach this place.

INES. This woman will bring trouble on his head—she who wanted to give her confessor to the king. Imagine, father, she wanted His Majesty to use her own confessor. She said so herself in a story I didn't understand. God almighty! Why did my husband receive her?

MENDO. He couldn't do otherwise. Hadn't they been friends?

INES. I'm afraid so. (*Knocking at the door*)— I hear noise at the great gate. Could he be back already?

(*Enter the corregidor with a number of armed men*)

CORREGIDOR. *Salutem omnibus.* We're back, but this time with reinforcements. The scofflaws will stop laughing. We'll see now who pays for the breakage.

INES. What is you want, sir? What are you here for?

CORREGIDOR. For nothing, except to apprehend and take into custody a Don Esteban, lord of Mendoza, and a Doña Serafina, Duchess of Montalvan. Nothing else.

MENDO. What are you saying? It's impossible.

---

15. At this point, Mérimée indicates a change of setting to "a low room in the chateau." As this change seems unnecessary, I have suppressed it.

CORREGIDOR. Kindly don't interfere with the law. I know my business. No resistance, or I'll put you all to the sword and raze this castle to the ground.

INES. Sir....the duchess...is gone...and my husband...is gone too.

CORREGIDOR. Do you take me for a fool? Nobody left by the great gate. The bird is still in its nest. (*To two constables*) You, prevent anyone from leaving. (*To the others*) You, follow me.

(*They leave*)

INES. I knew it, I knew it! This duchess will be the death of him! Mother of God, protect him!

MENDO. Don't worry. A rich man always gets out of a scrape.

INES. But where is he? When will they give him back to me?

MENDO. I hope to God he's coming back.

INES. You're saying this as if you thought he wasn't.

MENDO. No, no....I hope...he'll be here soon.

INES. You have something on your mind you daren't tell me. Yes, you know or you suspect something terrible.

MENDO. You're mistaken, daughter. Let's go to our rooms. All we can do now is pray God that he may keep your husband from harm.

INES. How you frighten me! A thousand horrible thoughts are crowding in my mind.

MENDO. Why stay here? Come with me, come away.

(*They leave*)

Act Three
Scene 1

(*An inn at Elvas, on the Portuguese side of the frontier. The innkeeper, soldiers and Portuguese citizens are sitting around a table and drinking*)

HOST (*rising with a glass in his hand*). To John of Braganza, king of Portugal, and down with Spain![16]

ALL. To John of Braganza and down with Spain!

HOST. A real Portuguese, thank God, a good king, a jolly fellow, the kind we need, not one of those hungry-looking Spaniards who pump the doubloons out of our country.

A SOLDIER. Let them come back; we're here to greet them.

HOST. You don't know the news, gentlemen? When our men threw the Spanish envoy—

---

16. I am taking the harmless liberty of adding these "down with Spain" shouts for the sake of immediate clarity.

SEVERAL. Vasconcellos!

HOST. Out the window in Lisbon, what do you think happened?

A CITIZEN. He broke his neck on the pavement.

HOST. A huge phantom appeared to all the people, shouting with a voice of thunder, "To the fray, men of Portugal! The yoke of Spain is broken!" And who do you think it was?

A SOLDIER. What a question? Who could it be except the ghost of King Sebastian![17]

HOST. Exactly....After speaking these words, the phantom melted into the air with a noise...a noise as if ten thousand cannons had been fired at the same time. And it's true, because I have the news from my sister who was in church when Vasconcellos flew out the window.

THE SOLDIER. And what's so extraordinary about that? Everybody knows that King Sebastian isn't dead. Look here. One day, when I was doing guard duty, it was as dark as in an oven; it was drizzling, and I was trying keep my musket dry when a great white shape, armed from top to toe, with a crown on its head, brushed right up against me, making a deep moan. Now I tremble before no man that's made of flesh and blood, but when I see a ghost, I lose my courage, so I fell to the ground and recited a litany that drives spirits away.

HOST. I know one that's often been of use to me.

(*Enter Don Cesar*)

A CITIZEN. Hey! Who's this coming in?

HOST. Gentlemen, this is a gallant young Portuguese, Don Cesar de Belmonte, who is in command at the siege of Aviz.

(*They all rise*)

DON CESAR. Greetings, friends, greetings.

HOST. This is an honor for my inn.

DON CESAR. It will enjoy a higher one presently. I am expecting a lady in flight from Castile, where she is being persecuted as a friend of Portugal.

HOST. All that we own is hers to command.

DON CESAR. She'll be arriving any moment.

HOST. My lord, I take the liberty of asking your Excellency how things are going for our side.

---

17. "Allusion to a popular belief in Portugal. Many people believe that King Sebastian (who was killed in Africa) is not dead and that he appears to his subjects on extraordinary occasions. I believe that his last apparition occurred during the French occupation of Lisbon in 1808-1809" [M]. Sebastian was killed in Morocco in 1578, but his body was never found. I have lightly elucidated the host's story so as to make it intelligible without going so far as to insert the legend of King Sebastian into the dialogue.

DON CESAR. Superbly, my friend. The Spanish garrisons are withdrawing in all haste. Everywhere John of Braganza is recognized and acclaimed by his subjects.

HOST. Good!

DON CESAR. Only on the towers of Aviz is the Spanish flag still flying. But we'll be planting our own on them before long.

HOST. I'll lead the assault myself if need be, spit in hand. I wish I could impale as many Spaniards as I've spitted turkeys in my lifetime!

(*Enter the Duchess and Don Esteban*)

DUCHESS. Hail, land of refuge! Hail, Portugal! And long live John of Braganza!—Ah, Don Cesar!

DON CESAR. I'm overjoyed, Doña Serafina, to see you safe on Portuguese soil.

DUCHESS. Yes, I am safe at last. (*She speaks to him aside. Don Esteban remains in a corner, looking uneasy. Then, in a loud voice*) Don Cesar, may I introduce my savior, Don Esteban de Mendoza. Baron, this is Don Cesar de Belmonte.

(*The two coldly salute each other*)

DON ESTEBAN. You need to rest, Doña Serafina; I don't know whether this inn—

DUCHESS. No. A while ago I was half-dead with fatigue, but now, surrounded by friends...(*Don Cesar bows, Don Esteban frowns*) rescued from the claws of Olivarès, I feel suddenly refreshed. I do believe I could dance!

DON CESAR (*low*). His Majesty will receive you in Lisbon with open arms.

DUCHESS (*low*). Do you think so? (*Aloud*) Do you realize how close I came to disaster, Don Cesar? Without the bravery of Baron Mendoza, I would have been caught and locked up in Segovia.

DON CESAR. God! If only I'd been there!

DON ESTEBAN. Sir, it was a business that didn't deserve your presence. (*Low to the duchess*). Kindly ask this man to leave the premises.

DUCHESS. Our carriage broke down on the road. While it was being repaired, here comes the Corregidor and his men. Pif, paf! Pistol shots...drawn swords...I almost died of fright, and I didn't open my eyes until Don Esteban came back to announce that the enemy was in full flight.

DON CESAR (*low*). Will he be staying here?

DUCHESS (*low*). Yes. We must keep him happy till we get what we need from him concerning what you know at Aviz.

DON CESAR. Doña Serafina, you need to rest after your painful journey. Allow me to withdraw. My Lord, if I can be useful to you in any way in this country, please call on me.

DON ESTEBAN. I am your servant.

DON CESAR (*low to the duchess*). The Spanish commander needs a letter...but you understand....

(*He leaves*)

DUCHESS (*merrily*). Well, Don Esteban, what's the matter with you? Are you sulking?

DON ESTEBAN. I, madam?

DUCHESS (*imitating him*). I, madam? Yes, you, sir. What's ailing you? What have I done to deserve this sour mood?

DON ESTEBAN (*coldly*). Madam, you jest so gracefully...you are always so lively (*she looks tenderly at him*). Ha! Don't look at me as you're doing now, or I won't be able to scold you anymore.

DUCHESS. Dearest Esteban, what on earth have I done to deserve a scolding? (*Tenderly*) Shouldn't *I* be scolding *you* for following me all the way to Portugal? And yet, how can I hold against you a disobedience that saved me?

DON ESTEBAN. You torment me, Serafina, with your innumerable acquaintances. The passion I felt for you in Madrid has returned...but, God help me, you have friends in every place. Even in Portugal!

DUCHESS. Well, what is so surprising about that? Don Cesar was in the conspiracy like myself.—Ye gods, I regret only one thing, namely that I implicated you too deeply in it.

DON ESTEBAN. Oh Serafina, you know the way to make *my* regret vanish.

DUCHESS (*pretending surprise*). Lord Mendoza!—But in fact, what's to become of you? If I were you, seeing that I was compromised and all but exiled from my country, I'd accept a post in Portugal.

DON ESTEBAN. What would they do with me here? And, besides, am I not a Castilian?

DUCHESS. What of it? Am I not a Spaniard? But they banished me, and I belong to the country that gives me asylum.

DON ESTEBAN. Let us change the subject.

DUCHESS. No, we must talk about it...otherwise you'll increase my remorse for having made you leave your country...for exposing you to resentment in Madrid without offering you compensation at the Portuguese court.

DON ESTEBAN. Is it for the Portuguese I fired my pistols? The compensation I look for—

DUCHESS. Of course you don't wish to *fight* at the side of Portugal...but there are positions....

DON ESTEBAN. I repeat, let's change the subject.

DUCHESS. But what's to become of you? You can't safely return to Spain at this time.

DON ESTEBAN. Do you wish to rid yourself of me so soon?

DUCHESS. You're driving me to distraction!

DON ESTEBAN. And is it up to John of Braganza to reward me for offering you my poor services?—No, Doña Serafina, I am rewarded enough by my happiness in seeing you out of danger.

DUCHESS. You are no longer a Spaniard. Why not become a Portuguese? Listen to me. I am in a position to promise you employment that will earn you the favor of John of Braganza without obliging you to bear arms against Spain.

DON ESTEBAN. Strange obstinacy!

DUCHESS. You can even do your compatriots a favor. For instance, the fortress of Aviz is under close siege. Don Cesar is launching an attack on it tomorrow. But, out of consideration for me, he will allow the garrison to withdraw. Write to the commander. You are his superior. Tell him to give up a useless resistance. Authorize him to yield the city.

DON ESTEBAN (*sternly*). Do you understand what you are asking me to do?

DUCHESS. Something utterly simple. You told me yourself that you are sure the fortress is untenable. Save Spanish lives, that's all.

DON ESTEBAN. And Spanish honor?

DUCHESS. Honor! Honor! Your word. With that word in your mouth you can cause a great deal of blood to flow. But say no more. What is it to me whether or not Don Cesar launches the attack? But I promise this scarf to whoever will be the first to plant the Portuguese flag on the towers of Aviz; and I'll be delighted if that man is Don Cesar.

DON ESTEBAN. Don Cesar! Always Don Cesar! That is *your* word. Serafina, since we've arrived in Portugal you've never stopped talking about Don Cesar.

DUCHESS. And why shouldn't I?

DON ESTEBAN. I don't wish to boast of what I have been able to do for you, but tell me, where will you find a heart that loves you like mine?

DUCHESS. Are you forgetting?...

DON ESTEBAN. Let me forget everything in your arms, Serafina; I adore you; why do you want to kill me with your flightiness?

DUCHESS. My Lord, you forget the tie that binds you.

DON ESTEBAN (*angry*). No, heart of stone, I do not forget. But my remorse wasn't enough; I still needed your reproaches, your sarcasms to finish me off.—That's right, I left everything for you: I sacrificed country, wife, honor...but you...you, who turned me into the basest of men, you, Serafina, you scornfully reject me and prefer Don Cesar's love to mine.

DUCHESS. Where is justice? Am *I* the guilty one? Did *I* commit perjury? Remember the orange-grove of Aranjuez, where you swore your eternal love a hundred times. You leave me...a few coldly polite letters have to be my consolation. They too come to an end. Then you strike the final blow: you take a wife, Esteban...and what a wife, what a rival!...That is how you remain true to your oaths. Go your way, liar, leave me to weep over my weaknesses in the past.

DON ESTEBAN. Serafina!...I never stopped loving you...I swear, yes, I swear....I left Inès...in order never to part from you...in order to live as your slave....Will you abandon me?...No! You're smiling, you're willing to open your arms to the man you once loved.

DUCHESS. Oh my Esteban!

DON ESTEBAN. I'm yours for life!

DUCHESS. If you are willing to defy the world's opinion, I'll live for you as you will live for me.

DON ESTEBAN. Forever!

DUCHESS. Forever! Oh my beloved, we will live happy, far from Spanish tyrants, by the side of a king we adore, John of Braganza.

DON ESTEBAN. Long live John of Braganza!

DUCHESS. We are Portuguese! Here is my scarf, dyed in Braganza's colors!

DON ESTEBAN. I intend to spread the news that I have died....I'll change my name...and then, in our retreat far from the tumult of the court, we will live blissfully in each other's arms....But if that poor—

DUCHESS. Idol of my heart!...Tell me, will you write to the commander of Aviz?

DON ESTEBAN. I beg you, Serafina, don't demand this of me!

DUCHESS. I don't, but I beg it of you.

DON ESTEBAN. You want me to....Yes, for you, I'll sacrifice everything....

DUCHESS. A kiss for the trouble?

DON ESTEBAN. But what am I to say?...I can't write....

DUCHESS. Say that there's no hope of help from Spain....Is that true or is it not?

DON ESTEBAN. It is...and yet....

DUCHESS. Don't you want me to clasp you in my arms?

DON ESTEBAN. Write it yourself....I'll sign. Are you satisfied?

(*The duchess writes*)

DUCHESS. My best, my darling! (*She kisses him*) Yes, now at last I believe in your love!

(*She rings; enter Pedro*)

DUCHESS. Let this letter be promptly handed to the military governor of Aviz. You'll find an ensign of the Beira volunteers downstairs who will take charge of it.[18]

PEDRO. My Lord, are you for the new fashion of wearing Portuguese colors?

DON ESTEBAN. Well, what about it?

PEDRO. If you are, I ask for my discharge. I don't feel like wearing a Portuguese scarf. I was born a Spaniard, and a Spaniard I'll die.

DON ESTEBAN (*low to Serafina*).[19] Oh, Serafina, what I have sacrificed for you!

DUCHESS (*low*). What! You're agitated because a servant wants to quit your sevice? (*To Pedro*) Here, my good man, is a purse: go drink to my health. Return to your home, and may Our Lady of Pilar assist you.[20] (*Whispers*) If anyone asks you what has become of Baron Mendoza, say that he died...that he died in a duel...do you understand?

PEDRO. Should I say it to everybody, even to Lady Mendoza?

DUCHESS. To everybody. Take this ring too; you'll give it to your wife if you have one. But first, deliver the letter downstairs. (*Exit Pedro*) Esteban, do you see the sun setting in that grove of orange-trees? It's the return of a certain thrilling evening in Aranjuez!

DON ESTEBAN. Oh, why did I ever leave you?

Scene 2

(*The Mendoza residence, as in Act One. Inès and Mendo are discovered*)

MENDO. He had to go into hiding because of that unfortunate fracas with the corregidor...but as soon as the matter is hushed up he'll return.

INES. But why hasn't he written? I could have had three letters from him by this time.

---

18. But what of the fact that Don Esteban has been recalled to Madrid and must be supposed to have no authority any longer over the commander of Aviz, who could hardly have been kept in the dark about this? (Even the corregidor knows.) Mérimée could easily have overcome this little difficulty, but seems to have remained unaware of it.

19. The stage direction here is mine; Doña Serafina's reply should also be *sotto-voce*.

20. "A venerated statue in the cathedral of Zaragoza" [M].

MENDO. Hm.

INES. I see only too clearly that you're not telling me what you think. Esteban is dead or unfaithful. God grant that he be unfaithful!

MENDO (*aside*). Yes, so I can avenge you.

INES. What did you say?

MENDO. I hope that he's alive and still loves you...but I've more than one reason—

INES. Mother of God! Isn't this Pedro?

(*Enter Pedro*)

PEDRO. Madam, I kiss your hand.

INES. Pedro...what have you done with my husband?...Speak....

PEDRO. Sad news, madam.

INES. He's dead!

PEDRO. May God have mercy on him and forgive his sins.

INES. He's dead and it's her fault! (*She faints*)

MENDO. Villain, you've killed my daughter!

PEDRO. Madam, madam! Come back to your senses! Don't believe a word I said...Lord Mendoza is not dead....

INES. Mendoza?

PEDRO. Lives and is well, but—

INES. Thank God, I shall see him again!

PEDRO. I don't know if you'll see him again....

INES. Pedro, tell me everything. Don't hide anything from me.

PEDRO. You wish to know the truth?...Very well, he's in Elvas, with that duchess he calls his dear Serafina. I saw him wearing a scarf with the Portuguese colors, and I heard plenty more from others. For myself, when I saw what I saw, I asked for my discharge. The duchess gave me money for spreading the word that he's dead, and your husband looked like he agreed. But I wish the ducats had melted in my hand and burned through to the bone! Because my lie almost killed my good mistress....

INES (*sobbing*). I won't survive this!

MENDO (*aside*). What I foresaw has happened. Inès!

INES. Father?

MENDO. Have you kept the clothes you wore in our village?

INES. Yes, father.

MENDO. Go fetch them. Take off everything this liar has given you. Keep nothing that was his. We won't stay another day under his roof. You'll come with me to Badajoz. The Ursulines will shelter you.

INES. Give me your arm...I'm so weak....

MENDO. Come...lean on my arm....I am strong....Let's go!

(*They leave*)

Scene 3

(The inn at Elvas. Don Esteban sits deep in thought. Enter the Duchess)[21]

DUCHESS. Why so sad, dear friend? Can your Serafina take your mind off your melancholy?
DON ESTEBAN. With a conscience burdened like mine...can a man be merry?
DUCHESS. You should go hunting; it will distract you a little.
DON ESTEBAN. Has the Aviz commander returned to Spain?
DUCHESS. I fancy he has.
DON ESTEBAN. Have you found out whether the conditions of capitulation were religiously observed?
DUCHESS. I'm quite sure.
DON ESTEBAN. I'm glad.—Serafina, let's leave Elvas. The memory of what has happened in this inn is killing me. Would to heaven that we were together in the deserts of America!
DUCHESS. For me, Elvas holds only memories of love. But, with your permission, instead of the deserts of America, let us leave for Lisbon.
DON ESTEBAN. We'll see.—I'll go out for a ride on horseback.—Will you join me?
DUCHESS. No, I'm tired...I'm going to take a siesta.
DON ESTEBAN. And Don Cesar...where is he?
DUCHESS. Incorrigibly jealous!...In Aviz, no doubt.
DON ESTEBAN. Can you think that I distrust you, Serafina?...After the proof you have given me of your love!—Well, let me go for a gallop. When the wind whistles and whirls at my ears until I am numb—that's when I am most at peace.—Adieu.
DUCHESS. Adieu, my love.
(He leaves)
DUCHESS *(alone)*. Poor simpleton! How contemptible is a spineless man! At first I believed that something could be made of him, but he has too narrow a mind ever to be Serafina's mate. Sometimes I pity him...but a person who worried over such weaklings would fail in her noblest projects. Olivarès! You drove me from Madrid. I shall enter Lisbon in triumph. Now I can unleash my ambition; I see no limit to my growing power.—*(The clock strikes)* So late!...He should be here!

---

21. Here again I have taken a slight liberty. In the original, the Duchess and Don Esteban are discovered in conversation as the curtain rises. But since Esteban almost at once begins to *question* Serafina, Mérimée must have imagined her as having recently left the inn and then returned to it.

DON CESAR (*entering*). And here he is.

DUCHESS. Come in, Caesar; Pompey has gone for a ride.

DON CESAR. My queen admires my punctuality. I arrive from Aviz at a gallop, and I'm snatching you away without giving myself time to breathe.

DUCHESS. Our good man is worried about the Spanish garrison in Aviz.

DON CESAR. With good reason, by God! Let me be demoted to a foot-soldier if our Portuguese peasants allow a single one of them to return to Spain alive!

DUCHESS. How perfectly awful, Don Cesar!—Hand me my veil.—Is the carriage ready?

DON CESAR. It is, my charmer.

DUCHESS. Good! Let's be gone. Give me your hand.

(*They leave. After a while, enter Don Esteban*)[22]

DON ESTEBAN (*alone*). The fatigue of the body gives no rest to the mind....She stands always before my eyes....Oh, how she must be suffering at this very moment!...Poor unhappy girl!...What had she done?...Serafina! (*He calls*) Serafina! Doña Serafina! (*He goes out and after a while returns, very agitated, with a letter in his hand*) She's not in her room. Where could she have gone? And what is this? "To be given to Baron Mendoza." It's her handwriting. "Dear Don Esteban, it pains me no end to leave you, but I must absolutely go to Lisbon. Since Portugal does not seem to be much to your liking, I urge you to return to your excellent wife, who must be longing for you. Adieu; be happy with her, and do not miss me. Don Cesar...." Oh! (*He throws the letter down. Silence*) I have what I deserve. (*He rereads the letter*) Yes, what I deserve....I left an angel in order to throw myself into the demon's maw....Avenge myself?...No, I no longer have the stomach....What will become of me?...How could I dare show myself again to old Mendo?...Because Inès...I am sure that she will be the first to open her arms...but Mendo!...If the servant I sent....He must have told her....Oh, monster that I am!...I may have killed her! Inès, Inès, is it you or your corpse that awaits me?...I can no longer bear this uncertainty! I must know!...Back to Mendoza, let my head fall if it must! (*Enter Pedro*) Pedro! What news?

PEDRO. My Lord, I've come back to you....I couldn't lie....When I saw my lady's grief, I confessed to everything.

---

22. The entrance of Don Esteban is given as Scene 4 in the original, where it takes place in Serafina's room at the inn. I have made some very slight modifications in the soliloquy and the stage directions in order to keep the setting unchanged.

DON ESTEBAN. And then?

PEDRO. They've left your estate. Her father decided to take her to the Ursulines in Badajoz.

DON ESTEBAN. I'll go at once. Pedro, was it they who sent you to me?

PEDRO. Sir...my lady gave me this letter for you...without her father's knowledge.

DON ESTEBAN (*after reading the letter*). Not a single reproach!...Angel of God!...How could I so wrong her?—Come, Pedro; we'll ride our horses to the ground; we must be in Badajoz before the day is over.

PEDRO. It may not be possible. We'll have to take side-roads, my Lord.

DON ESTEBAN. Why?

PEDRO. The whole province is in arms....The peasants have massacred the entire garrison of Aviz. Any Spaniard they catch is a dead man.

DON ESTEBAN. That too!—No matter, Pedro! If I die, say that I died repentant.

PEDRO. Oh, my lord, she is an angel. She never stopped justifiying you to Señor Mendo.

DON ESTEBAN. On our way, Pedro....—Don Gregorio, the commander at Aviz, is he safe?

PEDRO. No, my lord, they hanged him.

DON ESTEBAN. Another murder on my conscience!

(*They leave*)

Scene 4

(*The parlor of the Ursulines in Badajoz*)

MENDO. Adieu, Inès. We shall meet again some day.

INES. Adieu, father. My life will soon be over. The blow was too hard. If he ever leaves that beautiful Serafina...if he returns to his Inès...alas, I won't live to see it, but tell him that I have forgiven him...and that I died praying heaven to forgive him. Adieu, my father. (*They embrace, and Inès is led into the cloister by the abbess*)

MENDO (*alone*). Now I can devote myself entirely to vengeance. Thank heaven, I still have my left hand.

(*Enter Don Esteban, pale and disheveled*)

DON ESTEBAN. Inès! Inès my beloved!

MENDO. Respect the woman—

DON ESTEBAN. Inès! Inès!

INES (*off-stage*). It's Esteban! He has returned to me! (*She enters and flings herself into Esteban's arms*) You still love me!...Oh, I am happy at last! (*She faints*)

ABBESS. Make her sit on this chair, and give her salts to breathe. Someone bring water!

DON ESTEBAN. Darling Inès!...If my love can repair my crime!...Oh, answer me, for pity's sake!

ABBESS. Drink this glass of water, madam.

INES. Esteban!...Father!...Give me your hands, both of you. (*She tries to join their hands, but Mendo refuses*) Esteban, kiss me...adieu. (*She lets herself go in his arms*)

ABBESS. She is dead.

MENDO. Baron Mendoza, what do you say to this spectacle? It is your doing....Look at this mutilated arm. What memories does it bring back to you? And tell me, what did you do to my daughter to express your gratitude to her?...To this day I never inflicted death on anyone...but now I stand as your judge and your executioner....May the Lord forgive you! (*He shoots him*)

ABBESS. Help! Murder! Close the doors!

DON ESTEBAN. Let him escape. (*He places his head on Inès' breast*)

*

MENDO. I won't move, because the play is over. Yes, ladies and gentlemen, so ends the second part of *Inès Mendo, or the Triumph of Prejudice*.

INES. The author has told me to come to life again in order to beg for your indulgence. You can go home now happy to know that there will be no third part.

The End

Also by Oscar Mandel

A Definition of Tragedy (1961)
The Theatre of Don Juan: A Collection of Plays and Views 1630–1963
  (1963)
Chi Po and the Sorcerer: A Chinese Tale for Children and Philosophers
  (1964)
The Fatal French Dentist (comedy, 1967)
The Gobble-Up Stories (1967)
Seven Comedies by Marivaux (1968)
Five Comedies of Medieval France (1970)
The Collected Plays: 2 vols. (1970–1972)
Three Classic Don Juan Plays (1971)
Simplicities (poems, 1974)
Amphitryon, after Molière (1976)
The Land of Upside Down by Ludwig Tieck (1978)
Annotations to 'Vanity Fair' (1981; 2nd ed with John Sutherland, 1988)
Collected Lyrics and Epigrams (1981)
Philoctetes and the Fall of Troy: Plays, Documents, Iconography,
  Interpretations (1981)
The 'Ariadne' of Thomas Corneille, with an Essay on French Classical
  Tragedy (1982)
The Book of Elaborations (essays, 1985)
The Kukkurrik Fables: 41 Mini-dramas for All Media (1987)
Sigismund, Prince of Poland: A Baroque Entertainment (drama, 1988)
August von Kotezebue: The Comedy, the Man (1990)
The Virgin and the Unicorn: Four Plays (1993)
The Art of Alessandro Magnasco: An Essay in the Recovery of Meaning
  (1994)
The Cheerfulness of Dutch Art: A Rescue Operation (1996)
Two Romantic Plays: The 'Spaniards in Denmark' by Prosper Mérimée
  and 'The Rebels of Nantucket' by Oscar Mandel (1996)
Fundamentals of the Art of Poetry (1997)
L'Arc de Philoctète (drama, 2002)
Reinventions: Four Plays After Homer, Cervantes, Calderón and
  Marivaux (2003)
Le Pigeon qui était fou (Toutes les fables de Monsieur Oscar) (2003)
Amphitryon, ou le Cocu béni (comedy 2003)
Le Triomphe d'Agamemnon (drama, 2003)

Currents in Comparative
Romance Languages and Literatures

This series was founded in 1987, and actively solicits book-length manuscripts (approximately 200–400 pages) that treat aspects of Romance languages and literatures. Originally established for works dealing with two or more Romance literatures, the series has broadened its horizons and now includes studies on themes within a single literature or between different literatures, civilizations, art, music, film and social movements, as well as comparative linguistics. Studies on individual writers with an influence on other literatures/civilizations are also welcome. We entertain a variety of approaches and formats, provided the scholarship and methodology are appropriate.

For additional information about the series or for the submission of manuscripts, please contact:

Tamara Alvarez-Detrell and Michael G. Paulson
c/o Dr. Heidi Burns
Peter Lang Publishing, Inc.
P.O. Box 1246
Bel Air, MD 21014-1246

To order other books in this series, please contact our Customer Service Department:

800-770-LANG (within the U.S.)
212-647-7706 (outside the U.S.)
212-647-7707 FAX

or browse online by series at:

www.peterlangusa.com